Education for Rural Transformation in India

About the Editor

Prof. Karanam Pushpanadham is a Professor of Education at the Department of Educational Administration, Faculty of Education and Psychology, The M.S. University of Baroda, Vadodara, Gujarat, India. He was the member of the Senate, The Maharaja Sayajirao University of Baroda (2012-2013). Worked as a Dean of Students at the Faculty of Education and Psychology, the M.S. University of Baroda, Gujarat, India during 2007-2010. Visiting Professor (2007-2008) at the Institute of International Education, Stockholm University, Sweden on Swedish Institute's Guest Scholarship for Advanced Research in Educational Leadership and Development focusing on the Head Teachers Management Training in Sweden. Worked as a Director, Education E-Learning Programmes and Assistant Dean for International Affairs at the Assumption International University of Thailand during 2005-2006. Guest Editor of an International Journal on Teaching and Studies, American Scholars Press, USA. Associated with International Research Project on "Education for Rural Transformation: India and China" in collaboration.

Co-coordinating Education for Global Citizenship Programme in collaboration with Stockholm School Administration, Ministry of Education, and Sweden. Involved in capacity building for teachers and teacher educators in ESD and Eco System Services and its application for creating safe school environment. Project Director of IB school evaluation programme in India. European Union's Erasmus Mundus Visiting Professor at the Department of Education, Aarhus University, and Copenhagen, Denmark during 2012. Directed International Training Programmes on School Leadership for the DEO's of Afghanistan and ICT in pedagogic development for the policy makers of Asia and African countries with the support of Swedish International Development Agency.

Education for Rural Transformation in India

Realities and Challenges

Edited by
Karanam Pushpanadham

CONCEPT PUBLISHING COMPANY PVT. LTD.
NEW DELHI-110059

ISBN-13 : 978-93-5125-107-1

First Published 2014

Published and Printed by

Concept Since 1974

Concept Publishing Company Pvt. Ltd.
A/15-16, Commercial Block, Mohan Garden
New Delhi-110059 (India)
T: 25351460, 25351794, *F*: 091-11-25357109
E: publishing@conceptpub.com, W: www.conceptpub.com
Editorial Office: H-13, Bali Nagar, New Delhi-110 015, India.

Cataloging in Publication Data--*Courtesy:* D.K. Agencies (P) Ltd. <docinfo@dkagencies.com>

National Symposium on "Education for Rural Transformation: Realities and Challenges" (2010 : Stockholm University)
Education for rural transformation in India : realities and challenges / edited by Karanam Pushpanadham.
p. cm.
Includes bibliographical references and index.
ISBN 9789351251071

1. Education, Rural--India--Congresses. 2. Rural development--India--Congresses. 3. Rural development--Government policy--India--Congresses. I. Pushpanadham, K. (Karanam), 1970- II. Title.

DDC 370.917340954 23

Preface

Despite unprecedented growth in world economies and unparalleled improvements in global standards of living over the past few years, poverty and hunger are still realities in several countries. Indeed more than 70 per cent of the world's poor are rural poor. One of the major inequalities affecting the rural poor is their unequal access to quality education, which is very important for social and economic development. Any attempt to redress the challenges of increasing inequity, poverty and widening human development gaps is possible through access to relevant, equitable and effective education of our rural people. Education for Rural Transformation (ERT) is the only way to reduce the widening human development gaps within and between nations. The dynamics of rural transformation in the "globalized" world has created new educational imperatives that call for a re-evaluation of present educational policies and priorities, and the re-examination of the role of education and learning (formal, non-formal and informal) for rural people from rather new perspectives. Henceforth, education should be seen as a key instrument for shaping and fulfilling the goal of rural transformation. It should contribute to the well-being of the rural people including food security, health, and employment, protection of the environment and the management of our natural resources.

Rural transformation faces a key challenge to achieve both Poverty Reduction and Education for All. In order to achieve the Millennium Development Goals, specifically the first two goals, reducing hunger and poverty by half and ensuring universal primary education by 2015, there is a need to change the traditional working modalities and address the needs of the rural India. This can be achieved through new multi-sectarian and interdisciplinary alliances and partnerships in education and those working in agriculture and rural development. Food and Agricultural Organization (FAO) and the International Institute for Educational Planning of UNESCO (2003) emphasized the need for specific modalities to address the demand and supply issues that education faces in rural areas. The report highlights the challenge as missing link of education interventions with broader poverty reduction and rural development efforts. The report has also envisaged that Education for All will never be achieved in areas affected by poverty, high mortality, gender and other forms of discrimination.

India lives in its villages. Rural Transformation is one of the most important factors for the growth of the Indian economy. India is primarily an agriculture-based country. Agriculture contributes nearly one-fifth of the Gross Domestic Product in India. In order to increase the growth of agriculture, the Government of India has planned several programmes pertaining to Rural Development. The introduction of Bharat Nirman, a project set about by the Government of India in collaboration with the State Governments and the Panchayati Raj Institutions is a major step towards the improvement of the rural sector. The National Rural Employment Guarantee Act, 2005 was another significant step for improving the living conditions and its sustenance in the rural sector of India. Sarva Shiksha Abhiyan as a national initiation of Education for All has been addressing the contextual issues of primary education. However, there is a need to have a cohesive approach and concerted effort to bring significant changes in rural India.

In view of such concerns, the National Symposium was organized by the Department of Educational Administration, Faculty of Education and Psychology, the Maharaja Sayajirao University of Baroda in collaboration with the Institute of International Education, Stockholm University, Sweden to provide a platform to policy analysts, administrators, researchers and practitioners to critically examine the current scenario of rural education in India, identify the challenges and to develop a framework for rural transformation. The two-day National Symposium deliberated on the key issues of Education for Rural Transformation in India by examining the policies and programmes and addressed the following issues:

- What are the current situations and trends in ERT and what are the challenges that ERT is facing in the rapidly changing global socio-economic, cultural and political contexts?
- What are the success stories of education for rural transformation?
- Whether the developmental policies and educational programmes of the government are rural inclusive and empowering rural people?
- What is the role of education in the process of rural transformation and sustainable rural development?
- How can education and learning contribute towards training for rural youth using non-formal and informal educational organizations?
- Are there discrepancies between research, policy and practices in ERT?
- What are the specific contextual strategies for promoting skills in rural people for transformation?

The challenges for rural transformation in terms of access and equity, availability of flexible and lifelong learning system, multiple layers of discrimination, quality of teachers, and its need and ways for social change in rural context were discussed. Such suggested ways were strategic management systems, increasing civil society participation, and offering flexible need based lifelong learning opportunities to ensure access, and equity for education to the rural mass. A significant focus was given to the initiations made by the Government of India in her development programme and inclusive policies for rural upliftment. The paradigmatic shift occurred in rural development with the passage of time was explored. The process strategy for education for rural transformation was suggested as ways to bring awareness and awaken Indian rural youth through capacity building.

Prof. Karanam Pushpanadham

- What are the current situations and trends in ERT and what are the challenges that ERT is facing in the rapidly changing global socio-economic, cultural and political contexts?
- What are the success stories of education for rural transformation?
- Whether the developmental policies and educational programmes of the government are rural inclusive and empowering rural people?
- What is the role of education in the process of rural transformation and sustainable rural development?
- How can education and learning contribute towards harnessing potential of youth using non-formal and informal educational organisations?
- Are there discrepancies between research, policy and practices in ERT?
- What are the specific contextual strategies for promoting skills in rural people for transformation?

The challenges for rural transformation in terms of access and equity, availability of flexible and lifelong learning system, multiple layers of discrimination, quality of teachers, and the need and ways for social change in rural context were discussed. Success suggested ways were strategic management systems, increasing civil society participation, and offering flexible need based lifelong learning opportunities to ensure access and equity for education to the rural masses. Significant focus was given to the initiatives made by the Government of India for development programmes and inclusive policies for rural development. The paradigmatic shift occurred in rural development with the passage of time was explored. The process strategy for education for rural transformation was suggested as ways to bring awareness and awaken Indian rural youth through capacity building.

Prof. Karanam Pushpanadham

Acknowledgements

The present book is the result of my Visiting Professorship at the Institute of International Education (IIE), Stockholm University, Sweden in 2007-08, where the concept of ERT was thoroughly discussed and Prof. Vinayagum Chinappa, who was then working at UNESCO, provided direction to our thinking and later as the Head of IIE, exercised his academic leadership for developing a comprehensive research project on Education for Rural Transformation: India and China. The result of the pre-National Education for Rural Transformation (ERT) Symposium in India prior to the ERT International Symposium (2010) at Institute of International Education (IIE), Stockholm University, Sweden, is presented in this book.

I am thankful to Prof. Vinayagum Chinapah, Institute of International Education (IIE), Stockholm University, Sweden, for providing academic and financial support for organizing India-ERT Regional Symposium in Baroda. I am thankful to all the members of the team ERT-International for their support and encouragement. I sincerely thank Prof. Vinayagum Chinapah for his valuable suggestions and insights into the area and appreciate his broad vision and action in making ERT ideas into reality. I must put on records that this national symposium was organized under the ERT International Project with the intellectual and financial support by the Institute of International Education, Stockholm University, Sweden. I also sincerely acknowledge the contributions of our ERT International Team at IIE. I am thankful to my friend, guide and philosopher Prof. Holger Daun for his continuous academic support and encouragement.

I would like to express my deepest appreciation and thanks to all the contributors from all over India. I express my gratitude to Prof. S. Kumar, Professor Emeritus and Former Dean, Faculty of Education and Psychology, The Maharaja Sayajirao University of Baroda, Vadodara for providing logistic support for the organization of the ERT Symposium and for providing all the required support to make it successful. I also thank Prof. R.G. Kothari, Dean, Faculty of Education and Psychology for his motivation and encouragement in all our academic endeavours.

I would like to take this opportunity to thank my friend Prof. S.C. Panigrahi, Head, Centre of Advanced Study in Education, Department of Education, Faculty of Education and Psychology, The Maharaja Sayajirao University of Baroda, Vadodara for his association with this project right from the inception. In fact, conceptualizing ERT in Indian context was done by both of us in series of discussions over a long period of time with lots of arguments and consensus. I thank Prof. N. Pradhan, Head, Department of Educational Administration, Faculty of Education and Psychology, The Maharaja Sayajirao University of Baroda, Vadodara. I appreciate the technical support rendered by Mr. H.S. Mistry, UGC-Research Fellow, Centre of Advanced Study in Education (CASE), Faculty of Education and Psychology, The Maharaja Sayajirao University of Baroda, Vadodara in preparing this book.

Prof. Karanam Pushpanadham
Director, National Symposium

Message

Stockholm University

Professor Vinayagum Chinapah
Head, Institute of International Education
Stockholm University
SWEDEN

Distinguished Colleagues, Ladies and Gentlemen,

I am much honoured to address this highly-esteemed audience of decision-makers, scholars, researchers and educators of this important National Symposium on Education for Rural Transformation (ERT). I am very thankful to the Maharaja Sayajirao University of Baroda, and to our project coordinator at this University, Dr. Karanam Pushpanadham for the efforts made to bring together the Indian expertise in this field. The results from this ERT Symposium will serve as direct inputs to the forthcoming International ERT Symposium in Stockholm, Sweden, next November 8-10, 2010.

The movement of Education for Rural Transformation is for sure not new on the agenda of many of us. The present initiative is just a follow-up of the collective works we started in 2000 for the UNESCO International Research and Training Centre for Rural Education (INRULED). The 2001 commissioned INRULED's report serves as the foundation for our present initiative with the following background:

> Most of the world's poor are rural and will be so for several decades. In spite of the rapid pace of urbanization, three billion or half of the people in the world—a quarter in industrial countries and 60 per cent in developing countries—today still live in what are categorized by countries by their own varying definitions as rural areas. And seventy-five per cent of the estimated 1.3 billion people in absolute poverty, struggling to survive on a

> dollar a day, live in rural areas. Although the march to urbanization is set to continue in the 21st century, by 2015, half of the population in today's developing countries and 45 per cent of the world's population will still be rural. The proportion of rural inhabitants is the highest in the South Asian region with about 70 per cent living in rural areas. (pp. 1-6)

The 2010 Education for All (EFA) Global Monitoring Report has chosen to address our major concerns through its title "Reaching the Marginalized". A major conclusion from this report deserved our great attention, namely:

> There is no single blueprint for moving towards greater equity in education. When it comes to tackling marginalization, each country faces a different set of challenges—and it has to meet those challenges in the light of the resources available. Just as marginalization is sustained by unequal power relationships, so policies for combating it have to be rooted in political processes and alliances that challenge these relationships... Reaching those who are being left behind as a result of disparities linked to poverty, gender, ethnicity, language and other markers of disadvantage should be established as a first order of priority. (pp. 270-271)

Let me now take this opportunity to re-iterate the rationale of our ERT initiative as expressed in our ERT Working Document.[1]

I am sure that you will agree with me that any attempt to readdress our world's increasing inequity, poverty and widening human development gaps is only doable and realistic (IF) we can guarantee universal equitable access to relevant and effective education and related social and economic services for our rural people who sadly make our world's majority of illiterate, unhealthy, malnourished, marginalized, and oppressed population. Their numbers are increasing at a skyrocketing pace

---

1. An ERT Working Document has been prepared for the forthcoming November 8-10, 2010 International Symposium in Stockholm.

and yet very little research is looking at the causes and roots of such deteriorating situations.

I sincerely believe that Education for Rural Transformation (ERT)2 is the only way to reduce the widening human development gaps within and between nations. The dynamics of rural transformation in the "globalized" world has created new educational imperatives that call for a re-evaluation of present educational policies and priorities, and the re-examination of the role of education and learning (formal, non-formal and informal) for rural people from rather new perspectives. Henceforth, education should be seen as a key instrument for shaping and fulfilling the goal of rural transformation. It should contribute to the well-being of the rural people including food security, health, employment, protection of the environment and the management of our natural resources. ERT should be inclusive and should meet effectively and equitably the basic learning needs of children, out-of-school youth and adults in the perspective of reducing rural poverty and henceforth, assuring an improved quality of life.

Ladies and Gentlemen, Why ERT and WHY India?

The great majority of our rural people can be found in the most populous (E-9) countries like India, namely, Bangladesh, Brazil, China, Egypt, Indonesia, Mexico, Nigeria, and Pakistan. The so-called belief in education for development has been very unrealistic and irrelevant, if not totally obsolete, for the poorest of the poor rural people of these countries. As the recent 2010 EFA GMR report argues:

> Rural children face heightened risks of marginalization in education, especially if they are poor and female. Rural-urban divides in education often overlap with wider inequalities... The poorest households in many rural areas are the furthest from roads, markets, health services and schools. (pp. 176-177)

---

2. ERT is a concept that was used and further developed in a state-of-the-art review commissioned by UNESCO and INRULED in 2001 entitled "Education for Rural Transformation—Towards a Policy Framework" (INRULED, China).

When it comes to India, this same 2010 report cogently argues that "India's wealth divides in education are among the largest in the world—and they are reinforced by regional and gender disparities. While the richest 20 per cent average over eleven years in school, the poorest have an average education expectancy that places them just above the four year 'education poverty line'. Poor rural females are well behind that line." (p. 142)

The rural people's ever-pressing needs for an education which is relevant, equitable and effective are neither subject to any discourse of human development nor given priority-concerns, be it at international, regional, national or local levels. India has designed its own strategies to achieve the Millennium Development Goals (MDG) by implementing social inclusive policies and programmes. It should be noted that all goals of the MDG can be linked to some extent to the process of rural transformation, if taken from a holistic perspective of human development. Putting human beings, and in our case, the most vulnerable ones, at the centre of genuine educational interventions should serve our vision, mission, strategy and action for an education that can only lead to rural transformation and improved quality of life of our rural people. This is my sincere appeal to all of you who can make a difference along this way in your own personal and institutional capacity.

This National ERT Symposium in India is both strategic and opportune. It is an integral part of a series of such similar ERT forthcoming events (2010, Stockholm, Sweden; 2011, Beijing, China; and 2012, India, venue yet to be fixed). This National ERT Symposium is intended, first and foremost for stocktaking of up-to-date relevant experiences and lessons learned for the further promotion of Research and Development (R&D) programmes and activities as well as for future capacity development in this field.

I, therefore, strongly believe that this Symposium is a move towards this direction.

Prof. Vinayagum Chinapah
Head, Institute of International Education
Stockholm University, SWEDEN

Executive Summary

The Department of Educational Administration, Faculty of Education and Psychology, the Maharaja Sayajirao University of Baroda, India in collaboration with the Institute of International Education, Department of Education, Stockholm University, Sweden has organized a two-day National Symposium on "Education for Rural Transformation: Realities and Challenges" during 18-19 August, 2010. There were about 35 paper presentations and 6 keynote presentations on the theme "Education for Rural Transformation". It was an interdisciplinary dialogue between educationists, social workers, sociologist, policy makers, management experts, researchers and teacher educators. It was a rigorous intelligent exercise to conceptualize the Indian scenario for rural transformation in an Indian sub-continent. The basic underlying purpose for conducting such symposium was to investigate the instrumental application of education to solve the realities, and embrace the upcoming challenges surfaced due to the wide gulf of urban-rural divide.

The Inaugural session of the two-day National Symposium on Rural Transformation catapulted the audience immediately into this very relevant topic. With his welcome address Prof. S. Kumar, Dean, Faculty of Education and Psychology highlighted some of the significant achievements of the Faculty over the years. Since its inception, the faculty has been closely associated with the major developments in the field of education. In fact, he pointed out that the Modular Training programmes for teachers were initiated in

Baroda before that caught the fancy of other universities. According to him, the need of the hour was not only to carry out educational strategies in the rural areas but also monitor the impact and transformation in the lives of people. He advocated the need for concerted efforts and role of higher education institutions in this mission.

Dr. Karanam Pushpanadham, Director of the National Symposium articulated the need to mobilize resources to realize the Millennium Development Goals. He felt that development should take into consideration the welfare of the people at large keeping in mind environmental concerns and the economy. The empowerment of the rural pockets was a step towards minimizing the disparities that exist in the world today. Quoting Noble Laureate Prof. Amartya Sen, he stressed the need for contextually relevant strategies for rural transformation which would enable the people at large to the freedom to choose and also the capacity to fulfil those choices. He wanted the audience to keep in mind the regional variances that prevail throughout the country while embarking on projects for rural transformation. Any project of rural transformation would have to study success stories from all over the world, would have to include expertise from various disciplines, conceptualize and contextualize the challenges imminent in such an endeavour. He also felt that local traditions and wisdom would actually pave the way for a meaningful ERT. As Prof. Vinayagum Chinapah, Head, Institute of International Education, Stockholm University, Sweden could not attend the Symposium, Dr. Pushpanadham read out his message. In his message, Prof. Chinapah outlined that this event was the first part of a series of such exchanges on ERT worldwide. The role of education, both formal and informal, was necessary to reduce the widening gap between the rural-urban divide prevalent in the world today.

The Chief Guest of the Symposium Mr. Raju Narayana Swamy IAS, Secretary, Department of Parliamentary Affairs, Government of Kerala energized the gathering with his short but powerful speech. Quoting Ravindranath Tagore, Mr. Raju advocated for the world where knowledge is free and acquiring knowledge and skills does not have any barriers. The route to rural transformation meant the easy accessibility to basic facilities. This did not mean that we have to prevent urbanization but create opportunities for the rural section to develop themselves and become self-reliant. Any change cannot happen overnight but it needed perseverance and a need to go beyond traditional methods of education. It could also mean incorporating digital technology and ICT in a major way. He called this Symposium an alarm bell, a bell that warned people that something had to be done for ERT and that too quickly. He entreated the audience to act and realize and not just to dream. Mr. Raju Narayana Swamy has also delivered a keynote address on the Tribal Development in Wayanad district in Kerala and stressed the need for civil society participation for rural transformation.

Dr. Karanam Pushpanadham and Prof. Sudershan Panigrahi discussed the need to reduce hunger and poverty on the one hand and primary education on the other by 2015 as a goal towards which educators had to mobilize their forces. Over the years many programmes of rural development were initiated in India but the success rate was very modest. More and more rural people became dependent upon the governmental programmes and thus the burden started increasing. Between 70s and 80s many programmes of rural developments were initiated but the failure to reach the goods to the poverty stricken people still remained. The gap between practice and pronouncement widened because of the faulty implementation strategies. Notwithstanding the official ideologies and defence to uphold the success of the programmes it was implicitly realized by the government officials that a rethinking is required towards rural development; and thus the idea of rural transformation surfaced. An argument may be forwarded to support this idea, *i.e.* rather than making people dependent on the governmental policies, it would be better to make them self-reliant and hence the concept of rural transformation. This idea has an implicit assumption, *i.e.* it is possible to create a situation through some means (and in this case education) which will give rise to some generic skills in the individuals that will enable them to lead a full and productive life as an individual, as a member in the family and society.

Dr. Ranjit Singh Ghuman from Punjabi University deliberated on the situation of rural students in Punjab. The first premise, he worked on, was that the literacy level was well placed as far as other states were concerned but that was just the first step. Would this literacy level translate into employment opportunities or open avenues for higher education? This question was explored and the findings did not present a very rosy picture. The sad fact is that 85-90 per cent Punjabis cannot afford to pay the fees for higher education. The statistics provided by this economic professor gave a very clear picture of the scenario. The alarming fact was that the government allocation for higher education in the state had fallen from 22 per cent in 1980 to 12 per cent in 2010. Through his impassioned speech, he urged that education could not be left to the private universities. The government had to fulfil the responsibility of providing basic education as enshrined in our Constitution. In an interesting and exhaustive research, Dr. Ranjit Singh outlined that there was a definite progress in literacy levels as far as generations were concerned. In cases, where 57 per cent of grandfathers were illiterate, only 9 per cent fathers were illiterate in the next generation.

Dr. Anjali Kirwardkar and Mr. Praful dwelled on the use of ICT in rural transformation. Talking of projects like E-Suvidha, the speaker demonstrated how rural transformation can be a tangible reality with greater levels of communication. Technology could play a significant role as it could ensure that the lowest common denominator could have a chance to be heard and listened to. Even maintaining of records like birth register or growth rate could be faster and accurate with wider access to digital technology. Mr. K. Vishwa Bushan from Department of Social Work of Andhra University provided a radically new approach with his paper entitled—"Role of Civil Society for ERT". In his plea he appealed for the formation of a civil society to solve the problems of our country. Here, apart from NGOs, government organizations and institutions, even common people like you and me should involve in the reconstruction of rural India. Though an idealistic viewpoint, the speaker's argument did touch the minds and more importantly the hearts of the audience.

The second day of the symposium saw an electrifying audience as the atmosphere was charged with ideas and counter-ideas on the theme. An exhaustive analysis of the subject made one aspect very clear that each and every speaker had researched his/her topic in detail and indicated that the compiled version would definitely provide adequate guidelines for our policy makers.

Prof. K. Sujata from the National University of Educational Planning and Administration, New Delhi presented the success

story of Tribal Education in Andhra Pradesh on the lines of rural transformation. She stressed the need for contextually relevant educational programmes are needed to uplift the lives of marginalized. Gurukula schools which were established in the tribal areas have transformed over the years in their perspectives and programmes and empowered tribal population even to become the members of Legislative Assembly and Parliament. She was of the opinion that Education is the only hope through which rural transformation is possible to the greater levels. Prof. Sujata emphasized the need for micro level actions which can directly affect the lives of rural people.

Prof. J.B.G. Tilak from the National University of Educational Planning and Administration, New Delhi in his valedictory address tried to draw attention of the audience towards the Government's policy issues on education. He was emphasizing that there is need to bring quality in the elementary education. Today it is government's policy to spend 6 per cent of total national income on education, but rather there is need to spend 1 per cent of total income on each child in the country aspiring to gain elementary education. Only then can quality be assured in elementary education; Quality elementary education which is need of current time. Matter of enhancing the standard of education in India does not depend on policies on education made by the government, it is not the question of policies, he said, rather 'it is question of priority that government makes to spend on what'. No matter how much ever fund one has for education or no matter how one spends on education, the effect of this done can be seen only if it is rightly planned such that it reaches the needy once on right time. He further said that in rural areas or for the poor people there is no need for quality education, rather what they need is some education, moderate quality of education, this is so because they are illiterate people, they don't know the value of education, value of quality education—Hence, they need tolerable quality of education, which even in this modern era we are not able to provide in several rural areas of the country.

It is not, that rural areas lack education because they lack money, because there is poverty. He said 'people in rural area are ready to pay for education, so money is not matter avoiding education, it is something else, it is WILLINGNESS. This Willingness is to be cultivated in rural areas for education to 'flourish'. According to Prof. Tilak what matters the most in high drop-out rate in education is not the quality of infrastructure in school, is not the inability to excess the infrastructure, what matters is the type of teacher, the personality of the teacher, the number of teachers in school to interact, their quality education, what matters most is teacher availability, for children's not learning and for their drop-out from school.

Azim Premji Foundations and Deepak Foundations are the Non-Governmental Organizations working for the promotion of rural transformation. They had presented their success stories of Educational programmes and their impact on rural population. Dr. Pushpa Wadhwani and Ms. Fiona Fernandes of Azim Premji Foundation, Gujarat provided a brief outline of vision, objectives of Azim Premji Foundation, Gujarat, and presented their learning experiences during the implementation of projects for elementary education. It was a brief description of projects undertaken by NGO, Azim Premji Foundation, Gujarat as an educational intervention in transformation of society. The address explored the current practices observed during the project work, the problems, the widely practiced methods of teaching and assessment, teacher's action, health, sanitation related problems, situational specific problems. The terms 'social exclusion', and 'social inclusion', and sustainable development was discussed. It was also discussed what teacher can do wonder in building a transformed society and how education can be effectively employed as a tool to release its profound catalytic effect over to lead the rural people happy and prosperous life. The speakers gave overview of the strategies for ERT (Education for Rural Transformation), along with flexibilities and innovativeness in present education system, and effective use of technology for qualitative improvement.

While each of the keynote addresses and paper presentations were specific and focused on one particular aspect of ERT, certain generic issues and concerns arose out of the same. This part of the report to capture the overall observations and ideas aired during the Symposium.

It was felt that the first step towards ERT was a basic understanding of the current realistic rural situation in our country. A fast paced mobility of resources was the need of the hour in order to realize the Millennium Goals of Education. Education for All,

Primary education and Sustainable human development were the three cornerstones to guide the work of educators. Any seminar on ERT in India had to address the regional variances that prevail throughout the country before embarking on projects of rural transformation. Further, any project of transformation would have to study success stories from all over the world, would have to include expertise from various disciplines and conceptualize and contextualize the challenges imminent in such an endeavour. ERT could be a reality only and only when the local traditions and wisdom are incorporated in all levels of planning and implementation.

There are many government initiatives to provide access to primary education, but issues of uniformity, quality and accessibility remain areas of concern—particularly in rural schools. Some of the stark realities of the rural education continue to be inadequate committed teachers, lack of teaching materials and a high school dropout.

It is important for the survival of the human race that rural areas must survive; and for their survival rural development is essential. The size of the area and population involved in rural development is so enormous that the options exercised in their transformation will have a tremendous impact on world development; and unless the open options with education are wisely exercised and the advanced countries lent a truly friendly helping hand in enlightened self-interest, transformation may not take place in a manner which makes for a better and a more harmonious world.

India is primarily an agriculture-based country. In order to increase the growth of agriculture, the Government of India has planned several programmes pertaining to Rural Development. The introduction of Bharat Nirman, a project set about by the Government of India in collaboration with the State Governments and the Panchayati Raj Institutions is a major step towards the improvement of the rural sector.

The National Rural Employment Guarantee Act (NREGA), 2005 was another significant step for improving the living conditions and its sustenance in the rural sector of India. Sarva Shiksha Abhiyan as a national initiation of Education for All has been addressing the contextual issues of primary education.

Unfortunately, the situation even after such marked initiatives remains an area of concern. In view of these factors, an in-depth study of the realities and challenges for ERT become the need of the hour. In India, about 51 per cent of the population in the rural areas, and 38 per cent in the urban and about 98 per cent in the country as a whole, were estimated to live below the poverty line. The most dangerous aspects of the arithmetic of inequality in India, is the socio-political system of which the inequality is both a cause and consequence. The socio-political system provides to this inequality such entrenched power that ending it by the normal democratic processes is going to be extremely difficult though not possible. Region-wise, the central eastern region is the most poverty-stricken region of the country, both in terms of poverty ratio as well as concentration of the poor. The group of 4 major states Madhya Pradesh, Orissa, Bihar, and Uttar Pradesh together constitute more than 61 per cent of the rural poor in India.

Eighty-seven per cent of the schools in India are in the country's villages. Government statistics and independent surveys have revealed that over 90 per cent of the rural schools at elementary level are run by the government. It is noticeable that in rural areas there has been an increase in enrolments in government SE and HSE schools in recent years with a corresponding decline in enrolments in the government aided schools.

Levels of Education in India

There are levels/stages of education in India. These levels are early-childhood, elementary, secondary and higher secondary education. The detailed status of these levels of education in rural area is mentioned below.

The salient fact which emerges from the 47th and 58th rounds of NSS on Consumer Expenditure, Employment-Unemployment, Disabled Persons and Village facilities is the spectacular rise in the number of pre-primary schools available in rural India. The proportion of villages having pre-primary school facilities is seen to have increased from around 39 per cent to about 68 per cent in these eleven years. By contrast, the proportion of villages with primary schools has increased by only about 6 percentage points and the proportion of villages with middle schools by only 5 percentage points. The proportion of villages with secondary schools has increased by only about 1.5 percentage points.

The facts and figures speak for themselves but there are broad indicators which we need to recapitulate once more. They are:

- Regional variations in rural education across states.
- The reality of high school dropouts.
- Gender disparity which cuts across the other parameters like class, caste and religion.
- Need for trained teachers both in terms of quality and quantity.
- Progress towards self-reliance and transformation.
- Skill development and training.

Dr. Karanam Pushpanadham, Director of the National Symposium proposed vote of thanks to all the delegates for their active participation in the symposium and valuable suggestions to carry out this ERT mission further.

Contents

List of Contributors

Amit Choudhury, Registrar, Regional Institute of Technology, Guwahati, Assam.

Ankush, G.S., Assistant Professor, Department of Extension Education, College of Agriculture, Latur, Maharashtra.

Archana Tomar, Assistant Professor, Navrachna College of Education, Sama Road, Vadodara.

Avtar Singh, Assistant Professor, School of Education, DAVV, Indore.

Bharati B. Ganiger, JRF, Department of Education (CASE), Faculty of Education and Psychology, The M.S. University of Baroda, Vadodara-390002.

Daisy Nath, Assistant Professor, Department of Education, Karamsree Saikia College, Guwahati, Assam.

Deota Nilambar Prabhakar, Associate Professor, Department of Education (CASE), Faculty of Education and Psychology, The M.S. University of Baroda, Vadodara-390002.

Doss, M., Associate Professor, SCERT, Pondicherry, Tamil Nadu.

Hemendra S. Mistry, UGC-Research Fellow, Department of Education (CASE), Faculty of Education and Psychology, The M.S. University of Baroda, Vadodara-390002, Gujarat.

Hemlatta Rajput, Teacher, Jay Ambe Vidyalaya, Karelibaug, Vadodara, Gujarat.

Karanam Pushpanadham, Associate Professor, Department of Education Administration, Faculty of Education and Psychology, The M.S. University of Baroda, Vadodara-390002, Gujarat.

Karande, Y.R., Assistant Professor, Department of Extension Education, College of Agriculture, Latur, Maharashtra.

Kishori Dash, Assistant Professor, Government College of Teacher Education, Rourkela.

Mande, J.V., Assistant Professor, Department of Extension Education, College of Agriculture, Latur, Maharashtra.

Meera Subramanian, Research Scholar, Centre of Advanced Study in Education (CASE), Faculty of Education and Psychology, The M.S. University of Baroda, Vadodara, Gujarat, India.

Milind Sahastrabuddhe, Associate Professor, Department of Education Administration, Faculty of Education and Psychology, The M.S. University of Baroda, Vadodara-390002, Gujarat.

Monika Arya, Assistant Professor, B.P.S. Mahila Vishwavidyalaya, Sonepat, Haryana.

Pathy, M.K., Assistant Professor, Government College of Teacher Education, Rourkela.

Pramila Gururajan, Ph. D. Student, Department of Education (CASE), Faculty of Education and Psychology, The M.S. University of Baroda, Vadodara, Gujarat.

Pratibha Gupta, Assistant Professor, Navrachna College of Education, Sama Road, Vadodara, Gujarat.

Priyanka Kacker, Teaching Assistant, Department of Psychology, Faculty of Education and Psychology, The M.S. University of Baroda, Vadodara-390002.

Rajeev Rattan, D. Associate Professor, Department of Education, Jammu University, Jammu.

Rajesh Sharma, Assistant Professor, Kadi Sarva Vishwavidyalaya, Gandhinagar, Gujarat.

Raju Narayana Swami, (IAS), Secretary, Parliamentary Affairs, Government of Kerala, Kerala.

Ramesh, M., UGC-Research Fellow, Department of Education (CASE), Faculty of Education and Psychology, The M.S. University of Baroda, Vadodara-390002.

Ranjit Singh Ghuman, Prof. and Head, Department of Economics, Coordinator, CASE, Punjab University, Patiala, Punjab.

Rishi Raj Balwaria, Assistant Professor, Navrachna College of Education, Sama Road, Vadodara, Gujarat.

Sakesh Genni, Research Scholar, Centre of Advanced Study in Education (CASE), Faculty of Education and Psychology, The M.S. University of Baroda, Vadodara, Gujarat, India.

Sandeep Kumar, Research Scholar, Centre of Advanced Study in Education (CASE), Faculty of Education and Psychology, The M.S. University of Baroda, Vadodara, Gujarat, India.

Sudarsan, C. Panigrahi, Professor and Head, Department of Education (CASE), Faculty of Education and Psychology, The M.S. University of Baroda, Vadodara-390002, Gujarat.

Suradkar, D.D., Assistant Professor, Department of Extension Education, College of Agriculture, Latur, Maharashtra.

Suresh, K.P., Director, School of Pedagogical Sciences, Kannur University, Kerala-670 567.

Swaleha, Sindhi, Teaching Assistant, Department of Education Administration, Faculty of Education and Psychology, The M.S. University of Baroda, Vadodara-390002, Gujarat.

Thombre, B.M., Assistant Professor, Department of Extension Education, College of Agriculture, Latur, Maharashtra.

Tomba, Singh, Assistant Professor, Kadi Sarva Vishwavidyalaya, Gandhinagar, Gujarat.

Valli Pillai, Assistant Professor, Navrachna College of Education, Sama Road, Vadodara, Gujarat.

Vandana Talegaonkar, Assistant Professor, Navrachna College of Education, Sama Road, Vadodara, Gujarat.

Vikas Modi, Assistant Professor, Shah Govardhanlal Kabra Teachers' College (CTE), Jodhpur, Rajasthan.

1

Education for Rural Transformation

A Paradigm Shift

Sudarsan C. Panigrahi and *Karanam Pushpanadham*

Introduction

Despite unprecedented growth in world economies and unparalleled improvements in global standards of living over the past few years, poverty and hunger are still realities in several countries. Indeed more than 60 per cent of the world's poor are rural poor. One of the major inequalities affecting the rural poor is their unequal access to quality education, which is very important for social and economic development. Any attempt to redress the challenges of increasing inequity, poverty and widening human development gaps is possible through access to relevant, equitable and effective education of our rural people. Education for Rural Transformation (ERT) is the only way to reduce the widening human development gaps within and between nations. The dynamics of rural transformation in the "globalized" world has created new educational imperatives that call for a re-evaluation of present educational policies and priorities, and the re-examination of the role of education and learning (formal, non-formal and informal) for rural people from rather new perspectives. Henceforth, education should be seen as a key instrument for shaping and fulfilling the goal of rural transformation. It should contribute to the well-being of the rural people including food security, health, and employment, protection of the environment and the management of our natural resources. Rural transformation faces a key challenge to achieve both Poverty Reduction and Education for All. In order to achieve the Millennium Development Goals, specifically the first two goals, reducing hunger and poverty by half and ensuring universal primary education by 2015, there is a need to change the traditional working modalities and address the needs of the rural India. This can be achieved through new multi-sectarian and interdisciplinary alliances and partnerships in education and those working in agriculture and rural development. With this background, the paper attempts to address the following:

1. Conceptualizing and Contextualizing ERT.
2. Emerging Issues and Challenges for ERT.
3. Need for Paradigm in Education for Rural Transformation.
4. Framework for Action.

Conceptualizing and Contextualizing Education for Rural Transformation (ERT)

The term rural transformation subsumes two interrelated concepts, viz., development and social change. Before we elaborate on the concept of rural transformation, it would be pertinent here to have a brief discussion on the two related concept, viz., development and social change because of their varied meanings held by the scholars. There are a number of contending theoretical perspectives, which attempt to explain the process of social change, ranging from Spensor's ideas of social evolution, Durkheim's division of labour, Marx's theory of class struggle and conflict, to more recent theorists who exclusively stress that changes in the level of technology result in major changes in social super structure. Change is a social process and development suggests change in a given direction and it is generally assumed that there is a wide degree of community participation in determining the direction and means of change. Over the years, however, lot of political debates have taken place both at national and international level, as to what approach/s should be adopted for national development in particular context. Consequently, the concept of development remained largely the result of the political will of the power structure, to initiate designed changes. Stretching the argument further it can be observed that the conventional model of economic development, with the assumption that sustained increase in rates of economic growth, and GNP (now GDP) which it symbolizes, will automatically lead to the percolation of economic gains to all sections of society, has not proved to be correct. The distribution of economic gains has not proved to be correct.

The disparity in consumption levels, which follow from disparity in incomes, have continued and grown sharper. Many segments of the population and many spatial tracts have been by-passed by economic growth. Rural and tribal areas have particularly suffered the most. The traditional elite are often able to corner whatever benefits accrue from public investments, because of the political and other resources that they possess and can master. In many areas, the gap between the rich and the poor has widened. Large sections of the population live below poverty line. According to National Sample Survey Organization (NSSO) report of 2004-05, 28.3 per cent of households in rural areas were living below the poverty line. But, in view of the inadequacies pointed out in determining Below Poverty Line (BPL) people, the Ministry of Rural Development constituted an Expert Group in August 2008 to estimate BPL people. Accordingly, this Committee calculated the BPL households as 50 per cent. The following Table 1.1 indicates state-wise BPL households.

Table 1.1: Percentage of Rural Population Below Poverty Line—Current Levels and after Enhancement

State	*Present Figure*	*After the Increase*	*State*	*Present Figure*	*After the Increase*
Andhra Pradesh	10.83	19.13	Madhya Pradesh	37.67	66.35
Assam	21.79	38.50	Chhattisgarh	41.41	73.16
Bihar	42.53	75.14	Maharashtra	30.08	53.14
Jharkhand	46.46	82.08	Orissa	47.81	84.47
Gujarat	19.46	34.38	Punjab	10.04	17.74
Haryana	13.63	24.08	Rajasthan	18.76	33.14
Himachal Pradesh	10.87	19.20	Tamil Nadu	22.62	39.96
Jammu & Kashmir	4.51	7.97	Uttar Pradesh	32.88	58.09
Karnataka	20.05	35.42	Uttarakhand	39.87	70.44
Kerala	13.37	23.62	West Bengal	28.87	51.01
			India	**28.30**	**50.00**

Source: Report of Expert Group for BPL Census-2009, MHRD, Government of India.

From Table 1.1, it can be observed that more than 40 per cent of states have BPL households above the national figure. While such figures vary from time to time, it is a fact that poverty is a major problem for rural poor in India and prolonged existence of the widening gap between rural and urban poor in general and rural poor in particular has posed serious challenges for development planners. Thus, the development debate in the last few decades has thrown up several new formulations regarding alternative designs for living, and brought into sharp focus a number of new concerns. The accent now is on human-centred development, not as growth rooted is indicators of GDP and national income. This concept of development emphasises the quality of life not the pursuit of wealth; it takes note of deeply held cultural values, and seeks to promote indigenous creativity. The new concerns, among others, are focused on environment, energy and food security, all the three being inter-connected and inter-dependent.

Besides recognizing the nature of development it seems important to underline the current transformation of development thinking and its implications for education in rural areas. To a large extent, for about two decades, development policies at international level have been shaped by two contradictory approaches to development. On the one side, the specialized agencies of the UN put emphasis on social justice and human rights. On the other hand, the Washington consensus promoted a development model based on liberalization, deregulation, and privatization and decreasing role of the state generally to increased inequalities. Although, the associated prescriptions are much more complex, a significant result of this policy mix has been a reduced role for the state in development (Kydd and Dorward, 2001). It is perhaps this encouraging result that has paved the way for Rural Transformation rather than Rural Development.

Poverty eradication and ameliorating the conditions of rural people have been the major concern of many national and international agencies. Although these activities are not of recent origin but the initial nomenclature was different. Initially, in post-independent India—it began as rural development with an emphasis on social and economic welfare. Over the years many programmes of rural development were initiated but the success rate was very modest. More and more rural people became dependent upon the governmental programmes and thus the burden started increasing. Between 70s and 80s many programmes of rural developments were initiated but the failure to reach the goods to the poverty stricken people still remained. The gap between practice and pronouncement widened because of the faulty implementation strategies. Notwithstanding the official ideologies and defence to uphold the success of the programmes it was implicitly realized by the government officials that a rethinking is required towards rural development; and thus the idea of rural transformation surfaced. An argument may be forwarded to support this idea *i.e.*, rather than making people dependent on the governmental policies, it would be better to make them self-reliant and hence, the concept of rural transformation. This idea has an implicit assumption, i.e. it is possible to create a situation through some means (and in this case education) which will give rise to some generic skills in the individuals that will enable them to lead a full and productive life as an individual, as a member in the family and society. Thus this assumption has necessitated the idea of education for rural transformation. Rural transformation would mean:

- Pro-poor and non-discriminatory policy framework for promoting sustainable environment.
- Focusing on poverty reduction.
- Recognizing the potential of indigenous knowledge.
- Promoting the use of participatory approaches.
- Emphasizing community involvement.
- Adopting a holistic view of the development of rural space.
- Preparing rural people for off-farm employment by building knowledge and skills capacity.
- Understanding the complementality of urban-rural linkages.

Emerging Issues and Challenges for ERT

Rural Transformation through education is already initiated by the Government of India through various policies and programmes, such as Bharat Nirman, a project set about by the Government of India in collaboration with the State Governments and the Panchayati Raj Institutions towards the improvement of the rural sector. The National Rural Employment Guarantee Act, 2005 was another significant step for improving the living conditions and its sustenance in the rural sector of India. Data regarding employment growth in rural India indicate an overall satisfactory picture compared to total population. But when compared to growth rate in urban areas, the situation is far from satisfactory (See Table 1.2). Similarly, data pertaining to unemployment situation reveal that in rural areas approximately 12 to 15 per cent males and females are unemployed (See Figure 1.1). Although unemployment is very high among urban population, it is significant to note here that the type and quality of employment determines a great deal with regard to the economic status of people. In this regard rural people lag behind compared to their urban counterparts. Together these two facts drive home a point that much needs to be done to improve the economic status of rural people.

Table 1.2: Compound Annual Growth Rate (%) of Employment [Usual Principal and Subsidiary Status (UPSS)]

Employment Growth	*1993-94*	*1999-2000*	*2004-05*
Rural			
Male	1.93	0.80	2.20
Female	1.37	0.03	3.61
Persons	1.73	0.51	2.70
Urban			
Male	3.23	2.86	3.28
Female	3.78	1.50	5.41
Persons	3.34	2.58	3.71
Total			
Male	2.25	1.35	2.51
Female	1.67	0.19	3.90
Persons	2.06	0.98	2.95

Source: NSSO Employment and Unemployment Survey Reports.

In the field of education, Sarva Shiksha Abhiyan (SSA) as a national initiation of 'Education for All' has been addressing the contextual issues of primary education. Some significant achievements in the context of SSA are:

(a) Increase the number of schools from 8,53,601 in 2002-03

to 12,50,775 schools in 2007-08 (of the total schools, about 87.39 per cent schools are located in rural areas).

(b) The distribution of schools by type of building shows that 71.73 per cent primary schools have *pucca* (permanent) building as compared to 7.50 per cent having partially *pucca* and another 3.51 per cent having *kuchcha* (temporary) building.

(c) Student-classroom ratio has shown improvement on an average. About 37 students are sitting in one classroom in primary schools.

(d) The percentage of boys and girls enrolment in rural areas primary and upper primary classes (I-VIII) in 2007-08 were 52.07 and 47.93 respectively as compared to the overall enrolment of 52.12 and 47.88 for boys and girls.

(*Source*: Elementary Education in India—NUEPA, 2010.)

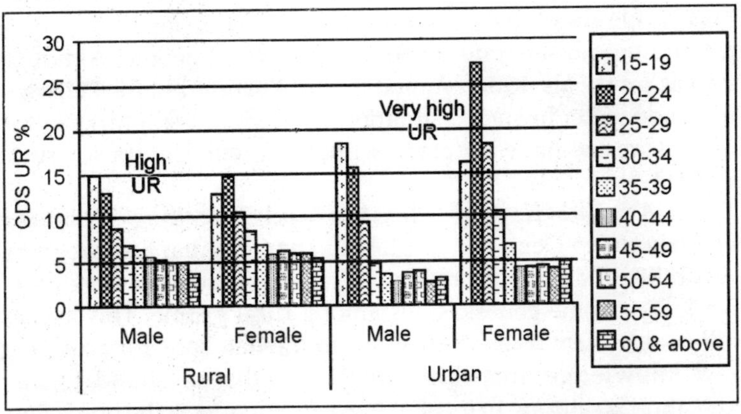

Source: NSSO Employment and Unemployment Survey Report.

Fig. 1.1: Unemployment Rates (UR) per cent among Males and Females in Rural and Urban Areas across Age Groups, 2004-05—Current Daily Status (CDS) Basis

But the national and international data on education in rural India still seems to be far from the satisfactory level. Some of the prominent emerging issues and challenges in this regard have been outlined below:

1. ***Contextualizing Education***: While attempting to do so, critical decisions have to be taken regarding the modalities. It is recognized

recognized that separate systems for education in rural areas or separate sets of policies for education in rural areas would undermine rural transformation. In the past, for the development of tribal people in India the policy of isolation and assimilation were followed. However, both the policies did not yield the desired result. Thus they were abandoned in favour of integration, because integration permits the various tribal groups to retain their separate identity by developing creative adjustments through which they become one and yet remain distinct (Panigrahi, 1993).

Accepting the fact that bringing rural people through integration into the mainstream Indian population would be a viable idea, what is required for their educational development is to have diversified curricula. In this direction, there exists a variety of curriculum managed by State, Central, International General Secondary Education (IGSE), Indian Certificate of Secondary Education (ICSE) and International Boards. Together all these boards cater to the needs of different segments of the population. It is also observed that special schools are set up for tribal people in India but no separate school exist for rural people. Although schools for tribals do accommodate rural people but their share is too inadequate. In such a situation the question still lurks in the mind: Can we have separate school and curriculum for rural people?

2. ***Availability of Flexible and Life-long Learning Opportunities***: Demands of globalization and the leap-frogging possibility of digital technology have necessitated the urgency of inculcating some generic skills among rural people. This in turn will enable them to learn to adapt to the demands for acquiring new knowledge and skills. While on the one hand formal education is catering to most of these requirements the one is now more on non-formal means. A variety of non-formal educational opportunities are available to cater to the needs of different types of clientele. The *Balwadies/Anganwadies* (Early Childhood Education Centres) acts as feeder and support programme for primary education. Primarily, these centres cater to the age-group 6-14, but children in the age-group 14+ are also enrolled. According to Fifth All India Education Survey (1978-86), out of 5,79,148 villages 93,763 (16.19%) villages had provision for non-formal education either at primary level or at the upper primary level or both. Out of these, 11,968 (2.07%) villages had NFE Centres for

girls. Further, 90, 988 (97.04%) villages with NFE Centres were catering to the primary level whereas only 6,079 (6.48%) villages with NFE Centres were catering to the upper primary level (See Table 1.3).

Table 1.3: Non-Formal Education Centres in Various Population Slabs in Rural Areas

Population Slab	*Total No. of Villages*	*No. of Villages with NFE Centres*			
		Total	*Primary Level*	*Upper-Primary Level*	*Separate Centres for Girls*
2000 and above	65257	20730	20171	1520	3598
1000-1999	105527	25606	24721	1991	3448
500-999	145515	23021	22272	1503	2658
Below 500	262849	24406	23824	1065	2264
Total	**579148**	**93763**	**90988**	**6079**	**11968**

With regard to the enrolment at the NFE Centres official statistics reveal that in the age-group 6-14 and 14+, 31,88,582 students were benefiting from 93,763 NFE Centres in rural areas. (*Source*: http://www.education.nic.in/cd50years/g'z/H7/oz/70BO/htm)

Besides these, the other non-formal mode is National Institute of Open Schooling (NIOS). It provides education inexpensively to remote areas. It enrolls about 350,000 students annually which makes it the largest open schooling system in the world. NIOS offers Open Basic Education Programme, which includes OBE 'A', 'B' and 'C' level course equivalent to class III, V and VIII respectively, secondary course equivalent to class X, senior secondary course equivalent to class XII, vocational courses and life enrichment programmes.

Depending upon the imperatives of a globalized world how far the formal and non-formal modes of learning will respond remains a major challenge for people in general and rural people in particular. Indeed, in the context of ERT whether these modes have adequate scope provide the much needed generic skills? If yes, how can they be? If not, what needs to be done?

3. ***Access and Equity***: Access to Education opportunities is a precondition to realize the Right to Education Act. A number of

problems surround the concept of access and equity in India. To mention a few, there is absence of schools in remote rural areas or schools located too far from home in dispersed habitats and difficult terrain (The 2007-08 DISE data reveals that 82 per cent of habitations have a primary school within a radius of one kilometres, there is an upper primary school within 3 kilometres for 75 per cent of habitations and 11.04 percentage of single teacher schools), attracting and retaining qualified teachers in rural areas (DISE, 2007-08 data reveals that there are about 5,84,000 para-teachers, constituting 10.48 per cent of the total number of teachers. About 68,186 schools out of 1,25,075 have para-teachers), rampant child labour (Although over the years, incidence of child labour in the country has declined from around 5 per cent in 1993-94 to approximately 3 per cent in 2004-05, the total magnitude of child labour is estimated to be approximately 10 million), a sense of uncertainty about the benefits of schooling [An NGO Pratham (2009) has pointed out that in class I-II, the percentage of children who can read letters, can recognize 1-9 numbers, can read English letters are 78.5, 78.7 and 54.6 respectively. Similarly, in class III-IV, the percentage of children who can read standard I text, can do subtraction, can read English sentences are 64.2, 56.3 and 16.7 respectively], and so on. Addressing these problems simultaneously is a herculean task and the problems get compounded by increasing spatial population. The crucial questions that we confront are: What should be our approach? Should it be only access or equity or both?

Although these problems mentioned above are not rural specific but nevertheless, they are very problematic in rural areas. A large number of initiatives like special schools for tribals, Eklavya schools, Sarva Siksha Abhiyan have been taken by the Governments; addressing these problems simultaneously is a herculean task and the problems get compounded by increasing spatial population. The crucial questions, therefore, we confront are: What should be our approach? Should it be only access or equity or both?

4. ***Multiple Layers of Discrimination***: Large scale disparity exists among different segments of population, especially between the main stream and various excluded groups characterized by high incidence of poverty and distinctive ethnic and cultural identity. The excluded groups are often disproportionately represented in rural populations. Gender discrimination introduces another dimension of disparity that cut across other forms of discrimination.

Whether the education and training that we envisage supercede the long standing traditions and prejudices existing in the rural life? How can Equity and Equality of opportunities be realized by surpassing the multiple layers of discrimination?

5. ***Quality of Teachers and Students Learning***: Availability of teachers, their qualifications and pupil-teacher ratio are important variables in determining quality education. Data pertaining to these variables indicate that in 2007-08, about 5.63 million (against 5.22 millions in 2006-07) teachers were engaged in teaching in 1.25 million schools. About 87.39 per cent teachers were located in rural areas in 87.34 per cent of schools in 2007-08. With regard to female teachers in primary schools, the data show that between 2004-05 and 2007-08, the percentage of female teachers had increased from 38.06 to 42.30. Although the rural-urban bifurcation clearly shows a vast difference 2004-05 (32.77), 2007-08 (37.73) in rural and 2004-05 (68.21), 2007-08 (69.63) in urban, the increase in female teachers is marginal.

Regarding pupil-teacher ratio, in 2007-08 it was 33:1 for all schools and 37:1 for primary as against 37:1 and 34:1 respectively in 2006-07, thus there a slight decrease in the ratio. It may also be mentioned here that out 624 districts in all the 35 states, 151 districts had above 40 pupil-teacher ratio.

Data pertaining to academic qualification of all categories of regular teachers reveal that during 2007-08, a significantly low percentage (2.58) of teachers have qualification below secondary level and a large percentage of teachers (43.54) have qualification up to higher secondary level. With regard to male and female teachers, the proportion is very similar 42.82 and 44.51 respectively. The same is with the rural teachers also. (*See* Table 1.4)

Table 1.4: Academic Qualification of All Categories of Regular Teachers: 2007-08

Qualification	*All Areas*			*Rural Areas*			*Urban Areas*		
	Male	*Female*	*Total*	*Male*	*Female*	*Total*	*Male*	*Female*	*Total*
Below Secondary	2.56	2.61	2.58	2.57	2.74	2.63	2.52	2.39	2.44
Secondary	16.11	17.75	16.81	16.72	18.84	17.47	12.39	15.79	14.61
Higher Secondary	24.15	24.15	24.15	25.40	27.89	26.29	16.55	17.42	17.12
Up to Higher Secondary 2007-08	**42.82**	**44.51**	**43.54**	**44.69**	**49.47**	**46.39**	**31.46**	**35.60**	**34.17**
Up to Higher Secondary 2006-07	44.27	45.32	44.71	46.28	50.39	47.71	32.10	36.55	34.99

Turning on to students learning, it can be observed that at the end of primary (classes IV/V), 95 per cent of students have passed in all areas with all types of management whereas the upper primary (Classes VII/VIII) result shows a minor variation between all types of management schools and Government managed schools—89.05 and 86.74 per cent respectively. Significantly, girls have done excellent in all types of schools (See Table 1.5).

Official data related to quality of teachers and students learning reveal an encouraging trend so far as rural education is concerned. Notwithstanding the official figures, it is still a reality that multi-grade teaching exists in rural areas (though a small percentage) lack of willingness among teachers and inadequate remuneration for working in a such an environment have pushed the education in rural areas a very insignificant and unrecognized level. Consequently, rural children are deprived of learner-centred pedagogy that promotes active learning methods, encourage critical thinking and inspires self-learning. What incentives can really attract both teachers and students to educational setting where teachers can act as facilitator and learner can act as knowledge constructor? Does this situation warrants specialized teacher preparation programme for rural areas? How far a unified curriculum for the country as whole can really address the diversified learning needs of rural people?

6. ***Strategic Management System***: It is observed that management is the key for success of any developmental programme. Strategic management provides overall direction to the programmes and policies by having "strategic alignment" between the Government and Society. Strategic management entails allocating the right amount of resources to the different areas so that those assigned to particular goals have what they need to meet their objectives. This ranges from providing the right supplies to enacting systems by which people receive the necessary training, all work processes are tested, and all informations and data generated are documented. Does strategic management revamp the rural systems and develop? Whether the alignment between the centre, state and local government develop the synergy for rural transformation? What managerial skills and competencies are required to instill strategic management system?

7. ***Civil Society Participation***: Community participation for rural management is essential for realizing the mission of rural

Table 1.5: Area-wise and Type of the School-wise Examination Results for the Year 2006-07

	Primary (Classes IV/V)						*Upper Primary (Classes VII/VIII)*					
	Boys Passed	*Boys Passed with 60% and Above*	*Girls Passed*	*Girls Passed with 60% and Above*	*Total Passed*	*Total Passed with 60% and Above*	*Boys Passed*	*Boys Passed with 60% and Above*	*Girls Passed*	*Girls Passed with 60% and Above*	*Total Passed*	*Total Passed with 60% and Above*
All Management	95.38	48.67	95.44	48.80	95.41	48.73	88.79	43.02	89.34	44.05	89.05	43.50
Government Management	95.04	44.57	95.06	44.94	95.05	44.75	86.50	38.95	86.99	40.67	86.74	39.78
Private Management	96.29	59.69	96.69	61.49	96.47	60.48	92.48	49.11	93.71	49.88	93.02	49.45

transformation. Enhancing community participation for ownership and accountability is a great challenge, especially in rural areas. In the recent times under the decentralized management of education, managerial structures have been evolved and it has been observed that the impact is not satisfactory. A concerted effort is needed to motivate the rural people by transferring certain powers and responsibilities that enable them to plan, execute and monitor the developmental programmes. How can the local political powers be tapped to strengthen community participation? What are the roles of corporate and educational institutions in empowering rural population? How to strengthen the VECs and local self help groups for monitoring development in their areas?

Need for Paradigm Shift in Education for Rural Transformation

Education has been recognized as a potential agent for social change and development and therefore, several interventions in this direction at the national and international levels have been planned and executed. For the past several decades, the dominant "education and development" paradigm has assumed a more or less direct and linear link between identifying overall rural development goals, selecting appropriate educational and training modalities, extending these to the rural sector through some planned mechanism through formal and non-formal institutions, and, finally, studying the impact on the lives of the rural people. This model is embedded in a notion that the governments both Centre and the State, provide the core from which any change to the periphery will take place. Educational institutions in the central places are seen as essential and primary elements to begin to bring knowledge and information to the periphery. This bringing of knowledge to less central regions has typically been attempted through some form of "extension". During 60s and 70s in India, several centres of Extension Education were established in the universities and other institutions of higher learning in order to address the educational needs of rural people. However, these assumptions make it difficult for any serious discussion as to how such an approach and peripheral knowledge bases can impact the life styles of rural people. Therefore, it has been increasingly realized that there is a need for paradigm shift in Education by understanding rural issues and challenges in a different framework and evolve different strategies that suit the local needs and demands. Education should be seen as a mechanism through which transformation can be made possible in rural sectors. To transform means to change in form, appearance or structure. Transformation in the context of rural people occurs first in individuals, and then, in the society. Transformation is the creation and change of a whole new form, function or structure. To transform is to create something new that has never existed before and could not be predicted from the past knowledge. Transformation is a "change" in mindset. It is based on learning a system of profound knowledge and taking actions based on reflections on that knowledge and leading to the generation of new knowledge and courage for action (Marcia Daszko and Sheila Sheinberg, 2005).

The approach for transformation through knowledge would include the systematic study of the nature of the social phenomenon, the notion that social transformation is linked—through knowledge—to a variety of "structured ideas" that are national and international in scope. More specifically, this knowledge is circulated through a complex network of communications that are not limited to the centre-periphery linkage system. The knowledge-transformation channels are characterized by the fact that they are highly diversified and differentiated. Finally, knowledge acquires its "transformed" nature due to the forward and backward linkages related to the utilization and adoption process—a process that takes place in a complex social, economic, cultural, and political context (John Hawkins, 1988).

Education for Rural Transformation means that a desired changes in individuals through knowledge and skills by continual questioning, challenging, exploration, discovery, evaluation, testing the social phenomenon. In transformation, there is no known destination, and the journey has never been travelled before. It embraces new learning and taking actions based on the new discoveries.

ACT: A Process Strategy for ERT

Education for rural transformation begins with individuals and their ideas and actions for life and living. It is an approach that requires certain essential pre-conditions. They are:

1. *Awareness and Awakening*: Information accessibility to rural people from all the sources can make them aware of the opportunities and prospects around them. Thereby they can reach to the state of awakening in order to grab those opportunities. Awareness and awakening help in deriving intentions and intentions provide constancy of purpose and create vision. Intention is the conscious choosing of a course of action.
2. *Competency*: In order to actualize the available opportunities, the required competencies are to be sought after by the people from the various means through which they are made available to them. Thus individuals equip themselves with necessary skills and competencies that enable their actions successful in realizing the vision. Here the input of training and development comes in. Providing lifelong relevant learning experiences based on rural needs and aspirations would enhance the competencies of people at large. Establishing institutions with high capacity which can identify the rural needs and scaffold programmes by tapping the local resources and talents. Honing the local talents for the productive utilization would certainly lead to transformation.
3. *Tenacity*: It is the quality of being determined to do or achieve something; firmness of purpose; "determination showed in every movement"; it begins with a purpose and then strong will to achieve it in dedication and determination. Tenacious people commit to three things. First, they take personal responsibility for their success. They know that they are responsible for their own life and career success. They are willing to do the things necessary to succeed. Second', tenacious people set high goals—and then do whatever it takes to achieve them. Third, tenacious people know that stuff happens as they go through life. They realize they will encounter many problems and setbacks. Tenacious people choose to react positively to the negative stuff that happens and move forward towards their goals.

Education for rural transformation becomes realistic when the above essential attributes can be imbibed in the rural people.

Framework for Action: A Thematic Model

The authors of this paper are of the opinion that no single strategy can work better in rural setting.

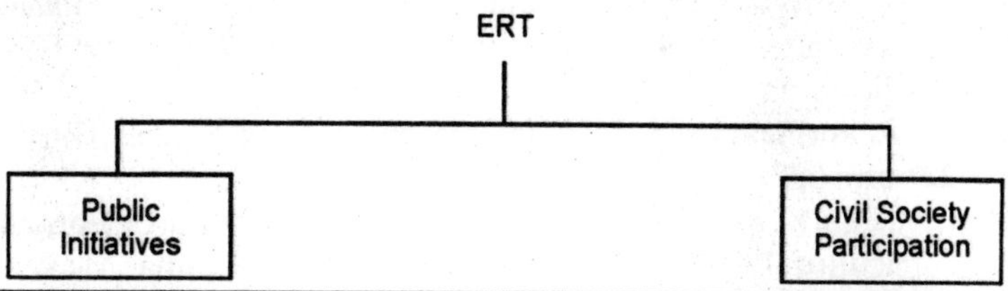

Public Initiatives	Civil Society Participation
Socially responsive and inclusive Policies and Programmes	Policy Implementation
Legal Framework and Protection of Human Dignity	Monitoring Growth and Impact
Institutional Capacity Building	Local Wisdom

The core of the rural transformation agenda is defined by the following major imperatives:

- Managing the complex and sensitive issue of rural-urban migration.
- Securing universal access by rural populations to basic public services including education, health, housing, fresh water, electricity, transport and communications, with improving quality standards.
- Creating systems that balance objectives of social equity, economic growth and environmental sustainability, and that can evolve rapidly as many young and better-educated people join new non-farm rural jobs or emigrate out of rural areas.
- Emerging innovation, research and development focused on the needs of rural people and rural producers and firms, and making much better use of the opportunities offered by the ICT revolution.

REFERENCES

Chaudhuri, S., and Ravallion, M. (2006). *Partially Awakened Giants: Uneven Growth in China and India,* World Bank, Development Research Group, Poverty Team.

Cohen, A. (1985). *The Symbolic Construction of Community*. Tavistock, London.

Desai, A. (2005). *Rural India in Transition,* Popular Prakashan.

Epstein, T.S., Suryanarayana, A., and Thimmegowda, T. (1998). *Village Voices: Forty Years of Rural Transformation in South India.* Sage Publications.

Flysand, A. and Jakobsen, S.E. (2007) *Journal of Rural Studies* 23, 206-221 and 207.

Gulati, A., Fan, S., and Dalafi, S. (2005). The Dragon and the Elephant: Agricultural and Rural Reforms in China and India. *Markets, Trade, and Institutions Division Discussion Paper, 87.*

Harper, S. (1989). The British rural and community: An overview of perspectives. *Journal of Rural Studies,* 5, 161-184.

Hawkins, J.N. (1988). The Transformation of Education for Rural Development in China. *Comparative Education Review,* 32(3), 266-281.

INRULED (International Research and Training Centre for Rural Education). (2001). *Education For Rural Transformation: Toward A Policy Framework.* UNESCO, Baoding, Zhengzhou, China.

INRULED (International Research and Training Centre for Rural Education). (2007). *Comparative Study on Diversified Learning Needs and Lifelong Learning in Rural Settings in Asia-Pacific Region.* UNESCO, Baoding, Zhengzhou, China. http://www.inruled.org/Templates/PDF/Comparative%20Report%20on%20Diversified%20Learning%20Needs.pdf

Liepins, R. (2000). New energies for an old idea: reworking approaches to 'community' in contemporary rural studies. *Journal of Rural Studies, 16*(1), 23-35.

Manniche, P., and Kjær, J. (1978). *Rural development in Denmark and the changing countries of the world: A study of Danish rural conditions and the folk high school with special relevance to the developing countries* (2., rev. and abbr. ed.). Copenhagen.

Marsden, T. (1995). Beyond agriculture: regulating the new rural spaces. *Journal of Rural Studies, 11,* 285-297.

Mehta, A.C. (2010). *Elementary Education in India—Analytical Tables 2007-08.* New Delhi: NUEPA.

Mehta, A.C. (2010). *Elementary Education in India—Analytical Report 2007-08*. New Delhi: NUEPA.

Ministry of Labour and Employment (2010). *Annual Report to The People in Employment*. New Delhi: Government of India.

Ministry of Rural Development (2009). *Report of the Expert Group to Advise the Ministry of Rural Development on the Methodology for Conducting the Below Poverty Line (BPL) Census for Eleventh Five Year Plan*. New Delhi: Government of India.

NCERT (2005). *National Curriculum Framework 2005*. New Delhi: NCERT.

Nyberg, A., and Rozelle, S. (1999). *Accelerating China's Rural Transformation*, World Bank Publications.

Oliver, L.P. (1992). Study Circles: Individual Growth through Collaborative Learning. *New Directions for Adult and Continuing Education, 53*, 85-97.

Panigrahi, S.C. (1993). A Study of Educational Development of Tribals in the Kalahandi District of Orissa. An Unpublished Ph.D. Thesis. CASE, The M.S. University of Baroda.

Shah, R. (2010). Primary Education: Gujarat cuts Sorry Figure. Ahmedabad (ed): *Times of India*. October 6th.

Suparman, M.R. (1983). *The rural co-operational education—a folk high school idea for Indonesia*. Linköping: FBA, University of Linköping.

Taylor, J.E., Rozelle, S., and de Brauw, A. (2003). Migration and Incomes in Source Communities: A New Economics of Migration Perspective from China. *Economic Development and Cultural Change, 52*(1), 75-101.

UNESCO (2001). Education for Rural Transformation Towards a Policy Framework, INRULED, Booding, China.

http://www.education.nic.in/cd50years/g/z/H7/OZH70B01.htm

2

Tribal Education as a Tool for Rural Transformation

A Case Study of Paniyas in Wayanad

Raju Narayana Swamy

Introduction

The "Kerala Model Development" has been the hypothesis of development that took shape in Kerala during the first three decades following the formation of the State. The characteristic feature of this model was the priority given to democratic culture in development. But the internationally acclaimed "Kerala Model" came under sharp criticism as it began to rust in the late eighties. The criticism was rooted in the perception that the model had outlived its purpose. It was criticized for its failure to produce enough wealth to satisfy the growing demands of a consumerist society. It was apprehended that the model would not even help to produce enough wealth and employment to sustain levels of living standards already achieved.

The results of Kerala Model of development are highlighted in the following indicators: a generally high literacy rate, a low population growth rate and high life expectancy and greater accessibility to essential services like health, water, electricity, public distribution system, roads, etc. These indicators are important because these are attributes available to, experienced by, a large section of population to show up significantly when measured on a spatial or per capita basis. The "Kerala Model" has in fact laid the foundations for the development of a new model based on knowledge-intensive industries and services and modernization of traditional agriculture and cottage industries. In the new "Kerala Model" education is the key of development. The state lays claim to the highest literacy rate in the country—90.92 per cent in 2001 as compared to the national rate of 65.38 per cent. However, the quality of education still needs to be improved. It is in this context that we are analysing the impact of the new model on the education of *adivasis* in Kerala.

The Scheduled Tribes constitute the most backward group among the weaker sections in Kerala. The social reality of the *Adivasis* in post-colonial Kerala is characterized by poverty, malnutrition, illiteracy, socio-economic and sexual exploitation by settlers and the depletion of their traditional resource base (C.P. Balan Vaidyar, 1997). The Scheduled Tribes lag behind the 'others' of Kerala Model of Development in their basic achievements like education and health, which has played a central role in Kerala's development process (Human Development Report, 2005, 2006). A review of literacy rates among ST population in comparison with that of the general population indicates a growing gap between literacy rates of these communities. In the recent past tribal education has achieved considerable progress in terms of primary education enrolment. But further analysis suggests that progress is lacking in terms of quality and in effecting the desired transformation. The following section will discuss about this in detail.

Statistical Profile of *Adivasis*

The Scheduled Tribe population is 3,64,189 (2001 Census), which is nearly 1.1 per cent of the state population. The highest percentage of ST is in Wayanad District forming 17.43 per cent of total population in 2001 census. The coastal district of Alappuzha has the lowest percentage (0.15%). More than 37 per cent of the ST is concentrated in Wayanad district, another 14 per cent is in Idukki. Thus more than 50 per cent of the total population of ST in the state is concentrated in the hilly districts of Wayanad and Idukki. There are 10 districts, viz. Kannur, Kozhikode, Malappuram, Thrissur, Ernakulam, Kottayam, Alappuzha, Pathanamthitta, Kollam and Thiruvananthapuram having proportion of ST to total population less than the state proportion of 1.14 per cent showing that southern districts have lower proportion of ST population. The 4 districts having proportion higher than the state average are Kasargode, Wayanad, Palakkad and Idukki. Kasargod and Palakkad together constitute more than 19 per cent of the ST in the state. The primitive tribes as recognized by the Government of Kerala are in the pre-agricultural stage of development with very low literacy rates. They together constitute nearly 4.8 per cent of the total Scheduled Tribe population in the State.

Literacy Status of *Adivasis*

At present the education sector as a whole in the state is characterised by the existence of a dual system: one segment comprising high quality institutions catering to the affluent 5 per cent of the population and the second consisting of low quality institutions meant for the masses. The state has never made any attempt at equitable distribution of quality higher education, the access to which is virtually barred to children of marginalized groups like SC/ST (Abdul Salim, 2008).

A review of literacy rates among ST population in comparison with that of the general population indicates a growing gap between literacy rates of these communities (Kerala Development Report, 2008). Our examination of recent trends in educational attainment of tribes and the trends in enrolment/drop-out for the children are empty by absence of relevant statistical data. The main sources which have been utilized are the Census, Statistical Publications of Tribal Department, the NSSO etc. We have also drawn upon active studies. It is found that the literacy rates of the tribes are far behind those of the other sections of populations. The literacy rate of the Scheduled Tribes population in the State is as follows:

Table 2.1: Literacy Rates—STs *vs.* All Castes

(in percentage)

Category	*1971*	*1981*	*1991*
General	60.42	70.42	89.81
Scheduled Castes	4.21	55.96	79.66
Scheduled Tribes	25.72	31.79	57.22

Source: Census of India, Series-10, Kerala. Paper-3 of 1971, 1981, 1991 Final Population Totals.

Even though a significant increase had occurred among the Scheduled Tribes a wide gap still exists between the literacy rate among STs and general population. Districtwise literacy rate in Kerala among ST shows that Kottayam has the highest tribal literacy and Palakkad has the lowest. A detailed literacy rate districtwise is given in Table 2.2.

Table 2.2: District-wise Tribal Literacy Rates

District	*1971*	*1981*	*1991*
Thiruvananthapuram	42.17	58.06	74.00
Kollam	32.59	50.30	62.42
Pathanamthitta	—	—	73.21
Alappuzha	60.23	53.71	74.48
Kottayam	38.44	73.63	88.69
Idukki	45.12	52.60	76.96
Ernakulam	—	43.35	62.78
Thrissur	25.06	29.90	51.40
Palakkad	7.13	12.04	34.87
Malappuram	13.67	16.33	43.93
Kozhikode	23.24	14.24	52.36
Wayanad	—	43.24	50.63
Kannur	25.52	33.18	58.61
Kasargod	—	—	66.38
Kerala	25.52	31.79	57.22

Source: Census of India, Series-10, Kerala, Paper-3 of 1971, 1981, and 1991, Final Population Totals.

About two-third of the districts in Malabar region have literacy rates lower than the state average. Malabar region has a tribal population of more than sixty-five per cent. The level of education among the ST and that of general population is discussed now.

Table 2.3: Level of Education among ST and other Social Groups

As on 1999-2000 (Rural)

Level of Education	*ST*	*SC*	*OBC*	*Others*
Illiterate	26.36	23.60	17.36	11.67
Literate without formal schooling	0.33	1.80	0.93	0.86
Below Primary	16.12	17.05	18.31	12.30
Primary	12.50	20.99	19.76	14.93
Middle	26.32	25.67	27.52	26.00
Secondary	8.22	7.49	10.72	19.50
Higher Secondary	5.26	1.67	3.20	7.44
Graduation above	4.90	1.73	3.20	7.30

Source: Human Development Report, 2005-2006, State Planning Board, Government of Kerala, p. 66.

From Table 2.3 it could be analysed that over a quarter of the ST population was illiterate compared to just a little over 10 per cent for others. However, it is at the higher levels that the differences are more striking, especially from 'secondary' level onwards. Hence, the deprived groups lag behind the 'others' in these basic functioning achievements, which has played a central role in Kerala's development process. Disparities in the literacy rate levels between STs and total literacy rate are continuing in spite of various educational concessions extended to Scheduled Tribes. There are three specific reasons for this, low enrolment ratio of Scheduled Tribes children at the school level, high drop out ratio of Scheduled Tribes as compared to non-Scheduled Tribes and poor economic conditions. The following sections will discuss these three factors in detail.

Economic Conditions

The backwardness and the poor living conditions of the Scheduled Tribe population are major concerns. Most of the tribal people have a low economic profile and lead a miserable life. The *adivasis* constitute 3 per cent of the total BPL population while their proportion to total population is only 1.14 per cent (*Economic Review*, 2009). It implies that the incidence of poverty among the Scheduled Tribes is about three times that of the total population of the state. The study of C. Krishnan points out that the major factor accounting for low educational achievements and low aspirations on the part of tribefolk in Wayanad (One of the 14 districts in Kerala) is their poor social and economic condition. They live in unhealthy environment, do low-paid physical labour, and own very little land (Krishnan, C., 1999).

Education and Enrolment

The percentage of Scheduled Tribe students in total enrolment also went up only marginally from 1.15 per cent in 2001-02 to 1.23 per cent in 2003-04. But the absolute number of Scheduled Tribe students enrolled went up from 58859 in 2001-02 to 60339 in 2003-04. Also the vast majority of these students are in government schools and government-aided schools. In 2004, 42.08 per cent of the SC/ST students were enrolled in government schools, 56.39

per cent in government-aided schools and 1.53 per cent in private unaided schools (Anjana, Alex, 2005). The proportions of Scheduled Tribe students in Lower Primary and Upper Primary schools during 2008-09 are relatively higher than their population percentage. In High School section the percentage of Scheduled Tribe students is little less than their population percentage.

Table 2.4: Enrolment of ST students at School Levels

(As on 1.10.2008)

Section	*Total*	*ST*	*Percentage to Total*
LP	1665993	33781	2.03
UP	1452540	24449	1.68
HS	1427293	15882	1.11
Total	4545826	74112	1.63

Source: Directorate of Public Instruction (2009), Government of Kerala, Thiruvananthapuram.

Also the proportion of enrolment of SC/ST students has been higher in general education than in professional education. In the professional stream at the post-graduation level, their proportion is nearly one-half of their corresponding shares at the degree level. The proportion of Scheduled Tribes enrolment in professional courses at the postgraduate level is almost half of that in the corresponding courses at the degree level (Abdul Salim, 2008).

Drop-out Rate

Among the Indian states Kerala has achieved the distinction of the state having the lowest dropout rate among school students. In the year 2006-07 drop-out ratio among school students in Kerala was 0.81 per cent. The drop-out rate in Lower Primary Section, Upper Primary Section and High School Section were 0.59 per cent, 0.52 per cent and 1.38 per cent respectively. Among the Districts, Wayanad has the highest drop-out ratio in the Lower Primary Section (1.89 %), Upper Primary Section (1.92%) and High School Section (2.56%). Drop-out ratio among Scheduled Tribe students is 4.18 per cent.

According to the report of SC/ST Development Department, the state never made any attempt at equitable distribution of quality higher education, the access to which is virtually barred to the children of the marginalized groups like Scheduled Tribes. The principles of equity and access are thought to be the concerns only of government-run and aided private institutions. Even here the SC/ST and other backward sections are unable to avail themselves fully of the facilities statutorily made available to them. Though the government has reserved 20 per cent (15% for SC and 5% for ST) of seats in the government aided Arts and Science Colleges in Kerala for SC/ST students, their annual quotas are seldom filled, not even as late as 2000 (Report on the Implementation of Safeguards and Development Programmes for SC/ST, 2000). In 2000 the share of SC/ST enrolment in Arts and Science Colleges was only 12.86 per cent. In a note prepared by the department in August 2000, it was pointed out that in the case of self-financing courses run by the University, the share of SC/ST students was marginal.

In all the Five Year Plans, priority was given to the educational development of Scheduled Tribes. The main reason for the very slow spread of education among STs is the peculiar nature of their dwelling. Majority of the STs are living in remote areas far away from educational institutions. Lack of sufficient educational institutions in tribal areas, poverty etc curtail effective educational development among STs. Moreover, the parents of the tribal children being generally illiterate, they neither attach much importance to education nor insist their children to attend classes regularly. The study of Sam Mohanlal highlights that the main reason for dropout is the total incompatibility between the students and the use of language in the textbooks, language used by the teachers in the school, and the contents of the text that are often not ecofriendly (Sam Mohanlal, 2001).

Role of Teachers

The representation of Scheduled Tribes in the cadre of teachers is very low. During 1997-98, out of 187088 teachers up to the High School level, there were 6642 (3.5%) belonging to SC and 354 (0.18%) belonging to ST. At the Primary, Middle and Secondary levels the representation of ST teachers was 0.1 per cent and 2.7 per cent and 0.18 per cent respectively. It is also seen that there is no inservice training for tribal teachers. The need for special training to understand the tribal traits for teachers in the tribal areas should be considered (Chapter X, 1998). The State Government should make efforts to fill up the prescribed percentage of reservation of 2 per cent for STs in the teaching profession.

State and Tribal Literacy Programmes

The government has been implementing several programmes for the educational improvement of the tribes for the past few decades. The levels of awareness and utilisation of these schemes are relatively low among the tribe-folk. In almost all the recent years, more than fifty per cent of the allotment under the State-level schemes of the Scheduled Tribes Development has been on education (Krishnan, C., 1991, p.44.). The total literacy campaign launched in 1991-92 did not fully succeed in incorporating tribes mainly because of non-easy accessibility to their settlements and dearth of qualified instructors to carry out the programme. A special project titled Tribal Literacy Project was launched for tribals once the total literacy campaign was over. This programme covered several programmes incidental to the cultural and socio-economic advancement of tribals. During 1995-96, the literacy programmes were transferred to the Panchayati Raj Institutions. The experience in Kerala shows that in spite of successful completion of the Total Literacy Campaign, a good number of literates and semi-literates relapsed into illiteracy mainly due to the lack of continuous and systematic follow up programmes (Environmental Literacy Programme: Evaluation Report, 2006).

Due to the gaps between and within education systems the current status of education prevailing is quantitatively inadequate, and qualitatively incompetent to address the education and training/skill needs of the *adivasi* population in Kerala. Internal inefficiency and lack of responsiveness of the societal requirements especially when it comes to the 'world of work', therefore, mean that the educational system has failed to benefit individuals who need to make a good living and to broaden their personalities with information and essential human qualities. Hence, the tribal youth should be equipped with necessary skills so as to enhance their contribution to the national economy and to increase their livelihood capacity. In addition to expansion of the formal education network, the non-formal and informal education networks need expansion to cover the greater rural population.

Tribal Education in Wayanad

The large influx of settlers during the first half of the 20th century transformed the socio-economic and cultural scenario of the district. The first school in Wayanad is the Upper Primary School in Mananthavady taluk established in the year 1869. By 1900 there were 6 schools in the region. After the formation of the present state of Kerala, 26 schools were begun in 1957 in several remote areas of Wayanad. In the process, the literacy rate among the *adivasis* of Wayanad has improved substantially. But still it has to go a long way to reach the height reached by the other sections of the populations in the district.

Table 2.5: Literacy in Wayanad District, 1991

Community	*Percentage*
General	82.73
SC	75.27
ST	50.63
Tribal literacy in Kerala	57.22

Source: Census of India, 1991, Series 12, Kerala.

The average number of students per school in Wayanad is 532 whereas in Kerala, it is 481. As majority of the ST lives in remote areas, the children find it extremely difficult to reach the schools. Paniyas are the single largest segment and they account for about 48 per cent of the habitats, 46 per cent of the families and 45 per cent of the population among major tribal communities in Wayanad. Adiyas form only 7 per cent of this population.

Table 2.6: Taluk-wise distribution of tribal communities

Taluk	*Adiyan*		*Paniyan*		*Kattunayakan*		*Kurichian*		*Kuruman*	
	H	*F*	*H*	*F*	*H*	*F*	*H*	*F*	*H*	*F*
Mananthavady	98	1344	257	2837	31	461	221	2089	24	340
Sulthan Bathery	1	16	291	3359	139	1790	2	28	234	3043
Vythiry	—	—	301	3118	31	372	101	930	52	501
Total	99	1360	849	9314	201	2631	324	3037	310	3884

H—No. of households, F—No. of families

Source: ITDP Survey, Wayanad, 1990.

Mananthavady taluk (taken for the study also) has a fair representation of all the five communities.

A General Profile of the Study Area

The field study was conducted among the *adivasis* in Wayanad, concentrating on a particular community, the Paniyas. The Paniya community of Mananthavady taluk constitutes the study. The total Paniya population in Wayanad is spread over in three taluks, of which Mananthavady has been purposefully selected for the study. This is located in the north-western part of Wayanad district. It touches the border of Coorg district in Karnataka. The total land area is 736.39 sq.kms. There are seven village panchayats in this block. The discussion in this chapter is only a part of the research work being done by the researcher in Wayanad. For the above study the researcher has concentrated on four hamlets selected from Mananthavady and Vellamunda panchayat of Mananthavady taluk. A total of hundred respondents from Paniya community are taken for the study by random sampling technique.

A Profile of the Hamlet under Study

Padachikunnu and Mandaikunnu Colony: These colonies belong to Mananthavady Panchayat, inhabited by members of Paniya community. The colonies belong to ward twelve with thirty six families in Padachikunnu and ten families in Mandaikunnu colony. The settlements are situated in close proximity to Mananthavady town, the nerve centre of Wayanad. Their accessibility to school, primary health centre, ration shop, post office, panchayat office and tribal office is within a radius of one kilometre. A few members of Padachikunnu colony have access to electricity. The colonies are situated on the fringes of agricultural land owned by non-tribes. Agricultural crops consist of mainly paddy, coffee and banana. The Paniya households of these colonies are working as agricultural labourers. They work in and around their colony or sometimes migrate to Coorg in Karnataka.

Mangalassery and Valaramkunnu colony are situated in Vellamunda panchayat. These two colonies are one kilometre apart. Mangalassery colony belongs to twentieth ward with thirty families and Valaramkunnu is in the nineteenth ward with thirty-

Table 2.7: Background Information of Paniya in percentage

Family size	*(No. of persons in one house)* *Up to 5 persons—62* *5-7 persons—32* *8-10 persons—6*
House construction	In %
Percentage with ST dept. provided houses	87
Percentage who built houses by themselves	13
Average No. of rooms	
1-3 rooms per household	84
Up to five rooms	16
More than five rooms	Nil
Electrification	Yes—13
No. of electric bulbs in the house	One—11%, two—2%, more than two—nil
Electrification	No—87%
Roof of house	Tiles—85% Thatched—3% Concrete—12%
Percentage of household possessing **radio/watch**	Yes—45% No—55%
Percentage of households with **bicycle**	Nil
Percentage of households with furniture	Bed—nil Table (for study purpose)—nil Chair (plastic)—72% Bench (small wooden stool)—89% Cupboard—nil Bookshelf—nil Almirah—3%
Fuel used in kitchen	LPG—nil Kerosine Stove—3% Fire wood—100%
Kitchen Utensils	Earthen vessels exclusively—nil Steel vessels exclusively—nil Earthen, Steel and Aluminium vessels—98% Crockery—nil Glass vessels (tumblers only)—35% Mixie—2%
Sanitation	Yes—14%, No—86%
Employment	Agricultural labourers—96% (men)/ 98% (women) Tribal promoters:— 4% (men) Anganavadi helpers—2% (women respondents)
Average working days of labour per month	Two weeks—91% Three weeks—9%
Whether participated in MGNREGP	Yes—93%, No—7%

Source: Survey Data.

two families. Being situated at a higher altitude reaching the colonies is very hard. The two hamlets are located at the extreme end of Banasura mountain ranges. The colonies are not provided with motorable roads. An *Anganavadi* (pre-primary school) is located near the Mangalassery colony while there is no provision for it near Valaramkunnu colony. The Paniya people living here depend on wage labour and also access forest products. Accessibility of tribal extension office, panchayat office, primary health centre, ration shop, telephone booths etc. are within a radius of four kilometres.

Broad Socio-Economic and Other Differentials

The most formidable problem, which is fairly common in demographic surveys relates to misreporting of age. Many household members have no exact record of the date of birth, and most of the reported ages are based on guesses and memory. Twenty-five men and twenty-five women respondents were selected for the study. Men respondents' age-wise reflects that respondents in a range of thirty to forty age formed sixty per cent, forty to fifty formed twenty per cent and in the age-group below twenty years formed twenty per cent. Distribution of women respondents' age-wise reflects that respondents in a range of twenty to thirty formed forty per cent and in a range of thirty to forty age-groups formed 26 per cent. The age-group of forty to fifty accounted for 15 per cent and fifty to sixty per cent formed 11 per cent. Up to twenty years age respondents formed 8 per cent. The availability of infrastructure facilities reflects the standard of development of any society. The infrastructure facilities which we are going to discuss here include settlement pattern, drinking water, sanitation, employment pattern, electricity, transportation facility, public distribution system, furniture, etc.

Education

Education is one of the most important prerequisites of human resource development. The Paniya communities by and large still are deprived of basic educational facilities. It was observed that three hamlets under study had *Anganavadies* (pre-primary schools) near to their hamlets. But the high school facility was not found in hamlets in Vellamunda panchayat. For the Paniyas in Vellamunda panchayat accessibility of high school is beyond their reach. The distance from the colonies to the schools is given in Table 2.8.

Table 2.8: Hamlet-wise distance to reach high school

Panchayat	*Hamlet*	*Distance to reach Lower Primary School (in kms)*	*Distance to reach Upper Primary School (in kms)*	*Distance to reach high school (in kms)*
Mananthavady	Mandaikunnu Colony	1.5	1.5	1.5
Mananthavady	Padachikunnu Colony	2.5	2.5	2.5
Vellamunda	Valaramkunnu Colony	3.5	3.5	6.5
Vellamunda	Mangalassery Colony	3	3	6

Source: Survey Data.

Drop-outs from Schools

Most of the Paniya parents prefer to stop their children's education in the mid-way itself. In the study we have found the Paniyas in Vellamunda panchayat are never even thinking of going to high school. They were even found not interested in sending their children to high school. 43 per cent of the respondents were illiterates and twenty three per cent had primary level of education. Thirty two per cent had high school education and two per cent had passed tenth standard. We failed to get a plus two passed respondent from any of the four colonies taken for the study. In the study it was also found that not a single woman had passed tenth standard. In fact female education is still lagging behind. It is so because every woman member in this backward community becomes an earning member and, therefore, lends their hand in any economic pursuit worth the name. In the Paniya community, as soon as the children attain the age of six or seven years, they participate in the income earning process and assist in some petty jobs like fetching water, collecting fuel wood, looking after infants at home etc. Boys will go for work as agricultural labourers. We have incorporated a slightly urbanized area also in our study. This we have done purposefully to understand whether urbanization has really helped these people in improving their educational attainment. Though in Mananthavady there is high school near the colony, we found no significant improvement in educational attainment among the respondents from this area. Hence, it could be concluded that distance to reach school is not the only reason for the low literacy attainment among the Paniyas. In Mananthavady most of the colony people had gone only up to seventh standard. Some of them had gone up to tenth standard. But while interacting with them, the quality of educational attainment was found to be very poor.

Since schooling of children in the tribal context is essentially a household decision, its variation should largely be the result of differences in awareness, responsiveness and motivations of the parents spaced out from the considerations relating to convenience of schooling. Most of the respondents gave vague replies as to the reasons for their dropping out of school. In the study it was found that sixty-two per cent of the respondents had no interest in studying while thirty eight per cent said they are interested in studying and financial crisis has restricted them form going to school. An interesting fact is that only thirty per cent of the respondents considered education as very important. Sixty per cent showed no interest, and in their opinion education is not at all significant. Seventy per cent of the respondents wanted their children to be sent to schools but the rest were found not interested in sending their children to schools. One important factor that hinders the development of education among tribal community is parental sluggishness. They give little importance to the education of their children. They do they insist on the regular attendance in classes by their children who happen to be enrolled. Ninety-two per cent of the respondents came with complaints on school facilities. They also complained about the partiality of teachers towards their children.

In the study we have also found that most of the tribal children's home environment is not conducive to education. Their dwellings lack facilities for study. Most of them have no electricity, no study room, no furniture, not even proper food (*see* Table 2.7). On an average, about 35 per cent of the tribal children in the district enrolled in standard I drop-out from schools before reaching standard VI whereas the corresponding dropout rate for non-tribal children was hardly five per cent (Krishnan, C., 1999).

Paniya Economy and Its Influence in Education

In the study we have found that the major factor accounting for low educational achievements and low aspirations on the part of Paniyas is their poor social and economic conditions. All the respondents were wage labourers. The total working days is limited to two weeks in one month (see Table 2.7). Of the 100 households taken for survey we have found that men in all the households are using liquor. Even we have found women taking liquor. Both men and women are taking betel leaves regularly. In the survey all the respondents said they are spending Rs. 20.00 per day for chewing. Children from the age of six or seven are even encouraged by the family members in taking pan. The youngsters are also using *hashish, ganja, pan, cigar,* etc. They are keen in spending their income for garments, cinema and liquor. Not a single household surveyed was found spending their income for buying books. None of them had gone to a library. Only the two tribal promoters incorporated in the study were found reading newspaper from Tribal Department Office. Non-enrolment in school is more due to poverty and general ignorance of the parents. Hence, the long-lasting solution to the educational backwardness of *adivasis* cannot be found without substantial improvement of their economic status. The following section will discuss on this.

Education for Rural Transformation

Education is essentially the process of awakening of the country's populace. Robert Chambers (1983), argued that 'putting the last first', was the only way to achieve rural development. Since then the acceptance of participation has become widespread. The rural poor live on the margins of subsistence—Illiterate, often malnourished, affected with serious health problems, sometimes stigmatised by ethnic prejudices, living often in remote, isolated areas and having limited access to productive resources. One out of five children in developing countries still does not attend primary school. A frontal assault on the citadels of situation is the need of the hour.

Herein lies the importance of rural transformation. The solutions to the problems of poverty and deprivation in rural areas do not lie in preventing urbanization. The inexorable forces of change have to be turned into positive development and enhancement of people's capacities to cope with change. A major development change is to manage a progressive transformation of rural areas, keeping in view the blurred boundary and the dynamic linkages between rural and urban areas. The said transformation no doubt seeks to convey a vision of poor active and positive process of change and development of rural communities in the context of national and global changes. Education in all forms as a means of equipping people which skills and enhancing their capacity is the heart and soul of agenda for such a rural transformation.

In the globalized world of twenty-first century, the dynamics of rural transformation has created a new educational imperative which go beyond traditional concerns. Increasing opportunities for post primary and secondary educations, alternative mechanisms for vocational and occupational skill development for changing rural needs, re-orienting tertiary education so as to serve the dynamic needs of rural development, and above all bridging the urban-rural digital divide and making better use of ICT for combating urban rural educational disparity is to be addressed in letter and spirit. In short, we should get out of the present scenario of resistance and self defeating neglect of the rural dimension in development, discourse and action. In spite of the overwhelming logic of numbers and intensity of problems the rural people represent (Eduction for Rural Transformation: Towards a policy framework, INRULED, September, 2001).

An approach to rural transformation in the context of Paniyas could be implemented by giving attention to the following matters:

(1) Tribal people in Kerala are now working mostly as unskilled labourers in the agricultural sector. They are not inactive, but they are also not incapable. For their survival they apply massive energy, potency and vitality on a daily basis. Education and skill development will enhance their ability to work better with much high return. But they have to be attuned to their needs.

(2) The present education provided by the government is not improving the quality of life of these people. It is neither helping in achieving the minimal economic growth nor resulting in significant decline in poverty. Education

though considered to be the major aspect related to economic growth and poverty elimination has so long been haunted by poor planning and functioning at the local level.

(3) In this context the issue which raises here is on how the education given to tribes could be reshaped to boost the proficiency of *adivasis,* which will promote the production structure and result in higher stage of their development. The workforce in rural areas will need to be highly skilled to quickly acclimatize to domestic requirements. In such a situation a redesigned general and technical education package will have to be offered before the adivasis in Kerala.

(4) The mission of having the *adivasis* out of poverty and putting them in control of their own lives is a composite concern. Provision of suitable education and skill development training in this situation would work as a means for it.

Education for Eradicating Poverty

Education should help to reduce poverty and provide better health. According to the Kerala Development Report (2008, p. 356.), the rural poverty among *adivasis* in Kerala persists and comes to more than two-and-a-half times that off the rural population of Kerala in general. The level of education is directly related to income and wealth, which in turn influence poverty. Education has to enhance capacities of people, expand the areas of competencies, and change people's practices and attitudes, which together can significantly improve their lifestyle. For eradication of poverty and attaining better living standards the education policy must be carefully designed at the local level.

Promoting Skills Through Education

There are many traditional skills and technologies practiced by *adivasi* people for generations. Many of them are locally specific which people learn usually through informal education. Some examples are mat-making using bamboo, pandanus leaf etc., vegetable preservation techniques for long term use (Bamboo seeds used for making 'Puttu' a favourite dish of Paniya community), meat preservation technique, seed preservation technique for the next crop (paddy) etc. These diverse skills serve up the local requirements. These usually include low cost or cheap process, with locally available natural raw materials and above all simplicity of the process. Most of these skills are now found to be in decline in the absence of support for production of commodities and marketing. Further improving these skills are necessary as the students can gather the necessary orientation and prepare themselves for wage and self-employment.

Rural Non-Farm Sector Development

Poverty situation in Kerala clearly suggests that the majority of the rural poor are marginal and landless farmers, agricultural labourers and other assetless non-agricultural workers. Agricultural growth is providing only limited possibilities for labour absorption and poverty continues on a massive scale in rural areas. In this context there is an obvious relationship between the rural non-farm sector income and the rural poverty. When the income from the rural non-farm sector sources are higher than that of the agricultural sector, access to the non-farm sector jobs represents an upward mobility improving wellbeing and reducing poverty. By diversifying their sources of income rural *adivasi* households can augment their incomes and minimize the extent to which they are affected by adverse income shocks from farm activities. The rural non-farm incomes increase the households' income. They can buy farm inputs more easily, thus increasing their farm productivity. Rural non-farm sector offers landless *adivasis* an important option for generating income. Biswajith Choudhurys' (2010) study on the rural non-farm sector in Bangladesh finds that the rural non-farm sector has played an important role in limiting rural poverty, particularly where land ownership is skewed and labour force growth remains high.

In the quest of diversification of the rural economy the significance of this sector in terms of potential for economic conversion has to be looked into. In the current overriding concern to have improvement in the rural economy, policy emphasis has to be laid on non-farm sector, particularly with its scope of contribution to accelerating the poverty reduction process.

Training the *adivasi* students in these sectors to some extent can help them to earn money from these sectors. They could acclimatise with the situation by trying to learn skills on the job, by which productivity and quality of rural small scale products will also remain high.

Conclusion

Education in Kerala is heavily biased against the Scheduled Tribes. Although a few ST students do benefit from education, they represent the cream of the community and not the masses. The children of the poor, less educated parents with low income occupations are only marginally represented. Decentralization of educational management is an aspect that needs special consideration in the context of tribal areas. In fact, considering the geographical terrain and communication problems in tribal areas, it is crucial to restructure the existing system of educational management. From the above study we can conclude that the present education system for *adivasis* is not a well planned one, although the government has succeeded in the enrolment of these people in primary school level. The education system has failed to meet the needs of *adivasis*. Shortages of trained teachers, reading materials, poor infrastructure facilities, etc. are the prime causes behind this. Finally, the study finds that educational system must suit with the rural and agricultural base, towards a knowledge skills-based economy. Overall, the available data evidence shows that importance to farm/non-farm activities in the rural areas can help in reducing poverty. The education system should also be moulded by giving priority to these sectors.

Rezaul Islam and Ahmedullah Mia (2007) in their study on rural people in Bangladesh find that the current life situations as well as the possibilities have influenced the rural poor to look for new opportunities and develop new aspirations. If people are equipped with more information, particularly science-based education and technical vocational training, they can shape their destiny to have a more satisfying standard of living. Skill development, competency building, and teacher's motivation also need to be strengthened for nourishing educational development. A remedy for educational backwardness of tribefolk cannot be achieved by neglecting their economic status. Careful and calculative measures must be taken keeping in view the cultural moorings of the tribals.

REFERENCES

Abdul Salim, A. (2008), 'Opportunities for Higher Education: An Enquiry into Entry Barriers' in Nair, K.N., and Nair, Gopinathan P.R. (eds), *Higher Education in Kerala: Micro-Level Perspectives*, Daanish Books, New Delhi, pp. 54-56.

Anjana, Alex. (2005), *Public Expenditure on School Education (Class I–XII) in Kerala, A Cost-Benefit Analysis*, Centre for Civil Society Summer Intership, Centre for Civil Society, p.13.

Balan, Vaidyar C.P. (1997), 'A Report on Adivasi Unwed Mothers in Kerala', in *Seventh Report of the 10th Kerala Legislative Assembly, Scheduled Caste Scheduled Tribe Social Welfare Committee*, Government of Kerala, December 19.

Chapter X, (1998), http://ncsc.nic.in/writereaddata/sublink2 images/98.pdf, Accessed on 1st March 2010.

Choudhury, Biswajith (2010), 'Poverty Alleviation through the Rural Non-Farm Sector Development: An Overview of Bangladesh Experiences', *IJSAS*, 3(1), January-June, pp. 77-79.

Economic Review 2008 (2009), State Planning Board, Government of Kerala, p. 371.

Environmental Literacy Programme: Evaluation Report (2006), AHADS, Government of Kerala, Thiruvananthapuram, p. 3.

Government of India (1991), *Census of India*, 1991.

Human Development Report 2005 (2006), State Planning Board, Government of Kerala, p. 67.

Islam, Rezaul and Ahmedullah Mia (2007), The role of education for rural population transformation in Bangladesh', *Asia-Pacific Journal of Cooperative Education*, 8(1), p. 20.

Kerala Development Report (2008), Planning Commission, Government of India, New Delhi, p. 40.

Krishnan, C. (1999), *Awareness and Utilisation of Educational Development Schemes by Tribesfolk of Wayanad, Kerala*, Kerala Research Programme on Local Level Development, Centre for Development Studies, Thiruvananthapuram, p. 17.

Mahendra Kumar, Mishra (1996), *Strategies of Tribal Education for Intervention*, CED, OPEPA, Orissa.

Mona, Sedwal and Sangeeta, Kamat, (2008), *Education and Social Equity: With a Special Focus on Scheduled Castes and Scheduled Tribes in*

Elementary Education, Research Monograph No. 19. www.create-rpc.org/pdf_documents/PTA19.pdf. Accessed on 5th January, 2010.

Radhakrishnan (2007), 'Nadinodu Inakkavumai (Malayalam)', *Deshabhimani*, 29th April, p.3.

Report on the Implementation of Safeguards and Development Programmes for SC/ST (2000), Government of Kerala, Thiruvananthapuram, p. 15.

Sam, Mohanlal (2001), 'Mother Tongue Education and Psycho-Societal Involvement in Tribal Communities: A Case of Paniya Tribe', *Language in India*, Vol. 1:3 May.

3

Rural-Urban Divide in Higher Education in Indian Punjab

Status and Some Best Practices

Ranjit Singh Ghuman

"...The need for an accomplishment based understanding of justice is linked with the argument that justice cannot be indifferent to the lives that people can actually live. The importance of human lives, experiences and realization cannot be supplanted by information about institutions that exist and the rules that operate. Institutions and rules are, of course, very important in influencing what happens and they are part and parcel of actual world as well, but the realized actuality goes well beyond the organizational picture, and includes the lives that people manage—or do not manage—to live."

[Amartya Sen, *(2009): **The Idea of Justice**,* p. 18].

Introduction

Tomorrow's world would demand highly qualified specialists and increasingly flexible generalists. Higher education needs to be ready to meet both these demands (The World Bank, 2000). Research and development, the ultimate guarantee of national self-reliance, can flourish only on the substrate of higher education. It provides people with an opportunity to reflect on the social, economic, cultural, national and spiritual issues facing humanity (Government of India, 1986). It contributes to national development through dissemination of specialized knowledge and skills. It is in this context that "the real wealth of a nation is its people" (UNDP, 1990).

Access to higher education and the broad range of services it can render to society is part and parcel of any sustainable development programme in which human expertise and professional skills are required (UNESCO, 1995). Tertiary education and research empowers nations to work on a level playing field among themselves. Negotiations with international institutions necessitates competency at all levels of tertiary education and research. A network of research universities and institutes is a natural mechanism of advancing the national research agenda. Development of tertiary education, is thus, in every country's interests and has legitimate claims on public funds (The World Bank, 2000).

The modern growth theory has established beyond doubt that economic growth and development cannot attain an optimum and self-sustenance path without the development of human resources (Romer, 1990; Lucas, 1993; Benhabib and Spiegel, 1994; Barro and Sala-i-Martin, 1995; Barro, 2001; Krueger and Lindahl, 2001). The ability of a nation to adopt and implement new technology from abroad is a direct function of its human capital stock (Nelson and Phelps, 1966). All those countries, who had focused on human capital formation in the past, have achieved high growth trajectory in their national and per capita income (OECD/UNESCO, 2002). Higher education is certainly associated with high economic returns and rising stock of human capital (Qian and Smyth, 2007).

The seminal work of Schultz and Becker have virtually revolutionized the main contours of development economics and led to resurgence of economics of education as the most important discipline of research in the knowledge economy (Schultz, 1961; Becker, 1964). Alfred Marshall, the great classical economist, also stated that although the nature's production system is subject to decreasing returns, yet the men's skills and knowledge have the capacity to produce increasing returns (Marshall, 1920). He further emphasized that all that is spent during many years in opening the means of higher education to the masses will be paid for if it called out one more Newton, Darwin, Shakespeare or Beethoven.

Many empirical studies have shown that a country would remain underdeveloped as long as her people are deprived of higher education (The World Bank, 2002; Tilak, 2004a, b). Kothari Commission also highlighted the key role of higher education in economic and social development of India (Government of India, 1968). Planning Commission of India (Government of India, 2008), emphasized the role of higher education in achieving better socio-economic development and emancipation of the individuals as well as the society. India's National Knowledge Commission (NKC) re-emphasized its commitment to promote higher education in India (Government of India, 2007).

Three great development waves (Japan: 1940s and 1950s; East Asian Economies, 1960s and 1970s; China, since 1980s) in Asia have taken place mainly by combining cheap labour with education and skill (Haq, 1998). "An intriguing question remains: Will the fourth great wave of development touch the shores of South Asia? Can South Asia become the next economic frontier in the 21st century?" (Haq, 1998).

Indian Scenario

India's total population increased to 1210 million in 2011 as compared to 1029 million in 2001 (Government of India, 2011). Literacy rate also increased from 65 per cent in 2001 to 74 per cent in 2011. The male literacy rate increased from 75 per cent in 2001 to 82 per cent in 2011. The female literacy rate, however, increased from 54 per cent to 66 per cent during the same period. As compared to 18.33 per cent literacy rate in 1951, this is remarkable achievement. But still there is a long way to go to achieve the Millennium Development Goal of 100 per cent literacy rate. At the same time, we shall have to go beyond literacy rate.

The Sarva Shiksha Abhiyan (SSA: Education for All) by the Government of India and the Right to Elementary Education (RTEE) Act are significant efforts towards achieving higher literacy rate and eventually higher gross enrolment ratio at all levels of education. The Mahatama Gandhi National Rural Employment Guarantee (MGNREGA) Act, 2005 is another flagship programme to provide livelihood to unskilled rural people of the country. This scheme shall have a positive bearing on the rural education by ensuring livelihood.

Though the rural-urban gap is narrowing down in terms of number of schools and teachers, yet, there remains a significant gap as far as the quality is concerned. It should also be kept in mind that India is still a country of villages as 72 per cent of its population lives in the rural area (Census of India, 2001).

The Gross Enrolment Ratio (GER) in higher education in India was 11 per cent in 2004-05, which has increased to 13.2 per cent in 2010. However, there is huge gap between rural and urban GER. During 2004-05, the rural GER was just 6.7 per cent against the 19.9 per cent in urban area (Government of India, 2008). The extremely low GER among the SCs (6.57%), STs (6.52%) and OBCs (8.7%) further highlights the huge rural-urban gap, as most of the people belonging to these categories are living in the rural area.

With high disparity between rural and urban India, in terms of GER in higher education, the inclusive education and inclusive growth seem to be an elusive target. This along with the high drop-out rate (overall 61.92 per cent, 60.41 per cent among boys, and 63.88 per cent among girls) from class I–X, shall put a strong hurdle in achieving the targeted GER in higher education (Government of India, 2008).

India has set a target of 15 per cent GER in higher education by March 2012, and 21 per cent by March 2017 and 30 per cent by 2020. This is good but affordability on the part of a large section of Indian population is going to be serious limitation as the cost of for-profit private institutions shall not be within their reach.

It is significant to note that nearly 80 per cent elementary schools in India are in the public sector. The proportion of such schools in the rural India is 85.51 per cent. Among the SC students nearly 87 per cent are enrolled in the government schools. Among the ST students 75 per cent are enrolled in the government schools. Clearly, the SCs and STs can afford to send their wards mainly to the government schools (Mehta, 2010). This trend shall continue in the higher education, too. Accordingly, the government shall have to be a major education provider if we wish to achieve the targeted GER and wish to bring SCs, STs and other weaker sections, especially from rural area, into the higher education.

The performance in examination at the elementary level is another significant indicator of rural-urban gap. In the rural elementary schools only 36.42 per cent boys and 37.35 per cent girls got first class (60% and above) marks during 2005-06. The corresponding figures in the urban area were 45.98 per cent and 47.35 per cent, respectively (Mehta, 2010). Besides, the percentage of single class room schools is much higher in rural schools (11.33%) as compared to urban schools (4.45%).

The employment opportunities in agriculture and allied agricultural sector are shrinking. As such a sizeable amount of workforce in agriculture is being rendered surplus (Bhalla, 1987 and 1989; Gill, 2002). The marginal and small size of operational holdings (62% marginal holdings—up to one hectare of land; 19 per cent small holdings—between one and two hectares of land) are not only economically unviable but are not providing year round employment to the cultivators and agricultural labourers. The development of Rural Non-Farm Sector (RNFS) is the only alternative to shift this surplus labour force from agriculture to non-agricultural employment (Chadha, 1986; Ghuman, 2005). The prerequisite to shift surplus labour force from agriculture to non-agricultural sectors is to equip this labour force with education and skill. Such a policy would not only make them employable in the RNFS but also raise their productivity as well as earnings levels. Thus, education and skill are *sine qua non* for rural transformation and thereby for overall development of the economy. Moreover, inclusive growth is possible only with education and skill for rural transformation.

Rural Urban Divide in Higher Education in Punjab

Tough higher education has expanded at a fast pace in Punjab, during the last about 40 years or so, yet, most of the rural population has been remained outside the higher education. The rural schooling got adversely affected in Punjab, mainly because of two reasons: the problem of militancy during 1980s and the withdrawing attitude of the government since 1980s. The share of budgetary allocation to education in the Punjab Government budget declined from 17 per cent in 1980 to 12 per cent in 2007-08. Compared to it, the share of general services (mainly public administration and the law and order) increased from 39 per cent to 51 per cent during the same period.

The higher education sector, within the education sector, is further facing a serious resource crunch. Consequently, the state funded universities, the government colleges and the government-aided-private colleges are facing a huge budgetary deficit. As a consequence, these institutions are facing a serious shortage of faculty. Significantly, the share of universities and higher education in the total budget allocation for education in Punjab has remained as low as 10 per cent during 2001-06. During 2006-07, it declined to 7.34 pr cent but increased to 9 per cent during 2007-08 (Government of India, Ministry of Human Resources, Budget Expenditure on Education for various years). Clearly, there is an urgent need to increase the budgetary share of education in general and higher education in particular. Higher education, being a social and merit good, deserves public funding (The World Bank, 2000).

It has been estimated that nearly 40 per cent of rural household in Punjab cannot afford the cost of graduate level liberal education in Punjab even for one child. In the case of urban households the proportion of such households is 31 per cent. Nearly, 85 per cent urban households and around 95 per cent rural households in Punjab cannot afford the cost of higher professional education given by the private service providers, for a single child, even if they spend their entire earnings on education (Ghuman *et al.*, 2005).

In view of the increasing cost of living and rising cost of education the issue of affordability is becoming more and more serious. The declining public funding to education sector, the rising cost of higher education and inequitable distribution of income would further exclude a large proportion of rural population from higher education. This would tantamount to exclusion of merit and creation of a mediocre society. This, in turn, shall become a serious constraint on the socio-economic development of Punjab.

Unfortunately, the proportion of rural students[1] in four universities (Guru Nanak Dev University, Amritsar; Punjabi University, Patiala; Panjab University, Chandigarh; and Punjab Agricultural University, Ludhiana) of Punjab was just 4.07 per cent during the academic session 2005-06. There were only 911 rural students out of a total of 22360 students in these universities (Ghuman *et al.*, 2006). It is significant to mention that the proportion of rural population in total population of Punjab was 66 per cent (Census, 2001). The share of rural female students, among the total rural students was 35.2 per cent. It is disappointing to note that even the share of rural students in Punjab Agricultural University (the product of which is to largely serve the agriculture and rural area) was 4.73 per cent.

The share of Scheduled Caste (SC) rural students among the total rural students was only 14.6 per cent. Significantly, the share of rural SC population in the total rural population is 33 per cent. Their share in the total population in Punjab was 28.85 per cent, as per Census 2001.

The share of rural students in the higher professional education was lower than their share in the liberal higher education. Out of 56240 students in the professional and technical higher education in the Universities and Colleges of Punjab, the number of rural students was only 2085 (Ghuman *et al.*, 2009) during the academic session 2007-08. It constituted only 3.71 per cent of the total enrolled students. Certainly, the other states in India would not be having a better scenario.

It has been found that a sizeable majority of rural students, in the liberal as well as professional courses, came from relatively well of parents. The parents were also educated and belonged to the upper social castes. They also had a relatively high level of income.

About 79 per cent and 89 per cent fathers of rural students in liberal higher education and professional education were having secondary and higher level of education. Nearly 54 per cent parents of rural students in liberal education were having annual family income above Rs. 100 thousand. The corresponding proportion of parents of rural students in the professional education was 75 per cent. Clearly, illiterate/lowly educated and low income parents were not able to send their children to higher education.

The collapse of rural school education, particularly in the government and government aided schools, along with the high drop-out rate, have been the main reasons behind exclusion of rural students from higher education in Punjab. It has been noticed that the drop-out rate from 1st to 10th standard was 48.10 per cent during the academic session 2002-03 in Punjab (Gill *et al.*, 2005). The educational attainment of poor households declined across all the grades from 1st to 9th during 1992-93 and 1998-99 (The World Bank, 2004). Another study based on the census survey of 36 villages of Punjab (located in 12 districts) found out that about 69 per cent of all the rural households and 90 per cent of all the rural labourer households did not have even a single member with matriculation level (Tenth standard) education (Ghuman *et al.*, 2007).

The under performance of education sector has crippled the education base of the workforce in the State. During 1999-2000, the education level of the workforce in Punjab was as follows: illiterate (33.50%); primary (22.10%); middle (13.00%); secondary and above (31.50%). Nearly 48 per cent of the agricultural workforce was illiterate (Chadha, 2004).

This sorry state of affairs has been the result of neglect of rural education by the successive governments in Punjab. The government schools in the rural Punjab have been facing a perennial shortage of teachers, and school heads, to the tune of around 40000, during the last about 25 years. The monitoring and regulatory mechanism has come to a naught (Ghuman, 2008). As a result, the relatively better-off and educated parents have started sending their children to the private schools in search of quality education. Some studies have revealed that a very high proportion (ranging from 60 to 85%) of students in rural government primary schools in Punjab belong to the SC (Scheduled Castes), BC (Backward Classes) and other weaker sections of rural society (Joshi, 2003; Kaur, 2004; and Rani, 2007).

Best Practices: Reaching the Excluded and the Under-served

The Yadvindra College of Engineering (YCoE) and Baba Aya Singh Riarki College (BASRC) for girls are the two best practices of inclusive education. The YCoE and the BASRC are located in remote and educationally backward rural areas in Bathinda and Gurdaspur districts of Punjab, respectively. Both these institutions are the best examples of reaching the excluded and the under-served. The YCoE is imparting technical education to the poorest of the poor rural students of Punjab and rest of India and the BASRC is imparting liberal education to the poor rural girls. The two best practices are aiming at inclusive education.

Yadvindra College of Engineering (YCoE): Golden Heart Scholarship Scheme

The Punjabi University established Yadvindra College of Engineering (YCoE) at its Talwandi Sabo campus (district Bathinda) during the academic session 2004-05. It was the pioneer effort to impart engineering education to the poorest of the poor rural people in Punjab and the rest of rural India, irrespective of caste, creed and gender.

The college admits students, after 10th standard examination, in the six year integrated course in three streams of engineering, namely, Computer Science, Electronics and Mechanical. The admission is done on the basis of the score in the qualifying examination, i.e. 10th class. Each engineering stream consists of 60 seats. Those who successfully complete their 10+2 (12th standard) examination are admitted in the engineering degree. In the six-year-integrated course the total number of students comes out to be 1080 over the period of six years.

The eligibility criterion for admission under golden heart scholarship scheme at YCoE for six years integrated course is as under:

(i) The student should have passed his/her matriculation examination with minimum 55 per cent marks (50% marks for SC/ST) category.

(ii) The students who fail in anyone of the subject English, Science and Mathematics shall not be eligible for admission.

(iii) The student should have passed his/her matriculation and previous four classes of study (i.e. from 6th to 10th) from a recognized school in a village which does not fall within the limits of municipal committee or corporation or under a small town/notified area.

(iv) The student should have done his/her study from the 1st to 5th class also from a school in a village which does not fall within the limits of municipal committee or corporation or under a small town/notified area.

(v) The annual fee and other charges of the school(s) from where the student have passed his/her matriculation and (his/her 6th to 9th classes) must be less than Rs. 600.

(vi) The student and his/her parents must be permanent residents of a village which does not fall within the limits of municipal committee or corporation or under a small town/notified area.

Every rural student fulfilling the above criterion is eligible to apply for admission in the YCoE.

Another unique feature of YCoE is that no tuition fee and funds (which are estimated to be Rs. 2.04 lakh for six years of the course) are being charged from the students. The university at its own level made a unique innovation to mobilize resources under the **Golden Heart Scholarships for Rural Students** from the benevolent individual donors and institutions. Each student under this scheme has been sponsored. The amount of stipend is a sort of interest free loan to the students which they are supposed to return in installments out of their earnings after getting into employment.

It is significant to note that the proportion of female students at YCoE is quite high. It ranged between 40 to 45 per cent. Given the proportion of girls in other engineering colleges of Punjab, this proportion is significantly high. This may safely be attributed to the abolition of entrance test, 100 per cent reservation for rural area students and sponsorship provided under the Golden Heart Scholarship Scheme. The proportion of girls in the engineering courses in the colleges affiliated to Punjab Technical University (PTU) was nearly 30 per cent (Ghuman *et al.*, 2009). Out of the total female students in the PTU, the share of rural female students was merely 3 per cent.

The share of SC rural students at YCoE ranges between 19 per cent and 28 per cent. Compared to it, the share of SC rural students in the total rural students in other professional/technical courses in Punjab is nearly 11.6 per cent. The proportion of SC students at YCoE is, thus, more near to the proportion of SC rural population (33%) in total rural population of Punjab.

The high proportion of SC students of YCoE has been mainly due to the admission criterion (100% reservation for poorest of the poor rural students, and that, too, without any entrance test) and cost-free education by way of arranging sponsorships. As a matter of fact, the non-SC rural households (poorest of the poor) and the SC rural households fall almost in the same economic category. The caste-neutral methods of reservation in higher education are more effective than the caste-focused reservation. It is in this context that the institution of golden heart scholarship scheme at YCoE is a path breaking endeavour of Punjabi University in reaching the excluded and the under-served people of rural area.

In the absence of Golden Heart Scholarship Scheme of the university, perhaps, none of these students could have even dreamt of having a graduate degree in engineering. This is an effort to use education for rural transformation.

Neighbourhood Campuses

Impressed by the success of YCoE, Punjabi University established a number of neighbourhood campuses in various districts of the typically rural areas of Punjab on about 300 acres of land, donated by the village Panchayats. At all these neighbourhood campuses, a high proportion of seats are reserved for rural students along with the constitutional reservation. However, unlike the Golden Heart Scholarship Scheme at YCoE, the students at these neighbourhood campuses are charged full fee.

The neighbourhood campuses are located in the remote rural areas and most of the students are getting quality education nearly at their door-step. They are commuting daily to the neighbourhood campuses and are, thus, saving huge expenses on the hostel/ paying guests. Only job-oriented professional and technical courses are being served at these neighbourhood campuses to enhance the employability of the youth in general and that of rural youth in particular.

During the academic session 2009-10, there were 3578 students at these neighbourhood campuses. Out of them 2145 (59.95%) were boys and 1433 (40.05%) were girls. Clearly, these neighbourhood campuses are doing a great job by imparting higher education and skill to those students who would otherwise have remained deprived of the higher education.

The YCoE and other neighbourhood campuses would, thus, catalyze rural transformation and enable the rural youth to compete at the national and international levels. It is indeed a path-breaking movement for equitable distribution of knowledge and for the upliftment of the rural poor. **Punjabi University is, thus, endeavouring to reach the excluded and the under-served.** In the process it is a modest effort to be in the role of Ambedkar.

Baba Aya Singh Riarki College

Baba Aya Singh Riarki College was the cherished dream of a saint-social worker, Baba Aya Singhji. Babaji knew the importance of the education for girls. He first founded a girls school, known as *'Putri Pathshala'*, with the help of local villagers, in 1925. Later, this school was renamed as Sri Khatagdhari Khalsa Senior Secondary School. With the continuous efforts of Babaji, this school was covered under the grant-in-aid by the Government of Punjab. Babaji was a widely travelled person as is evident from his foreign visits to nearly 12 countries. His foreign visits further added to his vision and commitment to the girls' education.

It was nearly eight years after Babaji's death (1968) that one of Babaji's student and a teacher in the Khatagdhari Khalsa Senior Secondary School, namely Mr. Swaran Singh Virk, that a girls college was established in 1976. The College, located in a village of district Gurdaspur of Punjab state of India, is named after Baba Aya Singh. The word 'Riarki' is after the name of the region in which the College is located.

Since the people, especially in the rural area, were least interested in the post-secondary education of their daughters, Mr. Swaran Singh, the founder Principal of the College, had to do a lot of efforts to motivate the parents to send their daughters to the College. He was inspired by Comrade Chanan Singh and Mr. Sampuran Singh in his endeavour to persuade rural parents for the higher education of their daughters. As told by Mr. Virk, he had to do a relentless campaign in the surrounding villages for this purpose and the parents of 34 girls promised to send their daughters to the College. Eventually, only 14 girls turned up for admission. Thus, the first batch of the College was started with only 14 girls in 1976. Thereafter, the number of students went increasing.

Till date the College continues to be a non-affiliated institution though it falls in the jurisdiction of Guru Nanak Dev University, Amritsar (a State University of Punjab province). At present there are about 600 girls studying in this College. Out of them nearly 250 are in +1 and +2 (11th and 12th class) and 350 are in B.A. I, II and III classes. Nearly 325 of them are staying in the hostel.

It is significant to note that this institution also runs school which has nearly 3000 students. One of the significant features of the school is that it has an exclusive wing for students from the down-trodden families from whom only Rs. 600 are charged annually.

The College and school are located in one of the interior village, namely Tughalwala, of district Gurdaspur in Punjab. It is situated right on the bank of a distributory of Upper Bari Doab Canal. The Canal is a perennial one and hence the surroundings are very green and beautiful.

The College serves the higher education need of the rural girls who otherwise might not have entered into any college. Because of the economic and socio-cultural inhibitions most villagers are still not willing to send their daughters to higher education institutions, particularly when they are located far away from their villages.

The tuition fee and the hostel expenses are kept to the bare minimum level. Only Rs. 800 are charged as tuition per annum and Rs. 5500 are charged for the hostel and mess annually, for the last so many years. It seems the inflation has no impact on the college expenses. And rightly so as the College has 8 acre agricultural land, one dairy-farm, a number of bio-gas plants, solar energy plant, flour mill, saw-mill, sugarcane-grinder, etc. which provide sufficient raw food items and other inputs.

The students do every work, from cleanliness to cooking, on their own, which minimizes the overhead costs. Further, the College has employed only 6 teachers, one for each subject, viz. English, Punjabi, Political Science, History and Economics. Most of the teaching work is done by the students themselves. The senior students teach the junior students, of course, in regular classes. This process further cuts down per unit cost.

In addition to teaching, the students manage all the works and activities of the College. These include management of accounts, admissions, library, hostel, kitchen, canteen, examinations, maintenance and up keep of the campus. All these activities are done by students by rotation and voluntarily.

The College is managed by a 16-member student committee which delegates duties to various sub-committees, such as, academic and admission committee, discipline and information committee, hostel committee, mess committee, reception committee, etc., etc. Thus, almost every student is involved in the management of the College.

The students are also taught agriculture and horticulture, apart from the preparation of food and beverages. The students also run cooperative store for books and stationary and a general store. The College offers nearly 50 per cent discount on most of the items.

Thus, in a very natural way the students learn dignity of labour, self-management and governance, management skills, simple and healthy life style, egalitarianism, frugality, self-confidence, cooking, responsibility, character building, etc. They also learn how to limit the wants and satisfy them with limited means. In this way, the students learn three basic tenets of Sikh Religion: recitation of hymns, honest labour and sharing with others.

The College does not observe festivals as holidays. Rather, the festivals, pertaining to different religions, are celebrated in the College itself. Even Sunday is not observed as holiday. Apart from syllabus teaching, the girls are taught value system, religious ideals, music, computer literacy, singing, painting, public speaking, and other co-curricular activities.

Besides being a low cost academic institution, the College gives free-ships to nearly 150 orphaned students. The College is self-financed institution and is managed by a trust. That way the College is doubly philanthropist. It does not take any grant-in-aid, or any donations.

Clearly, this is a unique example of self-governance, skill-updation, and a cost-effective education. Its uniqueness *inter alia,* lies in three areas, namely— (i) in imparting reasonably better quality liberal education at affordable cost; (ii) studying while teaching and teaching while studying, *i.e.* the senior class students teach the junior class students; and (iii) managing hostel and cooking/catering therein by the hostellers themselves. That way, this is the lowest cost institution in the entire state of Punjab and deserves appreciation.

The examinations are also conducted by the students themselves. No student does any copying during the examinations. The question papers and answer sheets are distributed by the students themselves. The University does not appoint any invigilators. However, occasionally the university's flying squads visit the examination centre. The College has kept Rs. 21,000 cash for awarding to flying squad if they detect any student doing copying. It is because of this that the University sanctioned its examination centre at the College, even though it is not affiliated to the University.

The evaluation of the answer sheets is, however, managed by the University. The result is also prepared by the University. The pass percentage of the College is nearly 100 per cent, with 60 to 70 per cent students getting first class.

While in College, one gets a feel of an unwritten motto: "yes, I can do it", finding no task too hard to handle. The management and the students of the College have proved the phrases true: "Where there is will, there is way" and "God helps those who help themselves".

After the completion of education from the College, the students come out with a wholesome personality and a value based life style. The College is, thus, making a valuable contribution to society and an excellent addition to human development.

The College is, indeed, doing a great social service to the rural and backward area of an otherwise prosperous state. It teaches how to make life rather than how to make money. The College is being run in a *'Gurukul tradition'*. It is indeed the *'Shanti Niketan'* of Punjab. The College is a movement in itself—the *'Tughalwala Movement'*.

Summing Up

Education, in general, and higher education, in particular, is *sine qua non* for the wholesome personality development of an individual and for the socio-economic development of the country.

In a vast country like India, with a very high proportion of rural population, the rural education is imperative for the inclusive education and inclusive and fast growth. There is an urgent need to bridge the rural-urban educational gap. India would have to do a lot more efforts to raise its GER in higher education so as to catch up with the world average.

The rural-urban divide in Punjab, one of the prosperous states of India, has been amply displayed by the meagre proportion of rural students in higher education. The rural people are virtually excluded from the higher education sector. Besides, majority of the rural households cannot afford to pay the cost of the higher education being provided by the private institutions. If this is the case of a prosperous state, one can well imagine the scenario in other states of India.

Punjabi University, Patiala has endeavoured to reach the excluded and under-served by way of establishing a cost-free college of engineering exclusively for the poorest of the poor rural students. The establishment of a good number of neighbourhood campuses in the rural area is another praiseworthy service by the Punjabi University.

Baba Aya Singh Riarki College for girls is another unique example for providing higher education to the rural girls. This is one of the most cost-effective, rather the lowest per unit cost institution.

The above mentioned best practices deserve appreciation and replication by others. Nevertheless a lot more needs to be done in order to address the widening rural-urban divide in education sector. The selfless efforts, like above, need to be supplemented by the governments, NGOs and individuals. As such, government must play its role in bridging the rural-urban gap in higher-education. The PPP mode and the private mode are no doubt significant ways to bridge rural urban gap. Both these modes, being largely driven by market may, however, not be adequate enough to bridge the rural-urban divide. They may continue to feel shy of reaching the excluded and the under-served as the latter have either very low paying capacity or no paying capacity. This, along with the high social and public returns of education, makes a sense of public funding to education.

NOTE

1. The students who pass their secondary (10th) or senior secondary (12th) or both the examinations from rurally located schools anywhere in India are considered to be the rural students. These rural schools do not fall in the area of any of the Municipal Corporation/Municipal Committee/Nagar Council/Notified Area Committee/Cantonment Area.

REFERENCES

Barro, R.J. (2001): 'Human Capital and Growth', *American Economic Review*, Vol. 91 (2), pp. 12-17, papers and proceedings.

Barro, R.J. and Sala-i-Martin, X. (1995): *Economic Growth*, McGraw-Hill, New York.

Becker, Garry S. (1964): *Human Capital: A Theoretical and Empirical Analysis, With Reference to Education*, Chicago, University of Chicago Press.

Benhabib, J. and M. Spiegel (1994): "The Role of Human Capital in Economic Development: Evidence from Aggregate Cross

Country Data", *Journal of Monetary Economics*, Vol. 34, pp. 143-51 and 158-61.

Bhalla, Sheila (1987): 'Trends in Employment in Indian Agriculture, Land and Asset Distribution', *Indian Journal of Agricultural Economics*, Vol. 42, No. 4, October-December, pp. 537-60.

Bhalla, Sheila (1989): 'Employment in Indian Agriculture: Retrospect and Prospect', *Social Scientist*, Vol. 17, Nos. 5-6, pp. 3-21.

Chadha, G.K. (1986): 'The Off Farm Economic Structure of Agriculturally Growing Regions: A Study of Indian Punjab', in R.T. Shand (ed.), *Off Farm Employment in the Development of Rural Asia*, Vol. 2, Canberra National Centre for Development Studies.

Chadha, G.K. (2004): 'Human Capital Base of the Labour Force: Identifying Worry Spots', *The Indian Journal of Labour Economics*, Vol. 47 (1), pp. 3-38.

Ghuman, R.S. (2005): 'Rural Non-Farm Employment Scenario-Reflections from Recent Data in Punjab', *Economic and Political Weekly*, Vol. 50, No. 41, pp. 4473-80.

Ghuman, R.S. (2008): 'Socio-Economic Crisis in Rural Punjab', *Economic and Political Weekly*, Vol. 43, No. 7, pp. 12-15.

Ghuman, R.S., Singh, Inderjeet and Lakhwinder Singh (2007): *Status of Local Agricultural Labour in Punjab*, The Punjab State Farmers Commission, Mohali.

Ghuman, R.S., Singh, S. and J.S. Brar (2005): *Unit Cost of Higher Education in Punjab: A Study of Universities and their Affiliated Colleges*, A Report Submitted to Association of Indian Universities (AIU), New Delhi.

Ghuman, R.S., Singh, S. and J.S. Brar (2006): *Rural Students in Universities of Punjab*, Punjabi University, Patiala.

Ghuman, R.S., Singh, S. and J.S. Brar (2009): *Professional Education in Punjab: Exclusion of Rural Students*, Punjabi University, Patiala.

Gill, Sucha Singh (2002): 'Agriculture, Crop Technology and Employment Generation in Punjab' in S.S. Johal and S.K. Ray, *Future of Agriculture in Punjab*, CRRID, Chandigarh, pp. 56-68.

Gill, Sucha Singh, Singh, S. and J.S. Brar (2005): *Financing of Secondary Education: Grants- in-Aid Policies and Practices in Punjab*, A Report Submitted to National Institute of Educational Planning and Administration (NIEPA), New Delhi.

Government of India (1968): *Report of the Education Commission (1964-66)*, Education and National Development, New Delhi.

Government of India (1986): *National Policy on Education, 1986*, Ministry of Education, New Delhi.

Government of India (2007): *National Knowledge Commission Report to the Nation 2006*, National Knowledge Commission, New Delhi.

Government of India (2008): *Eleventh Five Year Plan 2007-2012*, Vol. II, Government of India, New Delhi.

Government of India (2011): *Census of India 2011.*

Haq, Mahbubul (1998): *Dawn*, 27 April 1998; (quoted in *Human Development in South Asia 2007: A Ten Year Review*), Oxford University Press, Karachi.

Joshi, M. (2003), *Primary Education in Rural Punjab: A Case Study of Ropar District*, M.Phil. Dissertation (unpublished), Punjabi University, Patiala.

Kaur, Jaswinder (2004): *Changing Scenario of Primary Education in Rural Punjab: A Case Study of Ferozepur District*, M.Phil. Dissertation (unpublished), Punjabi University, Patiala.

Krueger, A.B. and Lindahl, M. (2001): 'Education for Growth: Why and For Whom?' *Journal of Economic Literature*, Vol. 39 (4), pp. 1101-1136.

Lucas, R.E. Jr. (1993): 'Making a Miracle', *Econometrica*, Vol. 61 (2), March, pp. 251-272.

Marshall, A. (1920): *Principles of Economics*, Eighth edition, Macmillan Publishers, London.

Mehta, Arun C. (2010): *Elementary Education in India: Analytical Report 2007-08*, National University of Educational Planning and Administration, New Delhi.

Nelson, Richard and Edmund Phelps (1966): "Investment in Humans, technological diffusion and economic growth", *American Economic Review*, Vol. 61, pp. 69-75.

OECD/UNESCO (2002): *Financing Education—Investment and Returns: An Analysis of the World Education Indicators*, www.oecd.org and www.unesco.org/publications.

Qian, X. and Smyth, R. (2007): 'Education and Economic Growth: Complementarities or Threshold Effects? Some Empirical Evidence from China', *The Indian Economic Journal*, Vol. 55(2), July-September, pp. 24-38.

Rani, Kavita (2007): "A Socio-Economic Analysis of Primary Education in Rural Punjab: A Case Study of District Bathinda, M.Phil. Dissertation (unpublished), Punjabi University, Patiala.

Romer, P.M. (1990): "Endogenous Technological Change", *Journal of Political Economy*, Vol. 94 (5), pp. 1002-36.

Schultz, T.W. (1961): 'Investment in Human Capital', *American Economic Review*, Vol. 51, January.

Sen, Amartya (2009): *The idea of Justice,* Penguin Books.

The World Bank (2000): *Higher Education in Developing Countries, Peril and Promise,* Washington, D.C., pp. 42-43 and 69.

The World Bank (2002): *Constructing Knowledge Societies: New Challenges for Tertiary Education,* Washington, D.C.

The World Bank (2004): *Punjab Development Report,* Poverty Reduction and Economic Management Sector Unit, South Asia Region, June 26, IBRD, Washington, D.C.

Tilak J.B.G. (2004b): 'Education in the UPA Government Common Minimum Programme', *Economic and Political Weekly,* Vol. 39 (43), October 23, pp. 4717-4721.

Tilak, J.B.G. (2004a): 'Public Subsidies in Education in India', *Economic and Political Weekly,* Vol. 39 (4), January 24, pp. 343-359.

UNDP (1990): *Human Development Report.*

UNESCO (1995): *Policy Paper on Change and Development of Higher Education,* www.unesco.org.

4

Quality Improvement Programmes for Tribal Children in India

The Challenges and Possibilities

K.P. Suresh

Introduction

The Government of India (GoI) and the UN system recognize that certain sections of the population remain marginalized. Therefore, it is the goal of the Joint GoI-UN System Educational Programme to target girls and the marginalized population of children in selected areas and to improve their attendance and performance in primary education. Children who are marginalized by the formal education system are usually Scheduled Tribes, Scheduled Castes, working children, those belonging to minorities, disabled children, and children in remote areas.

Who Are the Scheduled Tribes?

The term 'tribe' is nowhere defined in the Constitution and, in fact there is no satisfactory definition for the same. Although according to the Article 342, ST represents the tribe or tribal communities that are notified by the President. To the ordinary man the word 'tribe' means simple folk living in hills and forest; to better informed and knowledgeable persons, it signifies colourful people noted for their unique dance, music and art forms; to an administrator, it means a group of people whose welfare is the special responsibility of the President of India; whereas, to an anthropologist, it indicates a special field for study of a social phenomenon.

Tribes are not part of the traditional Hindu caste structure. ST's in India are more like the "indigenous" or "native people" in other parts of the world. The word 'tribal' or 'Adivasi' brings to our mind the picture of half naked men and women, with arrows and spears in their hands, feathers in their heads, and speaking an unintelligible language. Myths of savagery and cannibalism often encompassing their lives. However, one will be surprised and thrilled to see a peace loving, equitable, community living close to nature and with advanced cultural/social structure.

Scheduled Tribes are people who– (i) claim themselves as indigenous to the soil; (ii) generally inhabit forest and hilly regions; (iii) largely pursue a subsistence level economy; (iv) have great regards for traditional religious and cultural practices; (v) believe in common ancestry; and (vi) have strong group ties. However, all characteristics do not apply to all tribal communities.

Tribes are not homogenous groups. There are at least four groups of STs—hunting-gathering group, agricultural group, irrigation-agricultural group and industrial wage earning group. All these impressions are meaningful in their own particular ways. Therefore, we cannot accept any particular definition or explanation to describe the people who are classified as the people of the tribal origin.

However, various thinkers and writers have defined the term 'tribe' in different ways:

1. *Dr. D.N. Majumdar*: A Scheduled Tribe refers to "a collection of families or groups of families, bearing a common name, members which occupy the same territory, speak the same language and observe certain taboos regarding marriage, profession or occupation and have developed as well as assessed system of reciprocity and mutuality of obligations."
2. *Imperial Gazetteer of India*: "A tribe is a collection of families bearing a common name, speaking a common dialect, occupying or professing to occupy a common territory and is not usually endogamous, though originally it might have been so."

From the above thoughts we can ascribe the following characteristics to a tribe:

1. Tribe is a group of families.
2. Each tribe has a name.
3. Members of a tribe speak common language or dialect.
4. Members of the tribe reside in a common territory.
5. Members of a tribe observe taboos related to marriage.
6. Members of a tribe have a common occupation.
7. Members of a tribe have a well-developed system of reciprocal exchange.
8. A tribe has a common culture.
9. Members of the tribe work together at the time of war.

Thus we can see that tribes are a group of people with very unique culture and social structure of their own.

Challenges in Providing Education to Tribal Children

One of the challenges in providing education to tribal children relates to setting up school facilities in small, scattered and remote tribal habitations. The majority of the Scheduled Tribes live in sparsely populated habitations in the interior and in inaccessible hilly and forest areas of the country. Nearly 22 per cent of the tribal habitations have populations of less than 100 while more than 40 per cent have population of 100 to 300. The rest have population of 300 to 500.

Tribal Education—Issues and Problems

1. Attitude of tribal parents towards educating their child.
2. Superstition and blind beliefs.
3. Not accustomed to modern society and culture.
4. Poverty.
5. Health problem.
6. Unemployment.
7. No goal in life.
8. Exploitation by others.
9. Role of mediators, political leaders or agents.
10. Did not understand the importance of Education.

11. Attitude of peers in school.
12. Attitude of teachers.
13. Lack of proper guidance and counselling.
14. Shortage of learning materials.
15. Unaware of their rights and privileges.
16. Child labour.
17. Lack of nutritious food.
18. Irresponsible parents: Children have to lookafter their family.
19. Inferiority complex of tribal children.
20. Lack of hostel facilities and attitude of hostel wardens.
21. Lack of proper care at hostel.
22. Lack of motivation to tribal

Education of Tribal Children

The Constitution of India assigns special status to the Scheduled Tribes (STs). Traditionally referred to as *adivasis, vanbasis, tribes,* or *tribals.* STs constitute about 8 per cent of the Indian population. There are 573 Scheduled Tribes living in different parts of the country, having their own languages, which are different from the one mostly spoken in the State where they live. There are more than 270 such languages in India. According to the 2001 Census, the tribal population in India is 74.6 million. The largest number of tribes is in undivided Madhya Pradesh (16.40 million), followed by Orissa (7 million) and Jharkhand (6.6 million).

There were 16 million ST children (10.87 million of 6-11 years and 5.12 million of 11-14 years) as of March 2001, out of the total child population in India of about 193 million in the age, group of 6 to 14 years *(Selected Educational Statistics—2000-01, Government of India).* Education of ST children is considered important, not only because of the Constitutional obligation but also as a crucial input for total development of tribal communities.

National Policy Towards Education of Tribes

An important development in the policy towards education of tribes is the National Policy on Education (NPE), 1986, which specified, among other things, the following:

- Priority will be accorded to opening primary schools in tribal areas;
- There is need to develop curricula and devise instructional material in tribal languages at the initial stages with arrangements for switchover to regional languages;
- ST youths will be encouraged to take up teaching in tribal areas;
- *Ashram* schools/residential schools will be established on a large scale in tribal areas; and
- Incentive schemes will be formulated for the STs, keeping in view their special needs and lifestyle.

The NPE, 1986 and the Programme of Action (POA), 1992, recognized the heterogeneity and diversity of the tribal areas while underlining the importance of instruction through the mother tongue and the need for preparing teaching/learning materials in the tribal languages. A working group on Elementary and Adult Education for the Tenth Five Year Plan (2002-07) emphasized the need to improve the quality of education of tribal children and to ensure equity as well as further improving access.

The Interventions Being Promoted in States

- Schools, education guarantee centres and alternative schools in tribal habitations for non-enrolled and dropout children.
- Textbooks in the mother tongue for children at the beginning of the primary education cycle, when they do not understand the regional language. Suitably adapted curriculum and the availability of locally relevant teaching and learning materials for tribal students.
- Special training for non-tribal teachers to work in tribal areas, including knowledge of tribal dialect.
- Special support to teachers as per need.
- Deploying community teachers.
- Bridge Language Inventory for use of teachers.
- School calendars in tribal areas appropriate to local requirements and festivals.
- *Anganwadis* and *Balwadis* or crèches in each school in tribal areas so that the girls are relieved from sibling care responsibilities.

- Special plan for nomadic and migrant workers.
- Engagement of community organizers from ST communities with a focus on schooling needs of children from specific households.
- Ensuring sense of ownership of school committees by ST communities through increasing representatives of STs in VECs/PTAs etc. Involving community leaders in school management.
- Monitoring attendance and retention of children.
- Providing context specific intervention, e.g. Ashram school, hostel, incentives etc.

Tribals and the Kerala Model

Kerala stands out in the development history of independent India. There has been wide appreciation for its achievements in social developments (particularly with respect to education, health, literacy, sex ratio, women's status, implementation of land reforms and so on (Franke and Chasin, 1994; Ramachandran, 1997). These achievements have, however, not adequately filtered down to the weaker sections of society, particularly the tribals who have remained as outliers to the development process (GoK, 2003). Even the much celebrated decentralization process in Kerala has not been able to deliver development benefits to the tribal population. The lack of tribal participation in the development process has been pointed out as one of the important factors that contribute to the ineffectiveness of tribal development programmes in the state (Vijayanand, 1997).

As of 2001, the tribal population of 3.64 lakh comprised only 1.14 per cent of the total population of the state. A total of 38 tribal communities comprise the total tribal population in the state. These tribal communities are distinct from one another in terms of their cultural patterns, diversity of habitats, lifestyles, language, and livelihoods. In addition, they are spread over almost all the 14 districts of the state. Hence, numerically, culturally and socially, tribals constitute a very weak force in the state of Kerala. A close look at some of the indicators of social development indicates that tribals have been largely left out of the overall achievement of the state in this regard. For instance, while a high level of literacy is one of the defining features of the Kerala model, the tribal situation is markedly different. While the average literacy rate for the state is 89.81, it is only 57.22 per cent for the tribal sections, with female literacy among tribal amounting to only 51.07 per cent (GoK, 2005), as against the state average of 75.25 (Gulati and Ramalingam, 1997).

Integrated Tribal Development Programme (ITDP)

Integrated Tribal Development Programme (ITDP) was initiated in 1979 to enable tribal people to develop the capacities needed to effect sustainable improvements in their lives. Problems caused by erosion of land rights, geographical isolations, illiteracy and lack of political organizations have made tribal people vulnerable to many forms of exploitation and prevented them from asserting their basic rights. Through community organization, education and promoting secure livelihoods, the "software" of development, ITDP is helping communities to become self-reliant and adapt to the changing conditions of their environment. The people's organizations have been successful in freeing tribals from exploitative relations and in establishing claims towards realizing the rights of tribals in many villages.

Quality Improvement Programmes for Tribal Children

Development of Culturally Relevant Materials in Local Languages

Most of the states recognize the need to address issues related to teachers' attitudes, medium of instruction, textbooks and materials, curriculum and pedagogy and teaching-learning process in tribal areas.

An increasing number of researchers strongly advocate the use of the mother tongue or home language as medium of instruction in early stages of education. This assumes greater significance in the context of education of tribal children because their mother tongue is often quite distinct from the prominent languages in the state or regional languages. ST children face problems wherever teachers do not speak their dialect at all. From the perspective of language, it is desirable to have a local teacher from the same tribal community.

Although research evidence has demonstrated the positive consequences of bilingual or multilingual schooling on cognitive development and social interaction processes, tribal children would require special programmes to be able to cope. The Constitution of India allows the use of tribal dialect (mother tongue) as the medium of instruction if the population of the tribe is more than 100,000.

Use of Local Teachers

The acceptance of teachers by the community as one of them is critical for increasing schooling participation in tribal areas. An understanding of and respect for tribal cultures and practices and some amount of familiarity with the local language are important for teachers to gain this acceptance.

The presence of tribal teachers, especially from the same community, has shown and improved school participation of ST children. Coming from the same community, it is believed that the teachers would understand and respect the culture and the ethos with much greater sensitivity. Studies suggest that teacher motivation contributes more to teaching-learning process than teacher's competence.

Realizing the importance of having teachers from the local community, many states have appointed community teachers or para-teachers as they are popularly referred to. Different states have different schemes for appointing community teachers—Shiksha Karmi Scheme (Madhya Pradesh and Rajasthan), Shiksha Mitra Yojana (Uttar Pradesh), Lok Shikshak (Bihar), Andariki-Vidya Volunteer Scheme (Andhra Pradesh). Vidya Upasak Yojana (Himachal Pradesh), Shikshan Sevak (Maharashtra), Guruji (under EGS in Madhya Pradesh), Shikshak (under Basti Shala Scheme in Maharashtra) etc. It is estimated that there are about 220,000 para-teachers engaged in full-time schools in the country. The issues relating to classroom transactions are difficult as they deal with well entrenched attitudes and prejudices of teachers as well as seemingly intractable problems of the huge difference between home and school languages. Attempts have been made to address the first issue through training programmes for teachers. There may be a problem of acceptance of the tribal language as a medium of instruction in the tribal communities; therefore, adequate dialogue with tribal communities and their leaders is required to prepare them on this issue.

Conclusion

The discussion presented above gives us two important lessons. One is that the cognitive qualities of tribal children have to be viewed and evaluated taking into consideration their ecological and cultural contexts that place very different demands on day-to-day life. Because of differences in the demands of tribal ecology, the patterning of their cognitive abilities shows considerable variation from those of other groups. A related and more important lesson is that tribal children are neither culturally inferior nor cognitively less competent than the children of other groups. Instead many of their skills and abilities are highly developed and extremely sophisticated.

The implications of these findings for schooling of tribal children are clear. A programme of schooling, which does not pay attention to the ecological, cultural and psychological characteristics of tribal children, is highly unlikely to make any significant impact. The educational system of the dominant non-tribal population is of very limited value in the tribal cultural milieu because it does not match with the lifestyle of individuals and the needs of the tribal community. Linking school education with life in general and the needs of the tribal communities in particular is a most important step that requires serious attention.

The evidence suggests that tribal children do possess the basic cognitive abilities and psychological dispositions necessary for successful participation in school. Yet tribal children have very low levels of participation and success in school education programmes. This points out to our failure to develop a sensitive model of education that is rooted in the psychological strengths of tribal children. Studies indicate that, in comparison to other groups, hunters and gatherers possess a high level of visual and tactual differentiation; they demonstrate capacity for fine judgment of shape and size of stimuli as well as spatial relations and they produce fine categorization of an array of objects.

These abilities are required for success in science, art, music, dance, athletic activities, and vocations like carpentry, tailoring, wood and stone crafts. These skills need to be utilized not only for education of tribal children in schools, but also in the broader economic spheres of tribal life. Such attempts will be helpful in generating and promoting the sense of competence, self-efficacy, self-respect and positive self-image among tribal children in general.

This is possible only through sensitivity to tribal culture and life, recognition of the cognitive strengths of tribal children, and appreciation of their personality qualities. Efforts in these directions will be very helpful in organizing the programme of tribal education as well as promoting economic and other aspects of tribal development. Similarly, a clear policy for language use in schools has to be developed. Research evidence suggests that significantly fewer students drop-out of schools in which the language of tribal groups is used for instruction at the primary level. Development of primers in the tribal dialect involving content from the local context will go a long way in ensuring children's active participation in the learning process in school.

While there is a general need for improvement in physical facilities in all schools in remote tribal regions, change in perceptions and outlooks of teachers about tribal children are equally important. Teachers must be sensitized to the cultural and behavioural strengths of tribal children and motivated to do their best for them in schools. Incentives should be initiated to attract effective teachers to work in tribal schools and to retain them there. Only such motivated teachers are likely to generate interest among tribal children towards school education by attempting to link the contents of the curriculum with the existing realities of tribal communities through the use of innovative technologies.

REFERENCES

Aggarwal, J.C., (1992), *Development and Planning of Modern Education with Special Reference to Dalits*, New Delhi: Kranti Publishing House.

Chauhan, Brij Raj, (1975), *Scheduled Castes and Education*, Meerat: Anu Publications.

Elwin, Verrier (1963), *A New Deal for Tribal India*. New Delhi, Publication Division.

Majumdar, R.C. (2009), *The History and Culture of the Indian People*, Vol. 9, New Delhi: Sage Publication.

Reddy, Venkateshwara L., Narayana, Lakshmi M. & Rao, Bhaskara Digmarti, *Education For Dalits* (2004), New Delhi: Discovery Publishing House.

Sharma, Yogendra K., (2006) *Population Education Concepts, Principles and Approaches*, New Delhi: Kanishka Publishers and Distributors.

Singh, K.S. (Ed:) (2006), *Tribal Movements in India*, Vol. I, New Delhi: Manohar.

5

Accountability of Teacher Education for Rural Transformation

Issues, Concerns, Observations, Reflections and Suggestions

Avtar Singh and *Hemendra S. Mistry*

Introduction

What teacher education can do for the country is summarize in the lines that too much are expected and little is offered to them. Famous educator Chanakya once said that the construction and destruction of the society are in the lap of the teacher. If a teacher decides in goodwill a state can progress in an unprecedented manner but can ruin the same if decides otherwise. From the time immortal education is used as an instrument to bring desirable changes in the human behaviour in particular and the society in general. In the last century and so the multi-directed Industrial development put up a visible line in the living of the society which further demarked the society as Rural and Urban.

Rural are the people living in the vicinity less prone to the industrial wave or corporate sector with large landscapes having overcrowded dense population and more prone to agriculture, farming and small landscapes with less populated areas.

Further, UNESCO (2003) describes rural areas in its document *Education for Rural Development* as *Rural Areas:*

- a space where human settlement and infrastructure occupy only a small share of the landscape;

- natural environment dominated by pastures, forests, mountains and deserts;
- settlements of low density (about 5-10,000 persons);
- places where most people work on farms;
- the availability of land at a relatively low cost; and
- a place where activities are affected by a high transaction cost, having long distance from cities and poor infrastructures.

Indigenous culture, uniqueness, peculiarity are the basic pillars of the villages in any part of the world. Being a nation where the majority of the population lives in the villages, one can elicit India's spirit lives in its villages. Independency and efficiency, the indicators of development, utopian to the village transformation in any country and India is not an exception. The villages for its need fulfilment are dependent on the urban culture and *vice versa*. Further, the villages are the mirrors of development as far as the Indian scene is concern. India is growing since independence, 35 States/Union Territories, 640 districts, 5,924 sub-districts, 7,935 Towns and 6,40,867 Villages compared to 2001, the corresponding figures were 593 Districts, 5,463 sub-Districts, 5,161 Towns and 6,38,588 Villages. There is an increase of 47 Districts, 461 Sub-Districts, 2774 Towns (242 Statutory and 2532 Census Towns) and 2279 Villages in 2011 as compared to 2001; further emerged from the 16 states and more than 600 princely states at the time of Independence. According the population census (2001), out of a total population of 1027 million in India, about 742 million (or 72.2%) live in rural areas and 285 million (or 27.8%) live in urban areas (Government of India, 2011). There has been an increase of 2.1 percentage points in the proportion of urban population in India during 1991-2001 and is still increasing. The percentage decadal growth of population in rural and urban areas during the decade is 17.9 and 31.2 per cent respectively.

Today, Rural India presents a baffling dichotomy of images: poverty and growing potential of rural markets. The importance of rural sector has been on decline: Proportion of the GDP accounting from agriculture, industry and services have changed from 59: 13:28 (1947) to 24:25:51 (now); Proportion of the Workforce accounting from agriculture, industry and services have changed from 74:11:15 (1947) to 57:18:25 (now); Relative productivity ratios of 1:3.4:4.2 per unit of labour in agriculture, industry and services, respectively seem in conducive to equitable society and economic development. Clearly economic reforms have succeeded in transferring capital from inefficient to efficient sectors, but yet to achieve a corresponding transfer of labour (Mony, 2003). Further looking at the development of education in India since independence, India had received a good quantitative growth from 19 universities in India to 611 plus Higher education Institutions (including 44 central universities, 281 State Universities, 130 Deemed Universities, 90 Private Universities, 66 Autonomous Institutes of National Importance) and 26500 plus colleges (Desai *et al.*, 2011; www.ugc.ac.in; www.en.wikipedia.org/wiki/list_of_universities_in_India). The language of instruction at the better rated colleges is English. As far as the school education is concern India now have an elementary school in per kilometre radius.

Thus it can be easily elicited that the education in India have the quantitative growth and the efforts for making a qualitative changes in this sector is going on with the increasing need of time. Moreover, the rural habitats are too seeking the helping hands to bring the transformation in their situations. But the vital question is what change they want and what the intelligentsia coining the term Rural Transformation.

What is Rural Transformation?

> UNESCO describes term *Rural Development* in its document Education for Rural Development as: "...rural development encompasses agriculture, education, infrastructure, and health, capacity-building for other than on-farm employment, rural institutions and the needs of vulnerable groups (UNESCO, 2003).

Rural development aims at improving rural people's livelihoods in an equitable and sustainable manner, both socially and environmentally, through better access to assets (natural, physical, human, technological, and social capital), and services, and control over productive capital (in its financial or economic and political forms), that enable them to improve their livelihoods on a sustainable and equitable basis."

But as one talk of reform and development, let us not forget the particular qualities of education for rural people that could be exported to schools in urban areas and make the latter richer—pedagogically, intellectually and academically—precisely by being more practical in orientation. Rural life has fertilized education in many ways and this rich heritage should not be ignored and lost, but nurtured and enriched (UNESCO, 2003).

There are no universally accepted approaches to rural development. It is a choice influenced by time, space and culture. The term rural development connotes overall development of rural areas to improve the quality of life of rural people. In this sense, it is a comprehensive and multidimensional concept, and encompasses the development of agriculture and allied activities, village and cottage industries and crafts, socio-economic infrastructure, community services and facilities and, above all, human resources in rural areas. As a phenomenon, rural development is the end-result of interactions between various physical, technological, economic, social, cultural and institutional factors. As a strategy, it is designed to improve the economic and social well-being of a specific group of people—the rural poor. As a discipline, it is multi-disciplinary in nature, representing an intersection of agriculture, social, behavioural, engineering and management sciences (Singh, 1999).

In rural areas, the problems of access to education is acute and, in order to take on the enormous challenges involved in providing education for all, a more holistic view of education is needed. In particular, the issue of educational development in rural areas cannot be properly addressed without mentioning the issues emerging. The following section deals with the issues related with the rural setup as far as the teacher education area in India is concern.

Problems, Issues and Concerns for the Current Practices of Teacher Education in India

Taking synoptic views of the teacher education in India the following issues and problem emerges out clearing having its bearing on the rural transformation.

- *Unplanned growth of the teacher education institutions:* The mushroom growth of the teacher education institutions in India can be easily perceived as from just 315 institutions of teacher training in the country around 1998 to 10000 plus teacher education institutions in India in 2010 offering courses of D.Ed., ETT, PBTT, JBT, PTC, B.A. (Education), B.Ed., M.A. (Education), M.Ed., M.Phil., Ph.D., apart from the C.P. Ed. B.P.Ed. and M.P.Ed. courses, which in turn increases the number of institution near 50,000 plus, in India. And still the quality of education is at the stake (Singh and Desai, 2009). The quantitative growth had given a chance to access for training the un-trained teachers but the quality teacher education is still a mirage. The most of the teacher education institutions lies in the vicinity of the urban culture and give fruits to the population having the urban orientation. The teachers trained in this urban culture are far away from the problems and issues lies in lap of an Indian rural. The theoretical and pedagogical orientations in these urban simulated conditions give less cognition to the youth wishes to be the teacher.

- ***Lack of fair attention towards the rural educational practices and culture:*** As mentioned earlier that the peculiar, indigenous and complexities are diverse in the Indian villages and vary with reference to time, place and contexts. Further the issues in the periphery of the rural set up create a complex situation which need a farsighted approach with intellectual insight with proper experienced man power as far as the subject of education is concern. Although, the rural population too going to semi-urban and urban places to get the desired training but somehow the training lacks the perspective and unable to address the issues and problems of the Indian rural situations.
- ***Unbalanced and Lopsided development:*** Most of the teacher education institutions are in the urban set-up. For example under the western region committee of NCTE the Bhopal city itself have the 65 B.Ed. colleges, 68 D.Ed. colleges, 13 M.Ed., 14 B.P.Ed. and 2 M.P.Ed. Colleges out of the total 375 B.Ed., 280 D.Ed., 61 M.Ed. colleges, 45 B.P.Ed. and 8 M.P. Ed. The situation is similar in all the regional committees of NCTE. Somewhere the

situation differs than that mentioned above. Up to 2008, NCTE has approximately 8000 plus teacher education colleges and offering 7600 plus courses under its purview, which offers courses for the teachers from the pre-school to secondary level. The process of granting the approval to teacher training colleges is completely out of the sync with the demand for the teachers in that state. So while colleges are being granted affiliation with questionable regularity in states such as Tamil Nadu, Karnataka, Uttar Pradesh and Maharashtra, other states such as Orissa, Sikkim and Meghalaya are languishing. Sikkim has only two B.Ed. College and one elementary teachers training college as compare to the Uttar Pradesh has 700 plus B.Ed. colleges and 190 plus Basic teacher certification college (Singh and Desai, 2009).

As far as the demand of the primary teacher is concern it is always higher than that of the secondary teachers yet there are more colleges offering the secondary level courses for teachers. Also the examples of the multiplicity of the degrees at the same levels are also prevailing. For example, a primary teacher could go for a diploma in Education which is a two-year programme or for a BTC which is one year programme in some colleges and two-years in others or for a bachelor's degree in elementary education which is four year programme. On the other side as the country is on the verge of completion of the SSA (Sarva Shiksha Abhiyan) the forecast of the teacher needed in the near future to manage the institutions of primary education within the one kilometre radius is again a big question mark.

During the year the 2004-05, NCTE is reported to have granted approval to nearly 690 institutions in the country increasing the intake from 1,52,496 to 2,23,476 a net increase of 70,980 seats in the B.Ed. Programme. During the same period NCTE accorded approval to 22 M.Ed. Programme. NCTE has not explained so far how the increase of 70,980 students in the enrolment B.Ed. programme all over the country can be managed with an increase intake of 470 teachers keeping the ratio of 1 : 15 to students and the teacher educators. Can this is called a planned development?

Out of the total approved strength of 2, 23,476 the major chunk, 54,030 constituting 25 per cent of the total intake in this country is in Uttar Pradesh. During the year 2004-05 alone, 200 institutions have been granted approval with an intake if 20,000 additional seats in UP. Similarly in Karnataka, an additional 185 institution have been granted approval during 2004-05 taking the intake from 7,340 to 25,640. In Andhra Pradesh, however, there was only a marginal increase in intake from 34,121 to 36,221. In Kerela, 102 institutions have been granted approval during the same year and intake if 6,279 were nearly trebled to 18,174 (Singh and Desai, 2009). As on April 2006 the southern region constituted nearly 39 per cent, followed by the northern region with 36 per cent and the western region with 20 per cent, the remaining being the Eastern region. Can this imbalance be called a planned development?

Observations and Reflections on the Current Practices of Teacher Education in India

Apart from the quantitative growth the functioning of teacher educational institutions are need due attention. Some observations from the current practices of the teacher education institutions are (Bhatt, 2007; Pillai, 2007; Mehta, 1995; Singh, 1999; Govinda *et al*. 2003):

1. The institutions are rarely catered to the need of the lot coming from the rural set up.
2. Mismatch of the needs of Rural Youth and solution provided by the urban teachers.
3. The issues related with the rural youth are rarely addressed.
4. The gap between the rural-urban students widening at the sharp rate.
5. Adjustment and transition problems of the rural and semi-urban students are high that results in bad examination performance and low results, which further leads to stagnation and drop-out.
6. The rural and tribal youth faces more problems in understanding the content if the medium of instruction is in English which is not the language of instruction at the pre-college education level.
7. Peer-pressure and emotional adjustment problems are more prevalent in the transition groups.

8. The transited rural and tribal youth finds the personality issues with respect to the urban ones. Many a times they feel ashamed and shy against the urban ones.
9. The health related aspects are more likely to tackle as per the changing climatic conditions among the students coming from the rural background students.
10. Teacher education institutions rarely plan their activities in the rural set ups except the regional college of education (RIEs) where the internships are being organised in the areas from where the students are coming.
11. Issues and problems of the rural set ups are rarely discussed and resolved as the matter of concern.

Looking into the aforesaid mentioned issues, which need a great explanation, the observations are made in general rather than the particular one. The issues can be resolves in the collaborative manner mention in the section following the same.

Suggestions and Actions for Teacher Education in the Rural Transformation

What can the teacher education help out in the area of education apart from producing quality teachers?

1. ***Plan the Teaching Practice and Internship programmes in Rural Set ups:*** Few are the number of the teaching training institutions where the practice teaching and internship are organize in the rural and interior parts of the country. The lack of interest among the teacher educators, time-money involved, the efforts which lose the battle against the lazy and lackadaisical attitudes; non-co-operation of the urban schools for the teaching practice component; results in hurriedly conducted practice teaching/internship components. Student teachers are rarely confronted with the situations of real India. A need to conduct such practice in the schools of the rural vicinity. The teacher training institutions facing a situations where the schools in the urban set up rejects the permission for conducting the Practice teaching and internship in their schools due to the good result oriented mentality. In this

situation the rural school will give them edge to conduct a vital component and in return will take benefit of the teachers. Also the perspective teachers will get a real experience of rural life, problems and issues.

2. ***Organize multifarious activities for the wholistic development of the rural child:*** Once the teacher training institutions enter into the rural conditions the pedagogical, psychological, social and cultural issues wide open their mouths which can only be shut by conducting the activities resolving the same. The multifarious activities related with these issues like role plays, dramas, *nukkad nataks* (street shows), folks, dances, music will help to mingle with the students and people. The anthropological, sociological and philanthropic attitude will work there rather than the traditional one.
3. ***Prepare the teacher education programmes as per the need and contextualise to the villages:*** The adjustments in the subject curriculum will be the area now need attention for the rural transformation with respect to the responsibility of teacher education. The vocational, practical, work experience and job-oriented curricula attracts the rural habitats rather than the theoretical one. The syllabus and curricula contextualising the rural conditions helps in better understanding the basic issues of rural transformation. Make action plans on "Think global and act local" strategy.
4. ***Teacher education should reflect and directs its practices towards the issues of villages:*** Teacher education should reflect and directs its practices towards the issues of villages like Sanitation and Drainage, Dwelling-houses, Drinking Water, Agriculture and Industry, Educational facilities, Clinical facilities in the rural set up. Sensitize the community of teacher education towards the rural illiteracy, Casteism, Lack of services, Poor infrastructure facilities, Law and Order, Caste based judicial systems, Slow pace of modernization, Greedy Middle man shows, Lack of Information and services, Poor participation of the community in the village development programmes, Addiction of Liquor and other narcotics, Unemployment, Poor wage policies, Lack of access of the labour due to

Industrialization, Low rate of returns in terms of monetarily gains etc. are the issues need attention (Ahuja, 1996). Planning and Organization of the awareness-cum action plans for the health-care and sanitation will help the people of that habitat and the budding teacher educators. The basic orientation of such issues during the teacher training programmes will help the students to tackle the issues when perspective teachers will enter the field.

5. ***Producing teachers with positive frame of mind to work in village conditions:*** The future teacher coming out of these teacher training institutions dislikes to be posted in the rural and far-flung areas of the country. The charisma of the developing cities attracts the youth teachers to be the habitat of the concrete jungle. The basic mind set of the perspective teachers is narrow and of escapist nature. The inability of the teachers to fulfil the duties in the interior and deep school results in the low achievement of the students further hampers the quality of education. On the other hand the teachers do not have the pre-requisite training to face the challenges of the rural and interior areas as they have never undergone such situations during their teacher training programmes.
6. ***Give projects and assignments contextualizing village conditions:*** The assignments given in the teacher training institutions are lacking the perspective of bringing desirable changes in the individuals. The theoretical and bookish assignments lend them nowhere but rather push them near to the 'cut-copy-paste' technology. The assignments and projects given in these teacher training institutions given rise to the stress and fatigue among the students rather a joyful act. If a project and assignment on the themes concerning understanding and preserving the culture of the local context have been given would might had a positive change among the future teachers.
7. ***Give an ear to pronunciation and village language:*** Rarely an attention is paid on the language and pronunciation of the students. The accent and pronunciation of the students coming from the far-flung and rural dominated areas are often subjected to the peer teasing and further results in the timidity of individual from speaking in public. Such

treatment left the child nowhere but to either stagnate its performance or take a drop from the situations. The local dialect rarely finds its place to school or college curriculum. This gives a serious note for saving the indigenous culture as the languages and dialects are the building pillars of the civilisation and culture.

8. ***Pay attention to the indigenous and peculiar culture and promote the same:*** Promotion of the local handicrafts, small scale industry, manual labour and village women-oriented business plans will attract the rural and urban youth towards the indignity of the cultures. In the past the green-white-brown-pink-red, etc. colour revolutions had successfully made grounds for the rural development.
9. ***Keep a track on the village and urban achievement level and make efforts to reduce the margin between them:*** The discrepancy between the achievement level of the students from the rural and urban youth is increasing rapidly. The urban students due to ease of access to the guidance and tuitions outsides the rural counterparts with a significant margin results in the poor representation of the rural youth in the higher education level. Further, monitoring the same will result and finding out the weighted average results will equate the rural-urban dichotomy to some extent. The idea of standard scores can also be useful to compare the achievement of the students with respect to the different habitats. Methodology of computing the results and converting into the standard scores can be handed over to the teacher education elites to formulate the policy in this matter. Further the teacher educational institutions will monitor the achievement level of the students in the vicinity where they are located.
10. ***Adopt cluster of schools from the villages and nurture them:*** Adoption of the cluster or group of villages by the teacher education institutions will give solution to the problems of the rural education. A policy can be planned in a compulsory manner in which the teacher education institution should make compulsory to adopt villages and look into the progress of the villages. This will not only give cognition to the teacher educators about the

contemporary issues and problems but also helps in reaching and achieving the national goals of education.

11. ***Active participation in the Village Education Committee, School Management Council and Parent-Teacher Association for Planning and Implementation of the decisions:*** If adopting of the villages is done in a desirable manner then the collaborative and active participation of the teacher educators in the local level committees like the PTA, VEC, SMC etc. can easily be ensured. The much awaited and desirable thing expected by the elite planners of education to encourage the active participation of the local people can be ensure by this.
12. ***Rather than taking the theoretical issues the action research is to be given to initiate the mental processes for the young teacher educators:*** In the name of the theoretical researches the action research in the rural set up should be encouraged so as to bring small solutions to the big problems. The action research in its true sense should be implemented so as to tackle the issues emerging in the rural set up.

Concluding Remarks

With ever expanding areas of life results in shrinking the world to a global village, technologically all are villagers, the traditional issues are cease to eliminate themselves and individual initiation need a inescapable attention and boost. The teacher education cannot isolate itself from the reality of nexus between the rural-urban dichotomies. The development of the one without the other is impossible and keeping them together is the toughest task ahead on the shoulders of the teachers. The practices of the teacher education institutions need a paradigm shift from the traditional, monotonous, individualistic and partial to the wholistic, active, collaborative and harmonious. The spirit of India lies in the villages will be true to its mean if the some suggestions find its way to practical feasibility.

REFERENCES

Ahuja, R. (1993). *Indian Social System.* Jaipur: Rawat Publications.
Ahuja, R. (1996). *Social Problems in India.* Jaipur: Rawat Publications.

Bains, R.S. (1994). *Reservation Policy and Anti-Reservationist.* Delhi: B.R. Publishing Corporation.

Basu, D.D. (1970). *Dr. Ambedkar and Dalit Future.* Delhi: B.R. Publishing Corporation.

Bhatia, S. (2008). Ambitious 11th Plan on higher education may remain a dream. *Retrieved from the TNN news* of 20 October, 2010.

Bhatt, A. (2007). *Study of Transitional problems faced by the first year hostelite students of The Maharaja Sayajirao University of Baroda, Vadodara.* An Unpublished M.Ed. dissertation. Vadodara; CASE, MSU, Baroda.

Dash, S. (2006). Quality Improvement in Teacher Education: An Analysis of Present and Future: *Edutracks.* 5(10)

Dash, S. (2008). Plan Panel for Assessing Teacher Training Institutes. *Express News Service Posted*: June 27 at 2210 Hrs Ist.

Ghosh, J. (2006). Case for Caste-Based Quota in Higher Education. *Economic and Political Weekly*, June 17-23, 2006, Vol. (24).

Government of India (2011). *India-2011: A Reference Annual.* New Delhi: Publication Division, Ministry of Information and Broadcasting.

Govinda, R. and Diwan, R. (2003). *Community Participation and Empowerment in Primary Education*, New Delhi: Sage Publication.

Planning Commission of India (2007). *Draft Outline: Eleventh Five Year Plan*, New Delhi: GOI.

Malhotra, S.P. *Teacher Educators Can Only Improve Teacher Quality.* Retrieved from http.www.aiaer.net

Maheshwari, S. (2007)." Gurus Get it all Wrong". Article in *India Today* dated July 23, 2007. New Delhi: The India Today Group.

Mehta, A.C. (1995). *Education for all in India—Myth and reality.* Delhi: Kanishka Publication.

MHRD (2003). *Annual Report*, MHRD, *Government of India.* New Delhi: GOI.

Naik, J.P. (1965). *Educational Planning in India.* Bombay: Allied Publication.

NCERT (1966). *Education and National Development*, New Delhi: NCERT.

NCERT (1968). *Stagnation and Wastage in Primary and Middle Schools*, New Delhi: NCERT.

Pillai, T. (2007). *Peer pressure among the secondary school students.* An Unpublished M.Ed. dissertation. Vadodara; CASE, MSU, Baroda.

Rastogi, S. (2007). Meeting Challenges of Teacher Training Programmes through Globalization: *University News.* 45(3).

Singh, A. and Desai, R. (2010). UGC Minimum Standards and Procedure for the Awards of M.Phil./Ph.D. Degree Regulation, 2009: A SWOT Analysis, *University News*, 48(14)' April 5-11, pp. 10-18.

Singh, A. and Desai, R. (2009). Amalgamation of (Futuristic) Man power, Social Demand, Rate of Return, Cost-Benefit and Cost-Effective approaches to rejuvenate Teacher Education programme: Contextualizing to Indian situation. Paper presented in *National Seminar on Management of Teacher Education, MSU, Baroda.*

Singh, K. (1999). *Rural Development: Principles, Policies and Management,* New Delhi: Sage Publication.

Talesra, H. *et al.*, (2001). Agenda for Education-Design And Direction, New Delhi: Kanishka Publication.

UNESCO. (2003). *Education for Rural Transformation: Towards New Policy Reforms.* Italy: Food and Agriculture Organization of the United Nation.

6

Education for Rural Transformation

Realities and Challenges

Monika Arya

Introduction

In inter-dependent world, rural development can best be studied in the perspective of national and global development. The developing nations, having the predominant majority of the world population, are largely rural. In India, nearly 72 per cent of the people live in rural areas. The rural areas provide employment to around 60 per cent of the country's labour force through agriculture. Industry, the other main source of employment, is itself considerably dependent on agriculture for its raw materials and as the consumer of industrial products like fertilizers, pesticides, etc. The development of rural areas is important to industry and the urban areas also because of the vast and potential market that the rural population provides for manufactured goods. This demand can be converted into effective demand only by increasing the purchasing power of the rural people. The present condition of the rural poor is desperate. In the beginning of the new millennium, 260 million people were living below the poverty line in India, 75 per cent were from rural areas. This anger, frustration can any moment turn into violence, especially when disturbed by political parties. The traditional supports of the rural society-deep rooted traditional values etc.—are steadily changed by pseudo-modernization without anything significant replacing them. It further increases the problems of poverty, unemployment, diseases, population explosion, regional disparities in equality, etc. It is in the rural areas that major issues in the world's future transformation—population growth, energy, technology, etc. present their most serious challenge not only because of the dimensions of the problems involved but also because their solutions call for innovative approaches.

Current Situations and Trends in ERT

It is important for the survival of the human race that rural areas must survive; and for their survival rural development is essential. The size of the area and population involved in rural dėvelopment is so enormous that the options exercised in their transformation will have a tremendous impact on world development; and unless the open options with education are wisely exercised and the advanced countries lent a truly friendly helping hand in enlightened self-interest, transformation may not take place in a manner which makes for a better and a more harmonious world. We have the question of the role of education that can play in the process; the extent to which it is discharging that function and how it can do so more effectively the central fact in the present position relating to rural development is the extreme poverty of vast masses of human beings. The world may be divided into high-income, middle-income and low income countries. The situation or the plight of the low income group countries is grain and the future prospectus are given grimmer. In India, about 51 per cent of the population in the rural areas, and 38 per cent in the urban and about 98 per cent in the country as a whole, were estimated to live below the poverty line. The most dangerous aspects of the arithmetic of inequality in India is the socio-political system of which the inequality is both a cause and consequence. Region-wise, the central eastern region is the most poverty-stricken region of the country, both in terms of poverty ratio as well as concentration of the poor. The Ministry of Rural Development time to time has undertaken several programmes for implementation.

Some of the programmes are as follows:

- The Sampoorna Grammin Yojana (2001).
- Pradhan Mantri Sadak Yojana (2000).
- National Food for Work Programme (2004).

- National Rural Employment Guarantee Act (2005).
- Indira Awas Yojana (2010).

The major cause of poverty is the fast increasing population. The close link between rapid population growth and poverty has been clearly established by various studies. The world faces one of the most service challenges to growth and development from an exploding population. Nine states and union territories include Kerala, Tamil Nadu and Punjab, which accounts for 15 per cent of the total population, have already reached the replacement level of fertility. Other states such as Bihar, Haryana, Uttar Pradesh, Delhi, Sikkim, Nagaland, Chandigarh and Gujarat have shown an increase in the population growth rate during 1991-2001. Various studies have established the causes of rapid population growth; lack of education, especially among women; inadequate health facilities, which does not ensure the survival of children born. It covers practically the entire gamut of development.

Despite several steps taken by the Government of India to provide regular and productive employment in rural areas, the rural employment situation is far from satisfaction of workers in rural areas which are mostly engaged in low-paid agricultural activities, either as self-employed or casual labour. Rampant unemployment among the rural population, rural poverty alleviation programmes have been revamped to enhance their effectiveness.

- The Swarna Jayanti Gram Swarozgar Yojana.
- National Institutions.
- Special attention for providing technical support through education and technology.

Science and technology may be able to meet the challenge of increased food production, but it may not be able to affect its distribution in a manner as would ensure its reaching the vast masses that need it most but may not have the money, because of lack of adequate employment and education. Nearly half of all children in India, under three, are underweight, a quarter of all children are born with low weight and half of adult women are anaemic. Malnutrition is not only about hunger; its effect is linked with early marriage and consequently early motherhood.

Insufficient quantity of food is less to blame for child under nutrition than poor food quality and women's low social status. It is very ironical that people who produce food remain hungry. Improvement of agriculture and diversification of the rural economy is perhaps one of the most serious challenges that we have to face. Unemployment is the greatest insult to man's self-respect, who is rejected as useless, and the worst form of inequity and injustice.

For rural transformation, development orientation of social services, education at all levels need to provide the necessary transforming force. It requires reorientation of education, making it environmental and problem centred, using creative methodologies which would feed and sharpen curiosity, initiative, resourcefulness, spirit of cooperation and team work, which would lead the products of the education system to make rural areas more dynamic and productive.

Inculcation of scientific temper with education in the people so that the rationale of everything around them is sought, which would ultimately lead to the rationalization of every aspect of their lives—social, political and economic. The existing technologies, representing as they have centuries of experience and adjustment with the socio-economic environment, should receive the highest priority with a view to discovering the science behind them, thereby setting a clue to gradation and improvement. When new technology is introduced in an area, its impact on local communities, technically educationist people, social scientists and other concerned must, carefully assess especially the weaker sections. For example, a multi-purpose hall or an university or flyover as an industry set up in an *Adivasi* Area without providing them alternate residential accommodation and employment cause more problem than development. Education will need to provide not only trained manpower for handling various jobs required by this decentralized but highly efficient society. A very important step in education will be to link universities very closely with the rural development. That would create interest among students both of higher education and of rural development. Apart from the formal system, a comprehensive programme of non-formal education, with an immediate linkage with life's struggles and problems will be required to be organized. This ensures the necessary Research and Development input, which the transformation process requires. Education system enables the students to increase production and character building. Life in educational institutions should be based on co-operation, simplicity and self-government, of course, guided by teachers.

Some Strategies for Effective Delivery of Educational Services

Recognizing the importance of education in rural areas and adopting appropriate policies and operational strategies are necessary steps towards empowering the rural mass. Several strategies have been adopted for effective delivery of educational services in the countryside, also include expanding network of schools in rural areas, promoting gender and social equity, providing nutritional support to young children, ensuring participation in planning and management of education.

Promoting enabling skills of rural people to diversify their livelihood, such as literacy numeracy, farming skills for off farm activities and micro-business management are important for reducing poverty.

Students may be given an idea of global nature of energy, crisis and our own need and resources and this should be linked to local situation where carefully designed programmes would need to be launched for developing alternative sources of energy. Recycling of human, animal and vegetable waste effluent with compost pits, utilization of kitchen water for kitchen gardening, Gobar gas plants, etc. ought to energy creation and utilization. Like-wise, solar energy, as an in exhaustible source of energy ought to be a subject of study in our educational institutes. People will have to be educated with regard to nutritional standards and their present insufficiency as indicated by incidence of disease, death rate etc.

B.P.S.M. Vishwavidyalaya, Khanpur Kalan is the first women university in North India has been taken many initiatives and emerged as a pioneer in many aspects of higher education in rural area. The Centre for University Society Interface and Research is the latest innovative programme inaugurated by Chief Minister of Haryana on 14th August, 2010. It has been founded on the growing realization that there has to be a direct give and take between the universities and the society, which is a rich storehouse of knowledge that ought to be accessed wisely by the academicians. The Centre proposes to do exactly that through its innovative courses from the ensuring session 2010-11 by launching add on courses in these fields:

- Integrated Energy Resources Management.
- Micro-Finance Practices.
- Folk Medicine.

These are primarily fieldwork courses and the students shall be taken to the villages and surrounding communities to interact with them, learn from them, learn from, what they know and then plan how to put together what they learn and what use to make of that knowledge for lived life. Teaching will be done by teachers from different departments of the university and experts from NABARD, TERI, Ministries of State and Central Governments, and other Individual experts.

Some Developmental Policies and Educational Programmes

The Constitution of India has made a commitment to provide free and compulsory education for all children upto the age of fourteen. The NPE in 1986 and with its revised version in 1992, detail the policy measures and broad interventions for providing basic education for all, Government of India launched Sarva Shiksha Abhiyan (SSA) in the year 2000. By SSA, effective management of teachers and resources at local level, particularly at the sub-district level is recognized as extremely critical. Decentralization of planning and management of elementary education as a strategy has been given emphasis in Tenth Plan.

The most universities and colleges should be moved to rural areas. It will link modernity, through universities and tradition culture. Development agencies can be located on the campuses to promote close interaction between them and universities. Education and health facilities are so poor in rural areas that most academicians would hesitate to work in rural areas; they want turn out from rural areas especially for education of their wards. Electronic media like the Radio, Television, and Computer have already reached in rural areas but due to distance and communication difficulties, it will be difficult for universities to free flow of information, which is necessary for a university to remain up-to-date. Universities can help themselves effectively connects through internet and telecommunication for transformation new techniques in these areas. Just moving universities to rural areas may not achieve much for rural transformation. Changes in curriculum, methods of teaching and evaluation, etc. need to be effected before universities can become agencies of development and social transformation. Even areas, there affiliated colleges could be located right in urban area and would be visited by some of the best faculty and researchers of the university colleges in the rural areas would act as extension agents, transferring ideas and technologies to community and providing feedback to research centre and the university. For motivating students and faculty it is essential that they should be an integrated part of the curriculum a problem-centred, rather than a discipline centred approach, should be used. For evaluation a student credit should be given for his participation in rural development activities. Some research work in this regard should start activity. Considerable work needs to be done in this direction on priority basis before this can become a common practice in all universities.

Coordination among Government, Non-Government and Voluntary Agencies

There should be coordination of a university with Government, Non-Government and Voluntary Agencies. The experience of institutions attempted to work in rural areas shows that cooperation of voluntary organization is very helpful in identification of the needs of rural communities, which may be the basis for any active plan of action for rural transformation trough education. The coordination and cooperation between universities and Government agencies will, however, is not easy in view of the different cultures, thinking, concept prevailing in the academic institutions and government offices and require patience and understanding.

At the central level, a number of institutions/organizations are concerned with education. These include:

- Planning Commission,
- Ministry of Human Resource Development (its subordinate offices like the Directorate of Adult Education,

the autonomous organizations created by the Ministry-Research Councils, Academies),

- National University of Educational Planning and Administrations,
- National Council of Educational Research and Training (NCERT), and
- Central Advisory Board of Education (CABE)

Maximum results are to be obtained to be coordination among their policies should programmes. There is considerable scope for improvement in that direction. Either there are also other Ministries of the Government of India, with whom the Ministry of Human Resource Development must coordinate its functions, because they are also engaged in educational activities like the Ministries of Agriculture, Health Labour, etc. or they are economic Ministries whose programmes have educational implications.

The Divisions in the Planning Commission work more or less in an isolated manner and function as counterparts of Ministries. There is insufficient interaction between them, and especially with social services and social engineering divisions like Health Education, etc. with education, interaction of other divisions is confined to balance manpower availability with its demand since technical institutions train manpower which other Divisions utilize. Even this coordination is very imperfect at the moment. There is little realization that contribution of education to development is much more comprehensive than provision of skilled manpower. It has to provide the social climate, promote attitudes of people and their social organizations and reflect their aspirations and expectations. The result may be illustrated by one example.

Large river dams and flyovers have been built without adequate plan for all-round rehabilitation of thousands of displaced people with their social and economic life disrupted.

Another closely linked weakness of the Planning Commission is insufficient interaction among Human Resource Development Division. This departmental isolation exists in entire Government of India. It could be at least removed to some extent if the Planning Commission could take a collaborative and integrated view of Human Resource Development. Some of the elements of human resources development would include:

- Health (depending upon food, healthy environment, healthy occupational conditions, leisure time utilization, healthy social climate with a system of values preferring cooperation to cut throat competition, etc.);
- Education and training; and
- Social and political organization.

Human Resources Development is a much more comprehensive issue than mere workforce planning with which it is often equalized. An integrated view of development policies in this regard would reduce some of the absurdities, where we spend lots of money on education, while giving insufficient attention to nutritional deficiencies of children of ages five years and below, which make them permanently mentally deficient. Again, while there may be an advantage in keeping agricultural education with the Ministry of Agriculture and medical education with the Ministry of Health, etc. there are policies, which are as valid for agricultural and medical education as for the rest of education. Therefore, at least in the Planning Commission, there should be close interaction among education, Health and Agriculture Division.

Contribution towards Training for Rural using Non-formal and Informal Educational Organization

It may be worthwhile to have a Member in-charge of Social Planning Human Resource Development. A high-powered Social Planning and Human Resource Development Cell, consisting of very highly qualified social scientists, should assist him. Divisions of Education, Manpower, Health, Social Welfare, Labour and other Social Service Divisions should work to him through this high powered cell. Similarly, economic divisions like Agriculture, Irrigation, Power, Industries, etc. should secure views of this cell in regard to the social implications of their policies, programmes and projects and the safeguards, if any, which are needed while implementing them.

In the context of development, there should be frequent discussions between the Planning Commission and CABE, led by the Education Minister. At present there is hardly any contact between the CABE and the Planning Commission. The Deputy

Chairman or the Member for Education is generally invited to impress him with their united demand for more funds than for any serious discussion of the development and rural transformation through education and *vice versa*.

Educational policy formulation becomes fragmented the CABE confining itself mostly to school education—leaving higher education to the University Grants Commission (UGC), technical education to the All India Council for Technical Education (AICTE), youth and sports affairs to the Sports Council, cultural affairs to various Academies and State Ministers of Culture, and so on.

Education at State Level

Different educational activities in different departments are even greater in the States; and there is no place where an integrated view of education in respect of both policies and programmes, is taken except in the Planning Department, where many of these scattered activities are brought together for purpose of presentation of the State Plan to the Planning Commission.

Even in the Education Department, there is little coordination. There may be a Director of School Education, a Director of College Education, a Director of Adult Education, and Director of Technical Education, etc. Their work is supposed to be coordinated at the Education Secretary's level, which may be in-charge of other portfolios also. His secretariat, consisting of Deputy Secretaries, under Secretaries etc. cannot coordinate educational policies at technical level. For this purpose, a strong Planning and Statistical Cell, headed by a senior educational administrator and capable of taking a coordinated view of educational policies and programmes in the plan and their relationship with other sectors of development, should assist the coordinator. Another difficulty in the State Educational Department is the highly centralized character of administration and the consequent inflexibility of procedures, which adversely affect innovation management.

There is no linkage between the SCERT and research in the Education Departments of the Universities in the state. There is very little involvement of teachers in research. The potential of teachers for research remains uncxploited. Also in the matter of developmental linkage of education—as it requires school community interaction and the interaction of a school with local representatives and institutional units of other departments/ organization, which has to take place in field situations and the innovative ideas as to how to improve that interaction can also largely emerge only at the field level—it is most important to utilize and develop the capacity of the teacher, who is the field agent of the education department.

Conclusions

Rural areas and rural communities constitute the largest and most glaring example of inequity. They need most concern and attention of the world. On account of their large number, they pose the most serious potential threat to the world place and stability: yet they could become a productive force to world places and stability, if education for rural transformation is used. Apart from the formal system, a comprehensive programme of non-formal education, with an immediate linkage with life's struggles and problems will be required to be actively organized. This ensures the necessary research and development input, which the transformation process requires. The educational efforts, closely linked to research, science and technology must be intensified so that the people can understand, appropriate improve the new techniques and equipment introduced so that the village economy, instead of remaining in a stagnant state, becomes a growing and improving economy. The experience of institutions, universities to work in rural areas shows that cooperation of voluntary organization is very helpful in identification of the needs of rural communities, which may be the basis for any active plan of action for rural transformation through education.

REFERENCES

Cheidrn, C.P. (2010). "Micro Finance: A tool for Rural Development in India". *Pratiyogita Darpan*.

Conen, A. (1985). *The Symbolic Construction of Community*. London: Tavistock.

Desai, A. (2005). *Rural India in Transition*. New Delhi: Popular Prakashan.

Meena, G.L., Pant, D.C, (Eds.) (2010). "Agri-Business in India: An Overview". *Pratiyogita Darpan*.

Nayar, D.P. (1952). *Building for Peace*. New Delhi: Atma Ram and Sons.

Nayar, D.P. (2009). *Education for Rural Development*. New Delhi: Shipra Publication.

Satsangi, P.S. and Gautam, V. (Eds.) (1983). *Management of Rural Energy Systems*. New Delhi: Galgotia Publications.

University Education Commission Report (1949). New Delhi: Government of India.

Websites Referred

http://rural.nic.in/success.htm
http:/www.bps.womenuniversity.ac.in.
http:/www.worldbark.org.

7

Role of Vocational Education Towards Creation of Sustainable Livelihood Transforming Rural India

Amit Choudhury and *Daisy Nath*

Introduction

Vocational Education and Training (VET) is not new to Indian Philosophy in general and educational processes in particular. In *Geeta*, Lord Krishna accorded highest esteem to the path of *Karma*—standing for work, as compared to Gyan and Bhakti for attainment of truth and commune with the Lord. The roots of VET in India can be traced to the Vedic period say for example in *Ashramas* the disciples had to undertake all sorts of work for learning and living. According to the Vedas there exists four planes for the seekers of knowledge and these are—(i) Knowledge, (ii) Action, (iii) Devotion, and (iv) Wisdom. Knowledge, action and devotion have been regarded as three pillars necessary for the process of self-development. In fact the work-centred education was an integral part of the traditional Indian Education System.

The philosophy of VET for the present century should be laid on the foundations of Indian thoughts and traditions, with emphasis on 'sustainable development' and 'decent living'. The philosophy should suit the agrarian economy, keeping in view the needs of the technologically advancing world, globalization, market competitiveness and knowledge-based society.

What is Vocational Education?

Vocational education in India aims to develop skilled manpower through diversified courses to meet the requirements of mainly the unorganized sector and to instill self-employment skills in people through a large number of self-employment oriented courses.

Vocational education is imparted through Industrial Training Institutes (ITIs) and Polytechnics. Since 1980s the Vocational Education as a stream of learning apart from Science, Arts and Commerce has been adopted in certain Senior Secondary/Higher Secondary Schools of the country. Apart from these, the other providers of Vocational Education and Training are Industrial Training Centres, Jan Sikshan Sansthans, National Institute of Open Schooling, Colleges and Universities and IGNOU.

History of Vocational Education and Training in Modern India

The University Education Commission 1948-49 headed by Dr. S. Radhakrishanan rightly emphasized its importance in the following words: "Professional education is the process by which men and women prepare for exacting, responsible service in the professional spirit. The term may be restricted to preparation for fields requiring well informed and disciplined insight and skill of a high order. Less exacting preparation may be designated as vocational or technical education."

The Kothari Commission (1964-66) was of the view that for a majority of occupations, university degrees were not necessary; and these jobs could be competently performed by trained higher secondary students. This Commission felt that it should be possible to divert at least 50 per cent of students completing 10 year education to the vocational stream, which would reduce the pressure on the universities and also prepare students for gainful employment.

The National Policy on Education (NPE), 1986 further emphasized its importance and observed: "The introduction of systematic, well planned and rigorously implemented programme of vocational education is crucial in the proposed educational re-organization. Vocational education will be a distinct stream intended to prepare students for identified vocations spanning several areas of activity."

Where India Stands in Terms of Vocational Education and Training

While India has only 5100 Industrial Training Institutes and 1745 Polytechnics, China boasts of 500,000 Vocational Education and Training (VET) Institutes. Indian State Governments have 40 million educated unemployed on their musters, even as the domestic industry is experiencing severe shortage of skilled personnel. These 40 million youth are barely functional literates, unskilled in any trade or vocation. In India, there is a severe shortage of trained and skilled technicians as only 1.50 to 2.0 million (2%) students in the age-group of 15 to 25 are enrolled in VET every year, as against 80 per cent in Europe and 60 per cent in East Asian nations like Malaysia, Korea and Taiwan. Majority of Indian students are enrolled in general university programmes.

Importance of Vocational Education and Training in Indian Context

The skill shortage in the Indian economy today is largely due to neglect of vocational education The ASSOCHAM paper recently published revealed that nearly 300 million people of the 18-50 age-group are unemployed because they just do not have any marketable skill. At the same time, the scarcity of trained plumbers, carpenters and mechanics in Indian cities drains the economy of Rs. 100 crore a year.

In India every year, 6,50,000 engineering graduates and approximately two million graduates pass out of collegés. Nearly two-thirds of the 6,50,000 engineering graduates need to be re-skilled, so that they can get jobs in the industry. Meanwhile, the developed world requires knowledge workers and skilled professionals. By 2020, the developed world will have a shortage of 40 million working people, says a report. A recent study by Global HR Consultancy Manpower Inc. says that 41 per cent of employers worldwide are having difficulty filling positions due to lack of suitable talent in their markets. Manpower shortages can cripple economic growth. It can escalate wage rates, thereby reducing the competitiveness of these countries.

Need and Scope of Vocational Education and Training in India

According to a survey, 72 per cent of our population is under the age of 35 and it is estimated that 300 million people between the ages of 18 and 50 seek employment of some form. While 57 per cent are unemployable, 46 million are registered with employment exchanges with little hope of finding a suitable job. But there is a mismatch between the skilled manpower required and skilled manpower available and there is huge shortage of skilled talent. A majority of the youth passing out from our universities and colleges do not have the specific skill sets required by various sectors in the market. Vocational education is surely going to be an enabler to help India shine in the unorganized sector.

Recent Developments in the Field of Vocational Education and Training

The Government of India in recent years has laid a lot of emphasis on streamlining vocational education so that it fulfils the emerging need of the market by focusing on employability skills. Hardly 1.5 to 2 million students have registered for vocational education and training in India. In his recent Budget speech, Union Finance Minister Pranab Mukherjee said: "The demographic advantage India has in terms of a large percentage of young population needs to be converted into a dynamic economic advantage by providing them the right education and skills."

The National Knowledge Commission recommends for a model of imparting Vocational Education that is flexible, sustainable, inclusive and creative. It suggests for significant increase in public and private investment in vocational education and training.

Realizing the need for informal skilled workforce in the country, many private institutes are offering vocational training with accreditation from recognized industry bodies resulting in empowering employment. These institutes also assure better placements for their students.

A private institution VOCAD is one such institution which provides corporate and businesses one-stop manpower solutions for front end. A joint initiative of Collabrant Group and STRIVE (an incubation of and IFMR Trust), VOCAD's mission is to bridge the gap between rural, semi-urban and the urban areas through vocational education. The objective of this multibrand educational institute is to bridge the skill gap and provide trained manpower to various emerging service sectors in India Inc. and strive towards the development of skilled manpower for diversified sector through short-term, structured job oriented courses. VOCAD will put up over 600 centres in every district HQ of the country offering courses in the service sector verticals of lifestyle, telecom, hospitality, healthcare, travel, consumer durables, food and grocery, entrepreneurship management, banking, securities, insurance, mutual funds, basic accounting, basic commerce, BPO, construction management, auto mechanics, DTH, beauty care, etc. They have launched eight centres as of now all over India. Imparting vocational education and training would benefit all and also have the following advantages:

1. Prepare the youth for a vocation of their choice; Build up a formidable workforce of international quality, which would be in demand not only in India but also in all other countries.
2. In India, only IT training is of world class. In the manufacturing and service sector, there are hundreds of skills and vocations for which there is worldwide shortage.
3. We need millions of trained people in agriculture, floriculture, horticulture, sericulture, fishery, healthcare, tourism and in the manufacturing sector.
4. Reduce unemployment by supplying world-class skilled people.
5. Reduce cost and improve the productivity of services and manufacturing by providing skilled manpower to international standards.

Sustainable Livelihood and Development

The issue of development had been very significant and important till the last century. But it has been observed that the term 'development' has lost much of its importance and currency in recent times. For many the term development is too fuzzy and too easily disconnected from its goal of poverty alleviation. As poverty is one of the ticklish problems of any underdeveloped or developing country like India. Hence, the concept of creating sustainable livelihood has gained momentum in the line of attack of conceptualizing poverty alleviation for the poor people in the rural areas.

A livelihood is a set of capabilities and activities that provide the means of people to meet their basic requirements and support their well-being. It may be defined as ways of keeping oneself meaningfully occupied. The structure of livelihood reflects and looks for fulfilling both material and experimental needs of human being. Livelihoods are not simply confined to a small area, but connected by economic, political and cultural process and thereby have some casual relationship with natural environment, economic environment, political environment and cultural environment. The sustainability of livelihood is ascertained by its compassion, power of endurance and resiliency in the face of short term and long term challenges. According to Chambers and Conway, "a livelihood is sustainable when it can cope when it can cope with, and recover from, shock and stresses and maintain or enhance its capabilities and assets both now and into the future, while not undermining the natural resource base."

Rural Defined

In India Rural is defined as not "Urban" and "Urban" is defined as:

A. All Places so Administratively Notified.
B. Other places which satisfy all the following:
   - Minimum population of 5,000,
   - At least 75 per cent of all male workers in non-agriculture, and
   - A density of population of at least 400 per sq. km.

According to Food and Agricultural Organization (FAO), the definition of 'rural area' should meet two criteria: one related to unsettled land area and/or land used is for primary production (mining, agriculture, livestock, forestry, fisheries). Second, the residents of rural areas are largely dependent—either directly or indirectly—on these primary production activities as their principal, if not their only, source of livelihood.

A place where activities are affected by high transaction cost, associated with long distance from cities and poor infrastructures (Ashley and Maxwell, 2001). Some authors add to the list the prevalence of poverty, which remains higher in rural areas, in spite of often considerable urbanization (Wiggins and Proctor, 2001).

Rural-Urban Disparities*

- 55 per cent of rural females and 36 per cent of rural males are illiterate, as compared to 30 per cent and 19 per cent in urban.
- Infant mortality is 60 per cent in rural against 37 per cent in urban.
- 46 per cent of rural children are underweight and 41 per cent of rural women have low BMI, against 33 per cent and 25 per cent in urban areas.
- Only 50 per cent rural people have *pucca* houses and 60 per cent electricity, compared to 90 per cent in urban.
- 78 per cent rural households still use firewood for cooking.
- Less than 10 per cent of rural households own mechanized transport as compared to over 30 per cent in urban.

**Source*: Rural Transformation in India—Strategic vision from the Eleventh Plan.

Employment in Rural India*

- Rural India constitutes 71 per cent of India's population and 80 per cent of the poor.
- Growth rate of agricultural employment (1.1%) lower than that of total rural employment (1.6%) and total employment (1.9%), 1983 to 2004-05.
- But 72.6 per cent workers in rural India dependent on agriculture for employment.

---

* *Source:* Education, Skills and Development Dynamics in Rural India—Ravi Srivastava, Swati Sachdeva.

- 60.4 per cent rural workers are self-employed, principally farmers.
- Agriculture continues to dominate the employment landscape in India.
- Informal sector—92 per cent in rural areas—most of these workers are in agriculture.

The above given factual picture is partially responsible for the migration of rural folks towards the urban side in search of better prospect. And those who migrate, often happens to be the young and energetic one's thereby leaving behind the aged population to stick to farming and agriculture related activities.

Rural Transformation

The International Development Agenda: Millennium Developmental Goals (*Source:* UN Secretariat, 2002) come from the Agreements and resolutions of world conferences organized by the United Nations in the first half of 1990s, which was directed towards arriving at an agreement to reduce poverty and achieve sustainable development. Each of the seven goals mentioned below, addresses an aspect of poverty and the same be viewed together as they are mutually reinforcing:

1. Reduce by half the proportion of people living in extreme poverty between 1990 and 2015, and reduce by half the proportion of people who suffer from hunger;
2. Enroll all children in primary school by 2015;
3. Make progress towards gender equality and empowering women by eliminating gender disparities in primary and secondary education by 2005;
4. Reduce infant and child mortality rates by two-thirds between 1990 and 2015;
5. Reduce maternal mortality ratios by three-quarters between 1990 and 2015;
6. Provide access to all those who need reproductive health services by 2015; and
7. Implement national strategies for sustainable development by 2005 so as to reverse the loss of environmental resource by 2015.

Higher School enrollments, especially for girls, reduce poverty and mortality. Better basic health care increases enrollment and reduces poverty. Many poor people earn their living from the environment. As such progress is needed on each of the aforementioned goals. The discussion about education in rural areas is closely related to the broader rural development concept. Like education for rural people, rural development has been a very productive field in development studies (Stamoulis, 2001; Ashley and Maxwell, *op. cit.*). The following chart represents chronologically the dominant and sequential themes in rural development.

Chart 7.1

1950s	1960s	1970s	1980s	1990s	2000s
Dominant Paradigm and switches					
Modernization and dual economy					
	Rising yields on efficient small farms				
			Process, Participation, Empowerment		
			Sustainable livelihood approach		
Some sequential popular rural development emphases					
Community development					
	Small farm growth				
	Integrated rural development				
			Market liberalization		
			Participation		
					Poverty reduction strategy

Source: Ellis and Biggs (2001).

In the present context rural transformation indicates two things *sustainable development and sustainable livelihood* of the rural masses. Rapid changes in technology and fast paced globalization can reap in developmental benefits for a under developed region like Assam only when the population, majority of which is in rural areas, are properly educated and possess necessary skilful knowledge and competence to welcome the change.

On one hand the fast changing technologies and rapid globalization can be a boon towards creation of sustainable livelihood for the rural folk and thereby sustainable development, and on the other hand the same may adversely affect the very basic social fabric of the rural population.

Present Status in Assam

While most States in India are gradually shifting from traditional agriculture based economy towards industry or service oriented economy, Assam still is heavily dependent on this primary sector, i.e. agriculture. As compared to other states in India, Assam is a lesser developed State and a vast majority of the population resides in rural areas. Geographically too Assam portrays a mix of fertile plains, valleys alongside two mighty rivers—the Brahmaputra and the Barak—which sees perennial onslaught of floods, difficult hilly terrain etc. with villages scattered in far-flung and remote areas. Villages in Assam also project a diverse socio-economic, socio-political status. On one hand, Sualkuchi the largest village in the world happens to be the centre of Assam Silk, Sarthebari the centre of traditional brass and bell metal industry and on the other hand there are villages which do not have proper road connectivity and are housed in remote in accessible hilly terrain lacking the basic minimum social infrastructure like schools, dispensaries, etc.

The rural population in Assam comprises the hub of Assamese society and also represents the real Assam, where the rich Assamese culture and tradition flourished. The rural mass in Assam exerts a crushing influence on the socio-economic, cultural and political aspect of the greater Assamese society. Hence, the true development of Assam can only result through the development initiatives of its rural areas.

The significance or role of the activities of the rural people in the development process can be grasped from the fact that they contribute nearly half of total state income. Though Assam is rich in human resource as well as natural resources, she could not utilize for her betterment effectively due to lack of scientific know-how. Majority of the people live in rural areas and depend on agriculture and other allied activities and at the same time lag behind in intervention of science and technology due to mass illiteracy and ignorance.

As an old Chinese adage goes like *"while planning for a year, grow corns, while planning for a decade, plant trees and that while planning for life, train and educate people."* The same more aptly highlights the need for proper effective education both in formal and non-formal ways towards enabling the rural people gain sustainable livelihood in particular leading to sustainable development in general.

While the statistics as regards to education in Assam provides a bright picture in comparison to the national context, yet there is a situation of growing unemployment. The same in turn can also be seen as a prime factor for the social disturbances.

Vocational Education and Training in Assam

The vocational education was introduced in Assam in the year 1983-84 in 5 schools. But by 1985-86 only 2 schools continued the vocational education. Under the Centrally Sponsored Scheme (CSS) the vocational education was introduced in 50 Higher Secondary Schools as a separate stream with effect from 1987-88 academic sessions.

At present 200 higher secondary schools are being allowed to run the vocational stream in the State of Assam out of which 150 schools are presently functioning.

Table 7.1: The year-wise breakup in the State of Assam

Year	*No of Schools*
1987-88	10
1988-89	10
1989-90	30
1992-93	50
1994-95	50
1995-96	50

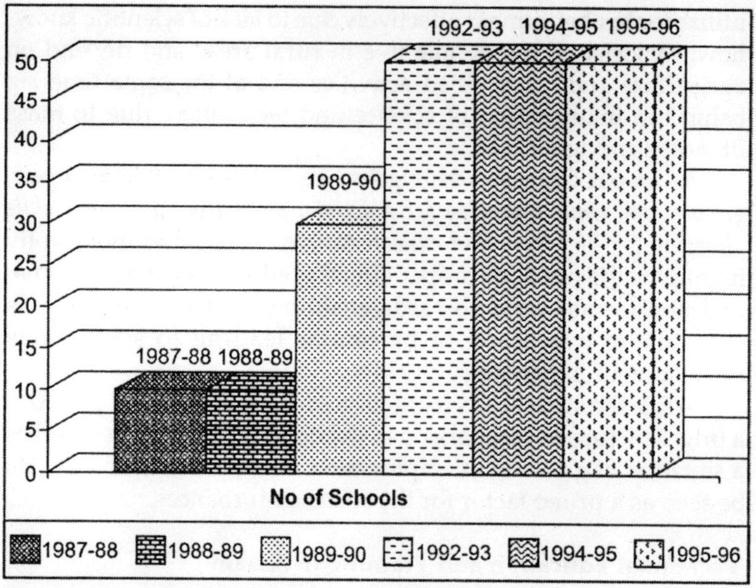

Fig. 7.1: Year-wise breakup in Assam State

The district-wise break up of Higher Secondary Schools offering Vocational stream of education.

Dhubri	*Kokrajhar*	*Bongaingaon*	*Goalpara*	*Barpeta*	*Nalbari*	*Kamrup*	*Darrang*	*Sonitpur*	*Nagaon*	*Morigaon*	*Jorhat*	*Sibsagar*	*Golaghat*	*Tinsukia*	*Dhemaji*	*Karimganj*	*Hailakandi*	*Karbi Anglong*	*N C Hills*	*Lakhimpur*	*Dibrugarh*	*Cachar*
4	2	2	3	5	5	9	3	5	8	1	7	8	3	4	2	3	3	3	1	3	2	3

The Vocational Stream in Higher Secondary Schools of Assam provided subjects such as:

1. Auditing and Accountancy
2. Office Management
3. Office Secretaryship
4. Commercial Art
5. Computer Technique

6. Inland Fisheries
7. Textile Designing
8. Auto Engineering Technology
9. Commercial Garment Making and Designing
10. Mechanical Engineering Technology
11. Maintenance and Repair of Power Driven Farm Machinery
12. Maintenance and Repair of Radio and TV Receiver
13. Maintenance and Repair of Domestic Electrical Appliances
14. Horticulture
15. Crop Production
16. Sericulture

Success Stories—From Assam and Its Neighbouring States
Asomi

A non-government organization engaged primarily in the field of Rural Development in Assam through effective conduct of innovative programmes targeted towards empowering the rural folks. Their present engagements are:

1. *Suoni Gaon* (Prosperous Village) Programme
2. Credit for Holistic Development Programme
3. Welfare Fund Scheme
4. Partnership with Government of Assam for World Bank aided Assam Agriculture Competitiveness Project
5. Dairy Development Programmes
6. Training
7. Implementation of Employment Generation Mission with Government of Assam

Within a short span of 10 years since its inception in year 2001, Asomi has made a mark for itself with contributions towards rural transformation. They have not only successfully convinced the urban daily wage owners to return to their primary activity of agriculture in their respective villages, but also helped them re establish themselves through proper and innovated approaches of training, mentoring and facilitating through the creation of 'community huts' wherein the farmers and other rural folks assemble to sort out and look for solutions to their problems.

Asomi's belief in micro finance and micro credit over 'grant-in-aid' programme paid rich dividends not only to Asomi but to all those families, villages where Asomi has ventured into.

Till date Asomi has successfully generated meaningful sustainable livelihood for 33000 families, created 2700 self-help groups with a total disbursements of Rs. 70.50 crore and an outstanding amount of Rs. 17.05 crore.

Asomi's magic wand being a well laid process of—

1. Awareness
2. Group Formation
3. Saving
4. Lending
5. Training/Skill Upgradation
6. Repayment

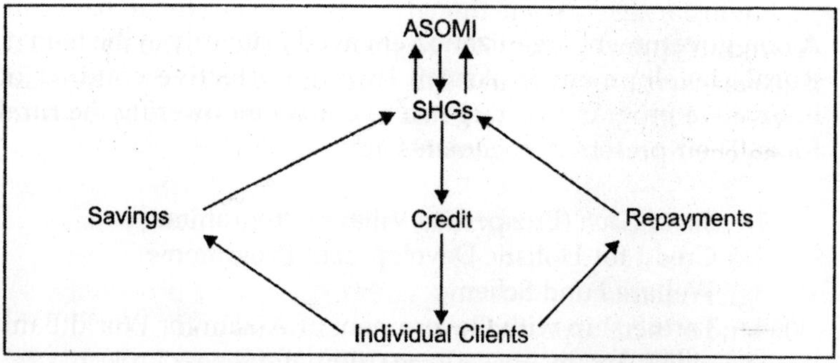

Rural Resource and Training Centre, Umran, Meghalaya

RRTC, Umran formerly known as St. Joseph's Agricultural Training Centre (SJATC), evolved into existence after several years of study and experimentation as an answer to the critical problems that challenge the vast majority of rural population of the North Eastern Region. RRTC was initially an extension of the larger network of Bosco Reach Out (BRO) and it continues to translate into reality BRO's vision and Philosophy "development through empowerment of people" focusing on vast natural resources.

RRTC has gained sufficient expertise in providing Skills Training in Farming, Livestock Management, Entrepreneurship Development and Appropriate Technology and has established its own model farm at a sprawling 175 hecters plus land area.

Hindrance—What Ails Vocational Education

One of the weaknesses of Indian education system is that it does not give due importance to vocational education. As a result there is a mismatch between the skilled manpower required and skilled manpower available. Every year we churn out millions of graduates who do not have the specific skill sets required by the market. If this trend continues it would hurt our economic growth in the long run. To change this situation first we need to change our mindset. In India, people are obsessed with attaining a graduation degree and generally look down upon vocational education. This has resulted in a situation where on the one hand there are scores of unemployed graduates and on the other hand there is a huge shortage of skilled workers such as plumbers, electricians, etc.

For instance in Assam, though the vocational stream has been allowed in approximately 200 Higher Secondary Schools, a total of 203 teachers are appointed full-time for the delivery of the said courses, which is highly insufficient at the first place. Moreover, the selected curriculum also fails to address the need of the industry. This is as a result of lack of industry interaction, non-involvement of location specific coursework which could have been well designed taking the needs of the industries as well as the region into consideration. A cumulative number of well over 5000 students have passed in the past 15years and ironically no record exists about their employment till date.

To sum up the failure of the VET Programme as such the following points may be put forward:

1. Lack of vertical mobility of the students.
2. Negative association of the term 'vocational' with 'manual labour'.
3. Lack of support from financial institutions to the successful candidates desirous to start entrepreneurial venture.
4. Lack of a well coordinated mechanism to impart knowledge and other vital inputs which promotes entrepreneurship.
5. The output from such programme falls short of expectation from the industrial employer as courses are not designed as per the requirement of the Industry.

6. Lack of proper follow up mechanism to make the programme a success.
7. Long duration of the courses.
8. Lack of coordination amongst various bodies/departments engaged in Vocational Education and Training.

Requirement

- Systematic reforms in Vocational Education and Training (VET).
- An Effective Public-Private-Partnership model that seeks to deliver the required thrust towards creation of avenues that shall serve as means for the rural poor to enjoy a decent sustainable livelihood through proper Education, Training, Skill Enhancement, Mentoring and Facilitating.
- The introduction of a 'special purpose vehicle' that shall carry forward the desired as well as planned policy initiatives of the Government both at the Central as well as the State level.
- The usage of innovative as well as cost effective approaches that shall ensure the positive outcome of all such policy initiatives targeted towards sustainable development through provisions of sustainable livelihood for the rural poor.
- To adopt a need based approach in design and development of all such curriculum which shall be location specific with respect to both industrial demands as well as local resource availability.
- Creation of clusters fostering optimum usage of resource for carrying forward all such development oriented schemes and programmes.

The Way Ahead

In order to make the Vocational Education and Training, an effective tool that will ensure the rural population a sustainable livelihood and in turn contribute towards sustainable development of the society as a whole, a well coordinated innovative approach should be adopted by all concerned Ministries/Departments in implementing such major VET Programmes.

Government's role should be that of a facilitator which shall empower Colleges and Institutions, NGOs, Panchayats, etc. to implement the VET Programme and to do the same an innovative approach is required to evolve a result oriented as well as accountable Governance structure.

Curriculum design, development and delivery should have active involvement of those stakeholders which needs skilful human resource so that the appropriate skill can be developed. During the designing of curriculum for all such VET Programmes, the regional needs, the availability of both natural as well as human resources etc. must be considered.

VET curriculum should be made such that it facilitates vertical mobility of the students. Introduction of Modular, Multi-entry, Multi-exit system should be expedited. For example, say a 1-year Programme on Poultry Management may be modularized into 4 independent quarterly modules with a popular nomenclature as cited below:

Module 1 duration 3 months → Broiler Management
Module 2 duration 3 months → Layer Management
Module 3 duration 3 months → Hatchery Management
Module 4 duration 3 months → Marketing Management

Where the students shall enjoy the flexibility of securing certification at any level on their exit and likewise may also avail the entry to the said programme at any level. A 2-year Construction Management Programme may be modularized into

Module 1 duration 3 months → Masonry
Module 2 duration 3 months → Carpentry
Module 3 duration 3 months → Fabrication
Module 4 duration 3 months → Electrical works
Module 5 duration 3 months → Plumbing
Module 6 duration 3 months → Paints and Varnish works

Final 6 months to involve 'on the job training' or 'apprenticeship'.

The said programme shall be inclusive of an 'on the job training' which will be arranged with the Industrial partner of the Programme. Necessary focus on the system of Assessment,

Certification, Accreditation of Institution and Teacher's Training should be given. The same would in turn go a long way to ensure the credibility of the VET Programme as well as ensuring the availability of well-trained teachers to deliver the same.

An effective institutional linkage between academic institutions, financial institutions, marketing and management Institutions, ministries etc. needs to be so developed that the absorption and/or vocational-entrepreneurial needs of all successful trainees from such VET Programme are adequately met.

REFERENCES

Education for Rural Development: Towards new policy responses—A Joint study conducted by FAO and UNESCO, coordinated and edited by David Atchaorena and Lavinia Gasperini. citeseerx.ist.psu.edu/viewdoc/download?doi=10.1.1.114.9056.

Report on All India Consultation Meeting on Vocational Education and Training: Setting Directions and Strategies for Eleventh Five Year Plan—PSS Central Institute of Vocational Education, Bhopal (a constituent of NCERT, under MHRD, Government of India).

Unpublished report on vocational education in Assam—R. Das, Academic Officer, AHSEC.

8

Education of Scheduled Tribes for Rural Transformation in India

Milind Sahastrabuddhe

Introduction

When we talk about, India we have to accept heterogeneities, which prevail. This is because we have Schedule Caste, Scheduled Tribe, other backward castes and people belonging to other castes. Not only is this but main thing to be noted that we have lot of disparities in rural and urban areas including education. It is said that real India resided in rural areas only. It has to be accepted that even after 6 decades of political independence, situation in rural areas is quite different than that in urban area, of course, with some exceptions. This is with reference to literacy rate, poverty, facilities for health, etc. One can say that education is one of the causes for the situation.

When we talk about rural areas of India, one finds that still large chunk of backward castes are there. Not only do this but we have Scheduled Tribes also which are lagging behind as far as economic development is concerned.

When we talk about their total population in India, it was 8.2 per cent according to Census 2001. However, at first glance, it may appear that it is not very sizeable portion of total population. However, it is a fact that we cannot ignore their contribution. When their overall position is not good (with some exceptions), we need to think about them.

One interesting factor is that before 1947, they were away

from our main stream of the society and they had their own customs, traditions etc. which they used to follow. When our constitution was drafted, these tribes were included in a "Schedule" and that is the reason why they are known as "Scheduled Tribe" one can find them in all nooks and corners of the country and they are known with different names in different parts of India like Bhil, Dubla, Rathvas, etc. One thing is that since we were interested in their overall development, certain percentage of seats were reserved for them with regard to admission in various courses or employment criteria's are relaxed for them. Not only this but they can avail advantages in terms of free ship, scholarship, free text books, uniform and stationery also. When our Constitution was accepted in 1951, one can see that the reservation was kept for 10 years only and it was expected that by 1961, they would attain 100 per cent literacy, which is still not there in all parts of our country. Some people have made use of these benefits and improved themselves but almost all have migrated to urban areas and the situation in rural areas is as it was. One can say that we can have different measures to improve their present position but a fact remains that education is the most powerful tool for their overall development and there by leading to rural transformation.

Present Scenario

Even today, the fact is that they are lagging far behind than over national literacy rate (65%). The situation is very dismal with regard to women and rural areas. The situation is worst where overall state literacy rate is not at all good like Bihar, M.P. It is dishearten to note that even in states like Gujarat and Maharashtra where overall position is not that good, situation for Scheduled Tribe has not considerably improved. Some people say that politicians have used them as their "Vote Banks" rather than showing real enthusiasm and they have made lot of money from various schemes meant for them. Establishing residential schools where staying and meal facility is free for whole year, some people have made money out of them or used them just as "Show Pieces" to capture lot of votes in elections at all levels. Situation regard to literacy rate has not improved due to such nasty acts. How

Education can contribute for their transformation especially in rural areas where it is not good at present.

Education and Economic Development are closely related to each other especially in 21st century. Education is cause and consequence for the poverty. At present, it is a crude fact that their economic condition is not at all good—especially in rural areas. When one (Boys and Girls) starts getting good education. Prospects for good employment are more and especially in the era of privatization where "Good Higher Education" is must for good earning. Getting education is not important (in terms of literacy alone) but good higher education like getting degrees for Technology, ICT, Computer Science, M.B.A. etc. would fetch more earning for them. Not only this but later on, after acquiring some experience, they can change their job for better earning also. They can also think of migrating to foreign countries at younger age for better earning. When their earning would improve, they would be able to improve their overall position in the society. Not only that they will be able to enjoy luxuries of the life alone but their own children would also get an advantage of "Good Higher Education". The process will go on and that is what is needed.

Apart from better earning, education will also help them to earn higher, most important thing is their awareness about personal health and health facilities provided by government to them. When one is educated one will understand their concepts like "Nutritious Diet" and one would implement them in own life. Further, it would also help them for what Do's and what Don'ts to be implemented in day-to-day life. This will help not only at the micro level but also at the macro level as we would have army of "*Healthy Citizens*". Education will also help them to decide at what age and at which economic level, one should marry. Concepts of family planning and proper gape between two children would also be understood in a real sense and implement in one's own life. This would go a long way in one's own prosperity in future and personal happiness. Unless and untill they are educated, they will not have idea about various medical facilities provided to them by government like primary Health Centres in rural areas. These people, in absence of proper education, will not take full advantage of such facilities. They will not approach such places at the right time and thus it would lead to wastage of resources. Not only this but instead of going to such places, they will remain in clutches of blind beliefs and traditions. They would take resort of those uneducated persons who would claim that god or goddess has given them divine power and they can treat them with the use of some water or *Prasad* which is totally unscientific. In this process, they would cause harm to their own health at the cost of their own money which is limited in natures. They would also mortgage their own property or borrow money from others but would not understood of a reality behind this. Sometimes, even it would go to an extent that they would allow those persons to do all sorts of evils with their own body.

Further, in absence of education, they would not be able to take full advantage of government loans and subsidies. Instead, they will go to private money lenders where they have to mortgage their property or have to pay very high rate of interest and some times, interest is more than the principal amount of money. Instead of this, when they are educated, they would take full advantage of whatever government loans or subsidies are available to them. With the help of these, they can better their own self-employment or business. If they are agriculturist, with use of this, they can enhance productivity. Not only this but in absence of proper education, they would not be able to reap benefits of all governmental facilities which are provided to them. They can take loans and pursue their higher education in abroad countries also. This will lead to higher educational qualifications and better prospects for higher earning. At school or college level of education, they would not show their ignorance towards various government facilities provided to them.

Most important thing is that their awareness for "Right to Information". Whenever, one is having something in a mind, one can get information related to it. People will sit silently because they do not have knowledge about this right. Once they are educated, they can always seek needed information. By this, if they have some injustice, they can raise their voice against this and can get needed justice for themselves. This, they can do either in person or collectively. Once they are citizen of this country they have right to know something which they want to. They would also have knowledge about fundamental rights.

The Scheduled Tribes: Social Context and Current Educational Situation

The Scheduled Tribes

A conspicuous trait of Indian culture is the survival of tribal society and culture in the midst of a rapidly changing society. Scheduled Tribes who inhabit isolated mountainous regions were not appropriated into the agriculture based kingdoms of the plains, in the absence of easy communication and transport facilities. Katsambis identifies the spread of Brahmanism and its rigid subordination of individual to social function with the spread of a more productive agrarian order. According to the Census of 2001, the Scheduled Tribes, constitute 8.1 per cent of the Indian population. In absolute terms, this comes to some 83.6 million people, classified under 461 different communities. They are spread over the entire country but are most heavily concentrated in central, eastern and north-eastern India. Two broad types scheduling, viz. area based and community based exist for tribes. Areas under the Fifth Schedule belong to nine major states of western and central region extending from Maharashtra on the West to Jharkhand in the East. Vulnerable tribal populations of some states are left out, however, such as in West Bengal, Karnataka, Tamil Nadu and Kerala. The Sixth Schedule applies to tribal areas in states of the North East. Unlike the relatively dispersed SC population, about 90 per cent of the Scheduled Tribes are found in a few states. Orissa and Madhya Pradesh have more than 20 per cent. More than 50 per cent lives in parliamentary constituencies where they form the majority. They are defined partly by habitat and geographic isolation but more on the basis of social religious, linguistic and cultural distinctiveness. The ST occupy a belt stretching from the Bhil regions of western India through the Gond districts of central India, to Jharkhand and Bengal where the Mundas, Oraons and Santhals predominate. There are also pockets of Scheduled Tribe communities in the south and very small-endangered communities in the Andamans. Northeast India contains a large proportion of the Scheduled Tribe population, including the different Naga sub-tribes (Sundar, 2006). Tribes represent differing levels opposing cultural principle of organizing life due to varying histories of assimilation and exploitation (Omvedt, n.d.). Colonialism marked a turning point in the history of trials. Economic interests of the colonists required large scale acquisition of natural resources, reducing tribal to positions of economic and cultural subservience to non-tribal communities. Forced absorptions have continued to take place at the behest of the aggressive dominant economic and political forces. Analyzing the post-colonial situation, Desai (1969) classifies the tribes according to various stages of cultural development which gives some broad idea of the variation. Class I are the "purest of pure" ST groups. Problems of the relatively isolated Scheduled Tribe populations are qualitatively different and demand different solutions; class II include those having contact with plains; class III—is the largest section in a peculiar stage of transition. They are looked upon as—"backward" Hindus, ST only in name, having been uprooted from the tribal mode by bonded slavery. Like the Scheduled Castes, the consequence of 'mainstreaming' through education and/or employment has occurred for them but largely at the lower echelons. Christian missionaries have been responsible for spreading education among tribal populations in various parts of the country—a development which had diverse social and political consequences for the tribes. Importantly, political assertion, middle class entry and like the SC, is the creation of a gap between tribal elites and the rest. Class IV tribes are an old autocracy—for example, the powerful Bhil, wealthy Santhal and Oraon, Mundas, who won historical battles of cultural contact. North Eastern tribal society, located in the peripheral extreme eastern region came under both colonial and Christian influences. However, the magnitude of the Christian impact as amative force to modernization has varied between these tribal regions (Ahmad, 2003; Bara, 1997). Overall, small sections of tribal groups have benefited while majority remain impoverished.

Capitalist onslaught on the tribal way of life by the Indian state and by national and global business interests have brought about further economic ruin. Large scale alienations and dispossession from land and natural resources, and displacement due to mega development projects such as big dams, power plants etc. have pushed the tribals into conditions of stark economic deprivation. Those who once led a bountiful existence now struggle for basic livelihood. As pointed out by Chalam (1993) scores of studies show how these processes have worked in tribal dominated regions (see also Pathy, 2000; Punalekar, 2000; Sundar, 2006). Post 90s the flow of funds for Tribal Sub-Plans are declining, worsening the bad situation created by a faulty implementation strategy, since its inception in the Fifth Five Year Plan (*ibid.*, 1993; Sharma, 1994). What is the contemporary educational status of the SC and ST groups? The following section reviews current state provision and quantitative achievements.

State Provision for Education for ST and Recent Trends in Their Educational Progress

State commitment to the education of SC/ST children is contained in Articles 15(4), 45 and 46 of the Constitution of India. Article 15(4) underscores the state's basic commitment to positive discrimination in favour of the socially and educationally backward classes and/or the SC and ST. Article 45 declares the state's endeavour to provide free and compulsory education for all children until they complete the age of 14 years. Article 46 expresses the specific aim to promote with special care the educational and economic interests of SC/ST. In its effort to offset educational and socio-historical disadvantage, the Indian state conceived range of enabling provisions that would facilitate access to and ensure retention of SC and children in school. In the initial Five Year Plans, the focus was on making available basic educational facilities such as schools especially in remote areas and providing scholarships and books. Both Central and State Governments took up the responsibility of special educational provision. The scope of enabling interventions expanded considerably after the Fourth Five Year Plan. Special schemes pertaining to school education of SC/ST children currently include: (i) free supply of textbooks and stationery at all stages of school education; (ii) free uniforms to children in Government approved hostels and Ashrams schools, and in some states also for children in regular schools; (iii) free education at all levels; (iv) pre-metric stipends and scholarships to students at middle and/or high school stage; (v) special scheme of pre-metric scholarships for children of castes and families engaged in unclean occupations like scavenging, tanning and flaying of animal skin; (vi) girls and boys hostels for SC/ST students and lodging facilities in hostels of backward classes including SC/ST; and (vii) Ashram schools for tribal children started with the intention of overcoming the difficulties of provision in remote regions and also rather patronizingly to provide an environment "educationally more conducive" than the tribal habitat. In addition, several states have instituted schemes such as scholarships to ST students studying in private schools, merit scholarships, attendance scholarships for girls, special school attendance prizes, remedial coaching classes, reimbursement of excursion expenses and provision of mid-day meals. The last has been recommended as an integral element in schooling by the Working group on Development and Welfare of the Scheduled Tribes during the Eighth Five Year Plan (Kamat, 1985; Chatterjee, 2000). Several studies carried out in the initial decades after independence and in particular, the landmark Report of the Commission of SC/ST of 1986-87 showed that educational progress till the mid-eighties was slow and uneven (Kamat, 1985; Government of India, 1990; Velaskar, 1986; Government of India, 1998).

Summing Up and Explaining the Situation of Persistent Unequal Access

Several crucial points directly emerge from the brief survey reported above. Regional studies which we have not reviewed here due to constraints of space have brought out the other points. Firstly, our analysis points out that a significant proportion of Scheduled Caste and an even greater proportion of Scheduled Tribe children continue to remain out of school. This is so even in the younger age-group, indicating that accessing basic school is still a problem, especially in certain states and regions which have suffered gross neglect by the polity and State. Secondly, and on a more positive note and notwithstanding the tendency of deliberate overestimation, there is an unprecedented rise in enrollment of both Scheduled Castes and Scheduled Tribes, which indicate a strong desire for education. Thirdly, and a dampener on the situation is that attendance rates at both primary and middle school and completion rates are far from satisfactory. This indicates that dropout, failure are problems that afflict SC/STchildren to a far greater degree than the rest and they thus continue to lag behind them in terms of educational attainment. Fourthly, there is great unevenness in the educational participation of the various states, and between regions/pockets. In some states progress is very good for both boys and girls but in others it is very poor. In most states girls are far behind the boys. There are also sharp disparities between rural-urban areas. Even in the relatively advanced states like Maharashtra, Tamil Nadu and Punjab there are marked regional, intra SC/ST and gender disparities on all educational indicators. Fifthly, though we have not done a systematic comparative analysis, Scheduled Tribes appear to lag behind the Scheduled Castes in most of the larger states barring, of course, the North East. Finally, there's a strong indication that specific regions and specific SC and ST groups face extreme and gross educational deprivation, within which the situation of girls is abominate is clear that the country still struggles to ensure equitable access to SC/ST, while resolve to universalize elementary education and equalize educational opportunity was to incorporate notions of equality of access, equality of survival and equality of learning achievement. Gender, caste, tribe and class inequalities exist in access, retention and years of completed schooling. Disparities in scholastic achievement—an area where we have little systematic comparative data—are even more glaring as revealed by a few micro studies. In sum, despite considerable quantitative progress, exclusion remains a depressing feature of the educational scenario of SC/ST children.

Impact of Structural Adjustment Policies on Educational Provision and Implications for Scheduled Castes and Scheduled Tribes

Structural adjustment policies have led to following developments in education: (i) privatization, i.e. the expansion of private funded educational institutions at all levels of education, (ii) narrow skill/knowledge based education geared to meeting the demands of the economy, (iii) budget cuts on education and slashing of teacher salaries in the interests of economy measures and positions, (iv) adopting narrow market oriented definitions and discourses of excellence, (v) advocating foreign borrowing for funding of basic educational commitments and making education a component of the safety net, (vi) involving NGOs as a support or replacement for the state delivery system, and (vi) avocation of a state withdrawal from all social sectors including the sector of education (Velaskar, 2003). Studies have noted that private schooling are playing a growing role in elementary education, a fact that government reports and statistics obscure (Kingdon, 1996). There is proliferation of private schools for the poor in urban, mofussil and rural areas. Unrecognised schools, which are not accounted in official statistics, have mushroomed in cities, towns and in the larger villages (Kingdon, *ibid.*). The NCERT survey estimated around 38,000 unrecognized primary schools in rural India (see NCERT, 1999).

The policy of privatization in education has enabled access of SC/ST children to private schools. However, the overwhelming majority of SC children continue to avail mainly of government schooling. According to the Sixth All-India Educational Survey, (NCERT, 1998), 91.3 per cent of SC children in rural primary schools and 64.6 per cent in urban areas were in schools managed by government and local bodies. At the middle stage, a relatively larger proportion of Scheduled Caste children were enrolled in privately managed schools, though expectedly this is more in urban (49.6%) as compared to rural areas (32.9%). There is a distinct trend towards SC enrolment in private elementary schools. As much as 32 per cent of the increase in primary school enrolment among Scheduled Caste boys was accounted for by private unaided (PUA) schools between 1986 and 1993. In rural areas PUA schools accounted for a relatively smaller proportion of the increase in enrolments during this period, around 7 per cent for Scheduled Caste boys and 4 per cent for Scheduled Caste girls (Tilak and Sudershan cited in Nambissan and Sedwal, 2002). However, the commercialisation and commoditization of education that privatizations entails, results in poor educational effects for SC/ST children. In a desperate bid to stay in the struggle for mobility, they avail private education in the faith that it is better quality education. In actuality, however, private education for the poor is largely of an inferior quality. The cost is exorbitant and the sacrifices made to meet them are not eventually worth them (Velaskar, 2003). State response to growing public demand for 'quality' education has been to launch innovative efforts on behalf of hitherto neglected segments, such as Lok Jumbos of Rajasthan, EGS of Madhya Pradesh etc. They have had some visible positive impact. In Madhya Pradesh for instance, the number of formal primary schools increased from 16,548 in 1990-2001 to 18,716 in 1998-99. During the same period Alternative Schools, 10,626 EGS schools, and 1133 TWD schools have been established. As a result number of schools nearly doubled from 19,295 in 1992-93 to 34,131 in 1998-99. There is also the case of West Bengal, however, where the state government sponsored alternative system of Shishu Shiksha Kendras is having encouraging results (Jha, 2002). However, impacts of alternative school and educational innovations need to be continuously and carefully assessed. Leclerq's critical evaluation of functioning of the Education Gurantee Scheme in SC and ST dominated districts of Madhya Pradesh sounds a worthy caution.

Conclusion

Lastly, one must admit a bitter fact that enrollment among this group has increased in standard one. However, later on, rate of dropout is high. One of the reasons for this is high rate of failure of stagnation. It ultimately leads to high rate of wastage (drop-out). It implies wastage of money, time and energy. Students at secondary education and further at higher education stage are few.

Therefore, Education is must for "Rural Transformation" and when we talk about "Rural Transformation" we can't sideline Scheduled Tribes which are one of the components of rural population.

REFERENCES

Abraham, L. (2004). "Building Cultural Capital to Combat Poverty: Globalisation, Education and the Urban Poor", in Ruzicka, Richard; Ballantine, J.H. and Jose A. Ruiz San Roman (eds.) *Education Participation Globalisation*, Prague, 2004.

Acharya, Poromesh (1981). "Politics of Primary Education in West Bengal: The Case of Sahaj Path", *Economic and Political Weekly*, Vol. No. XVI, No. 24, pp. 1069-75.

Acharya, Poromesh (1987). "Education: Politics and Social Structure", in Ghosh, R. and Zachariach, M. (eds.), *Education and the Process of Change*, New Delhi: Sage, pp. 65-79.

Acharya, Poromesh (1988). "Is Macaulay Still Our Guru?" *Economic and Political Weekly*, Vol. XXIII, No. 22, May 28, pp. 1124-1130.

Acharya, Poromesh (1998). "Bengali Bhadralok and Educational Development in Nineteenth Century Bengal," in Shukla, Suresh Chandra and Kaul, Rekha (Eds.), *Education, Development and Underdevelopment*, New Delhi: Sage, pp. 25-38.

Acharya, S. (2001). Access to Primary Education: Rural Maharashtra andMadhya Pradesh, in Vaidyanathan, A. and Gopinathan Nair, P.R. (eds.) *Elementary Education in Rural India: A Grassroots View*, New Delhi: Sage Publications, pp. 49-85.

Agarwal, Sapna (2003). "CINI ASHA: Building bridges for urban children", in Ramchandran, V. (ed.), *Getting children back to school; case studies in Primary Education*, New Delhi: Sage.

Aggarwal, Yash and Sibou, Sarika (1994). *Educating Scheduled Castes: A Study of Inter District and Intra Caste Differentials*, New Delhi: National Institute of Educational Planning and Administration.

Banerji, R. (1997). "Why Don't Children Complete Primary School?: A Case Study of a Low-Income Neighbourhood in Delhi", *Economic and Political Weekly*, Vol. 32, No. 32, pp. 2053-2063.

Banerji, R. (2000). "Poverty and Primary Schooling: Field Studies from Mumbai and Delhi", *Economic and Political Weekly*, Vol. XXXV No. 10, March 4, pp. 795-802.

Bara, Joseph (1997). "Western Education and Rise of New Identity, Mundas and Oraons of Chotanagpur, 1839-1939", *Economic and Political Weekly*, Vol. XXXII, No. 15, pp. 785-790.

Behera, D.K. *et al.*, (1999). "Contemporary Society: Tribal Studies", Vol. IV, *Social Realities*. New Delhi, Concept Publishing Company.

Berntsen, Maxine (1987). "Obstacles on the Path to School: Educational Problems of Backward Class Children", *New Quest*, July-August, (other details not available).

Berntsen, Maxine (1990). "Collapse at the Foundation—A Study of Literacy among Third standard students in Western Maharashtra", Phaltan, Unpublished Manuscript.

Berntsen, Maxinen. D. Kunachya Khandyavar, Kunache Oze (Marathi), unpublished paper.

Berntsen, Maxinen. D. Shoshitanche Shikshan (Marathi), unpublished paper.

9

Economically Correct Education for Rural India

Hemlatta Rajput

All men are born equal and must have the Right to Rise. Today they do not and people of conscience must fight till they do.
—Abraham Lincoln, 1859

Economic Reforms are not about rich guys buying Fancy bags or fancy cars. Reforms are about creating access and opportunities for the poor; the child who has power in his village to study at night, the mother who can use formal healthcare and the farmer who can reach his market via roads.
—Nandan Nilekani, Co-Chairman, Infosys

Introduction

In India we as a nation develop our nation in terms of big corporate houses, where a corporate world recognized at the world level for their quality in terms of production of goods and services, where we have maintain our economy safe from the world painful economic depression. Our corporate houses recognized at the world level for their remarkable performance at the corporate level. Even people of India enjoying every taste of the world in terms of their consumption basket at their doorstep, even Indian space programme had first found water at the moon which makes us proud to be an Indian for long period of time, even we have sustained our democracy after 63 years of independence though there were number of hurdles against the politics of the country, even we have achieved great success in the area of research and development, sports, politics, etc. all are representing our strength as well as future opportunity of India as a nation.

But within this joyful, colourful India the real shadow of India we can see in the rural India because whatever we have discussed it was enjoyed by the small group of urban population of India. That is only 20 to 25 per cent population are living in this strata and 70 to 75 per cent population are living in the rural area where we can say that they are using different products like branded butter, mobile, colour television, automobiles, as well as many well-known products. But they do not receive healthcare and education facility, electricity, drinking water, even they don't receive proper road and railway facility for their transportation, they don't have proper organized banking service so that they can receive financial support for their different social and economic needs. It means our government and corporate have provided the product or services which give profitability to their business and sustainability to their government in terms of the political power or lion's market share in terms of sales and profit. Even the government has started number of economic and social projects for the rural India. But, we have still not achieved our objective in terms of overall growth of the society as a whole. Why is it so?

Now-a-days everyone has concern for the rural transformation and development of the rural areas in terms of healthcare, education, and other peripherals of the welfare for the rural man. Because now-a-days the world at large has seen tremendous market for their product and service in the population of India and China due to demographic dividend and that's why all the strata of the society somehow rationally thinking for the transformation of the rural India well it is good enough that at least now time has come for rural development.

And this transformation will be possible only through education which provides enough solution for their different problems as well as it will provide economic return to the corporate as well as government at large for doing so we don't want simply an education reform for the rural India but we want economically correct education for rural transformation.

It means education which gives return for the rural people of India as well as economic return for the corporate world and sustainability for the government in the country. It means we want that type of education which will bring multiple demographic dividend for the overall component of the society. Because simply providing education doesn't solve problem of rural India as well as if the education will not give any indirect interest to the corporate as well as government they are not ready to participate actively in the growth of the nation and if we want the rural transformation in India than we have to think about the economically correct education for the rural transformation. The reason is that if rural India gets education than income of the rural people will increase and if income will increase they will demand more and more products and services from the corporate sector as well as they will provide raw material for the other industries in terms of agriculture and milk production. This circle of economically correct education will bring fruits for the rural community as well as synergetic impact on the corporate and government. Before going to discuss about the rural transformation we have to focus on the meaning of economically correct education.

Meaning of Economically Correct Education

The author wants to explain the term with the help of the economics and education:

- It means the education which will increase the long-term investment return for the society at large. In other words it will give positive result for the corporate and politics both.
- It will provide broad opportunity for all the sectors of the economy in terms of growth and development.
- It will help in terms of reducing unemployment, poverty, and population growth.
- It will empower rural people for taking their own decision for their life as well as for their nation.
- It will empower the rural people to generate thinking for the new innovation and research in their area.
- It will provide solution for their different problems related to health, financial, social, etc.
- It will generate more and more working opportunity in the rural India so that migration of rural people will be reduced.

- The education which will encourage corporate participation in the development of the rural India.
- The education which will make the people aware about their social responsibility and accountability for the society.
- The education which will provide more and more opportunity for the rural people.

Why We Want Economically Correct Education

The reason is that present education system has produced only more and more inequality in the society at large rather than creating multiple opportunities for the individual it will generate may be unwanted stress or may be directional less competition. In the present education system if we compared at large section of the society it will create only rate race among the students as a result they are just marks oriented rather than skill oriented as a result we have seen that after taking higher education also people are not able to generate employment opportunity for themselves. If the student has taken the degree in the form of different disciplinary subject from the university the job opportunities are very limited. But if we talked about the professional courses like MBA, IIT and MBBS than they really creating tremendous opportunity for the youth but as we have seen that this education is not available to all, only marginal section of the student groups are taking such type of professional degree as a result only one of the strata of the group in the society are enjoying major perk of the consumption basket and all others are just getting only bread and butter for themselves. Up to what limit it is beneficial not only this if we introduce the same model of education for the rural transformation it will only generate more unemployment, stress, unnecessary competition, more and more slums, as well as it will give frustration to the rural people because once they received education and if that education will not give them employment or solution for their problem they are not ready to participate in the educational transformation in the rural India. Similarly, even corporate are also not ready for such type of marks oriented education model because it will generate only problem of scarcity of skilled labour in the market and as a result they have to suffer in terms of quality of work or the problem related to the increasing labour turn over.

From the interview given by Dean of Delhi University the author wants to share the information that 80 per cent of students who have taken degrees in the area of science, arts and commerce are not able to get the jobs in the current market, only 20 per cent are getting employment opportunity in the market due to lack of application of knowledge in the real field. Therefore, for the rural India we want economically correct education which provide employment, solution for the problems in daily life as well as enhance the research and development activity at the rural India so that all the sections of the society will take participation in the society whether they are corporate or may be government.

Drawbacks of Current Education Model

- Our focus is on the things which we want to learn for passing the exam not for finding the solution for real life problem.
- Learner has no flexibility in terms of learning hours.
- It will generate more and more income inequality.
- Still it has not achieved 100 per cent literacy after the independence of India.
- It is increasing unemployment rate. Current unemployment rate is 7 per cent.
- It is just theory oriented rather than practical oriented.
- It did not fulfil present corporate requirement.
- It will not generate leadership quality among the individuals.
- It will not develop unique visionary approach in the mind-set of individuals.
- It is not able to develop soft and analytical skill among the students.

Why Present Education System is Not Appropriate for Rural India?

The author wants to pose the question against the Indian education system because as we are citizen of the country we have to ask as well as find the solution for our nation. Now why am I saying like that because as we all know that Government of India spending crores of rupees on the education system in terms developing schools, providing teachers, providing different infrastructure to the society, as well as by giving materials in terms of books, and different equipments of education. and also appointing different bureaucracy for the administration of the education programme but still after 63 years of independence India is unable to achieve 100 per cent literacy for the Indian education system even our government introducing different yojanas and schemes for the rural education but still we have not achieved our goal. Not only this in our country we are spending only 4 per cent of GDP on the education which is very less as compared to other developing nations even than we are unable to use available fund for the education programme. In the contrast whatever the amount used for the different education schemes it will just generate marginal impact on the part of quantitative data, for example, increase in percentage of enrollment ratio, decrease in the percentage of drop-out ratio. But, it will never show that how much social and economic welfare is generated out of that. Our government always said that in a primary education we are doing well by showing number of enrollments, but it will not show that how much knowledge they are getting for their daily life problems. Because present Indian education system provides the education which generates only thousands of data on enrollment or drop-out but it failed in generating employment opportunity out of the present education system.

Table 9.1: Growth in public expenditure on education in India

Year	*Percentage of GDP*	*Percentage of Budget*	*Per capita (Rs.) (1993-94 prices)*
1990-91	4.07	13.97	329
2000-01	4.26	12.23	509
2001-02	3.82	10.80	470
2002-03	3.97	12.60	495
2003-04	3.74	12.31	498
2004-05	3.49	12.27	—

Source: Tilak (2006).

Challenges of Education Systems for Rural India

- Today, India's education system is designed to overload the pupils with too much 'knowledge' or theory and the focus is to enable them to improve their memory skills rather than enabling them to be innovative/creative/ practical. Because, in the rural area we don't require education which generate only theoretical knowledge but we required the education which provide multiple solutions for the available problem.

- The current system is designed to create a hierarchical society, with only a small section scoring very high marks; the remainder gets fed up with the monotonous and irrelevant education system, forcing them to discontinue their studies.
- Current education system in the rural India does not provide scope for the professional as well as vocational courses so the rural people earn enough bread and butter out of practical learning.
- India has made giant leaps in the field of telecommunication and technology. There is hardly any village in India which is left out from this excitement. This technology has not touched the education system to provide 'remote teaching' facilities or online knowledge sharing.
- The urban sectors are more concentrated on, whereas technology can touch lives and enable education across the rural sectors as well.
- The cultural differences between the urban and rural sectors of people in India; this creates barriers for people in the rural sector, who are more docile in nature and it takes great efforts for them to open up, answering in class, or making their ideas heard.
- The access to uniform teaching content, especially video and multi-media content will enable removal of disparities. This will neutralize the ill-effects of absentee teachers (which is also a major problem in rural India).
- Limited access to technology, where only a few can afford.

Disparity Within the Education System for Rural India

In our country we have seen that there is great disparity or difference in our education system. On the one side, we have institutions which can compete with the best in the world, on the other side, we have "starving and staling institutions" both in terms of infrastructure and resources from the elementary school education to the higher and professional education level, why is it so? And answer of this question is available from the following reasons:

- Lack of willingness of our politicians to do work for the rural education system. They are just making the grants and reservation policy for the rural education system but there is no fundamental changes done by them.
- Resources for rural education which are mostly consumed on paper and cleared by audit well known method but in real terms they are not reaching to the real rural institution.
- Corporate sector take the advantage of the skilled and educated youth from our country's best IIMs and IITs but does not play any active role which really make the rural education system healthy for all.
- Lack of Public-Private Participation (PPP) in rural education system.
- There is no link between rural education institutions motive and government motive for the education.
- Rural people do not take the active interest in the education decision taken by the government, because they are unaware about the advantages of the economically correct education.
- There is no fixed accountability from the government side, institution side, teacher's side and not from the public at large for the rural India.
- Teachers are working in the rural area because they want only permanent government job. They are not interested in the rural development of transformation.

Before discussing the proposed model for the economically correct education for rural India we have to focus on the different aspects of the rural population at the world level.

Demographic Structure

From Table 9.2 we can see that in the year 2030 expected rural population will be 3.29 million in the world out of which 3.08 million belongs to only less developed regions of the world, which

Table 9.2: Rural population trends by region and development group—1950-2030

Development group	*Population*				*Growth rate (%)*	
	1950	*1975*	*2000*	*2030*	*1950-2000*	*2000-2030*
Rural population (in millions)						
–North America	62	64	71	61	0.28	–0.49
–Latin America and the Caribbean	97	124	127	116	0.55	–0.33
–Oceania	5	6	8	10	0.98	0.61
–Europe	261	221	193	131	–0.60	–1.31
–Asia	1155	1805	2297	2271	1.37	–0.04
–Africa	188	304	498	702	1.94	1.14
Rural population (in billions)						
– World	1.77	2.52	3.19	3.29	1.18	0.10
• More development regions	0.37	0.31	0.29	0.21	–0.45	–1.09
• Less developed regions	1.40	2.21	2.90	3.08	1.46	0.20

Source: United Nations Secretariat, 2002.

shows that in term of rural population how the less developed country will be the main target group of the world. Which we can observe from the following facts:

- An estimated 1.2 billion péople world-wide are classified as poor. In practical terms this equals the current population of China, is more than the population of India and more than four times the population of the United States. A startling fact is that over 70 per cent of the poor, or 840 million in developing countries live in the rural areas. They are caught in the vicious cycle of being unable to access the services and opportunities that might take them out of poverty—education, gainful employment, adequate nutrition, infrastructure and communications—because they are poor.
- 75 per cent of the world's poor are rural and most are involved in farming.

- 840 million undernourished people;
- 1.5 billion people who live without access to safe drinking water;
- 2 billion people who live without electricity;
- 860 million illiterate adults, more than half of whom are women;
- 130 million children out of school;
- 14 million children who have lost their mothers or both parents to AIDS; and
- In the 21st century agriculture remains fundamental for poverty reduction, economic growth and environmental sustainability.

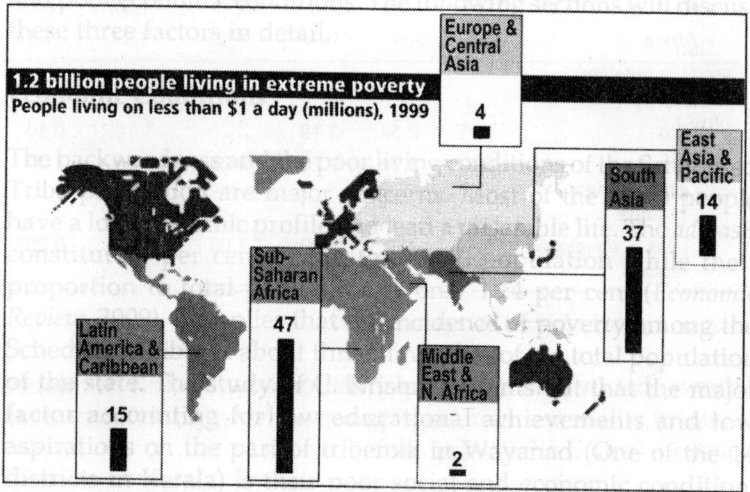

Fig. 9.1: Poverty Map
Source: United Nations Secretariat, 2003.

From the above poverty map we can see that at the world level 1.2 billion people living in extreme poverty and as per this map only south Asia comprised 37 per cent people living in extreme poverty.

From Table 9.3 we will find out that percentage of rural population is highest in case of India but if we see the GDP per capita which was lowest as compared to other nations, which shows that how crucial rural transformation is for the rural India.

Table 9.3: Comparison of India's rural population at the world level

2001	*Rural population (% of total population)*	*Rural population Density (rural population per sq. km of arable land)*	*GDP per capita (constant 2000 US$)*	*GDP per capita, PPP (constant 2000 international $)*
Brazil	18	55	3456	7351
China	63	560	1021	4233
Germany	12	86	23354	25785
France	24	77	22895	26142
India	72	465	466	2480
Indonesia	57	579	820	3146
Japan	35	993	37405	26117
Korea, Rep.	20	565	11220	16627
Mexico	25	100	5842	8876
Pakistan	67	438	528	1922
Poland	38	105	4398	10600
Russian Federation	27	31	1870	7383
South Africa	44	134	3046	9644
Thailand	69	268	2022	6362
Turkey	35	100	2690	6038
United Kingdom	11	116	24729	26868
United States	21	34	34484	33983

Source: World Development Indicators.

Food Industry as a Strength of the Rural India

According to a study by McKinsey & Company, the Indian food market is poised to grow from US$ 155 billion in 2005 to US$ 310 billion by 2015 and US$ 344 billion in 2025—at an approximate compounded annual growth rate of 4.1 per cent.

The development of the food industry in India stems from the consistently increasing agricultural output. With the second largest global arable land area, India is one of the key food producing countries in the world, second only to China.

- Currently, India ranks second in fruit production and third in vegetable production in the world;
- In 2007-08, foodgrain production in India had registered a 4.6 per cent growth with 227.32 million tonnes as against 217.28 million tonnes in 2006-07, according to estimates by the Ministry of Agriculture;

- The output of coarse cereals in 2007-08 was 39.67 million tonnes, 17 per cent higher than the 33.92 million tonnes in the previous fiscal;
- The total output of oilseeds is estimated to have risen to a record 28.2 million tonnes, about 16 per cent higher than the 24.29 million tonnes in 2006-07;
- The production of pulses has risen to 15.19 million tonnes, registering a year-on-year growth of 7 per cent and touching a new high;
- According to estimates by the agri-trade promotion body, the Agricultural and Processed Food Products Export Development Authority (APEDA), India's exports of agricultural and processed food products in 2007-08 has grown by 38 per cent, which, in absolute value terms, is US$ 6.59 billion, against US$ 4.79 billion in 2006-07;
- India's food processing industry is one of the largest industries in the country—it is ranked fifth in terms of production, consumption, export and expected growth. India is one of the world's major food producers but accounts for only 1.7 per cent (valued at US$ 7.5 billion) of world trade in this sector—this share is slated to increase to 3 per cent (US$ 20 billion) by 2015; and
- The Indian food processing industry is estimated at US$ 70 billion. According to the Ministry of Food Processing, this industry contributed 9 per cent to India's GDP and had a share of 6 per cent in the total industrial production. The industry employs 1.6 million workers directly.

Sustained by high agricultural output, international demand and a strong domestic market, the Indian food industry offers ample scope for large investments in processing technologies, skills and equipment, packaging, refrigeration of frozen food and thermo processing.

Currently, only 6 per cent of the country's fruit and vegetable produce is processed and India's share of the global market stands close to a dismal 0.03 per cent. While the size of the global processed-food market is estimated at US$ 3.2 trillion and nearly 80 per cent of agricultural products in the developed countries get processed and packaged (as suggested by 'India Food Report 2008', released at the Food Forum India, in Mumbai), there is huge scope for export-led growth in this particular sector. Recognizing this, in the next few years India aims at raising the share of processed food to 20 per cent in comparison to total agri-produce, on the one hand, and enhancing export of these items to 3 per cent on the other.

The domestic food market, according to the 'India Food Report 2008' is estimated at over US$ 182 billion accounting for about 2/3rd of the total Indian retail market.

If we see below two Tables 9.4 and 9.5 in which Table 9.4 shows that India secured 1st, 2nd or may be 3rd position in the food processing in the year 2005 but if we see its growth as compare to other sector of Indian economy from Table 9.5 we can see that for the year 2005-06 it was growing at 5.8 per cent rate but after that this rate was continuously falling at the increasing rate in the year 2008-09 it was just 1.6 per cent as compared to the other sectors of the economy which shows that something is wrong with agricultural sectors.

Table 9.4: India's Competitive Advantages in Food Processing

Content	*India*	*Global Rank*	*Share in Global production*
Arable Land (million hectares)	161	2	–
Irrigation land (millions hectares)	55	1	–
Major food crops (MT)	35	3	4%
Fruits (tonnes)	47	1	10%
Vegetables (tonnes)	82	2	10%
Rice/Paddy (tonnes)	132	2	22%
Wheat (tonnes)	65	2	12%
Milk (tonnes)	88	1	16%
Sugarcane (tonnes)	289	2	21%
Pulses (tonnes)	12	1	21%
Tea (tonnes)	0.88	1	28%
Edible Oilseeds (tonnes)	25	3	7%
Cattle (Millions)	226	1	20%

Source: Cygnus report, India Food Processing Sector, 2005.

Problems in Rural India as Weaknesses of Rural India

In India, where 70 per cent of population lives off the land in remote villages, each with an average population of about fifteen hundred people, the effect was amplified. Rural India has been crippled by policy-makers' comprehensive neglect since the

Table 9.5: Rate of growth of different sectors of Indian economy at factor cost at 1999-2000 prices (%)

	2003-04	*2004-05*	*2005-06*	*2006-07*	*2007-08*	*2008-09*
Agriculture	10.0	0.0	5.8	4.0	4.9	1.6
Mining and quarrying	3.1	8.2	4.9	8.8	3.3	3.6
Manufacturing	6.6	8.7	9.1	11.8	8.2	2.4
Electricity, gas and water supply	4.8	7.9	5.1	5.3	5.3	3.4
Construction	12.0	16.1	16.2	11.8	10.1	7.2
Trade, hotels and restaurants	10.1	7.7	10.3	10.4	10.1	*
Transport, storage and communication	15.3	15.6	14.9	16.3	15.5	*
Financing, insurance, real estate and Business services	5.6	8.7	11.4	13.8	11.7	7.8
Community, social and personal services	5.4	6.8	7.1	5.7	6.8	13.1
Total GDP at factor cost	8.5	7.5	9.5	9.7	9.0	6.7

* Trade, hotels and restaurants, transport and communication (together) grew at 9 per cent, 2008-09.

Source: Central Statistical Organisation.

country became independent. Among rural households 89 per cent do not have telephones and 52 per cent do not have domestic power connections. The average power breakdown in India is three hours per day of seventeen hours daily during the monsoon. Twenty per cent of rural habitations have partial or no access to safe drinking water. The average village is more than a mile away from an all-weather road. People living away from the main village do not have access to any such roads.

Symptoms of this government underinvestment are everywhere. India export food and grains, yet large sections of Indian society still have the lowest per capita caloric consumption in the world, India wastes more grain than Australia produces and more fruits and vegetables than the United Kingdom consume. As we have already seen than government has no proper ware housing facility to protect the produced foodgrains.

Why Rural India Becomes More and More Poor?

- Excessive dependence on the nature: if we talked about the rural India than we can say that for each and every demand they mainly depend on the agricultural sector and this sector's growth mainly depend on the monsoons as a result due to the scarcity of water approximately 53 per cent of agricultural area is un-irrigated.

- Lack of knowledge about the different welfare schemes introduced by the government.
- Unable to use financial facility because they are not able to understand the different complexities involve in the borrowed finance available from the government banks.
- Lack of use of capital intensive techniques: majority of Indian farmers are using traditional methods of farming because of lack of awareness and finance.
- Low factor productivity because of division of land from one generation to other it will reduce farm size and as a result land productivity as a factor of production is reduced day by day.
- High incidence of poverty and unemployment. Of the total 26 crores people Below Poverty Line in 1999-2000, 19.3 crore (74%) were in the rural sector. Similarly, the proportion of unemployment in rural areas is much more than urban areas.

Threats from the Rural India

From the statement that treats from the rural India which shows that now rural India has already bared a lot in terms of exploitation so they are use to with the different threats comes from different aspect in their life it means. If such a large number of population are not handled for the productive purpose. It will generate number of complexity for the over growth of the society.

This is the theory proposed by the sociology that if large sections of the society does become part and parcel of the growth process it will generate revolution against the hierarchy of the society and fight for their right. It means now there is high time to think and implementation of the rural transformation in India.

Opportunity of the Rural India

No doubt there are tremendous number of complex and multiple problems belong to the rural India. Still Indian rural economy has tremendous opportunities for the growth and development.

Indian agriculture sector and food processing industry rank among the major three ranks but their growth in the overall growth of other sector is continuously decreasing at the increasing rate if this rate of growth increasing at the increasing rate for the agriculture and food processing industry. Rural India becomes a strategic key component of the development process.

Not only 70 per cent population belong to the rural India and as we know that more than 55 per cent population in India belong to young age-group it means more proportion of youth generation belongs to rural India.

As we know that rural India also becomes the untapped market for the corporate sector and if we provide economically correct education which generate employment opportunity as a result consumption basket of rural India will test different products of the corporate world at the more and more competitive rate.

Role of Economically Correct Education in the Transformation of the Rural India

If we want that rural India will get their glory at the national and international level, we have to make education as our means of transformation but here education means economically correct education. We as a nation develop such type of education system which provide multiple employment opportunity to the rural people at their door step and for that we required different model of the education because present education system does not solve problem of rural India. So that we have to prepare a model for the rural India which provide employment opportunity within the rural area as well as in the urban area.

For rural India government has to initiate corporate partnership also so that they will generate more and more demand in the rural India by providing employment opportunity.

Step 1

- Primary schools more focused on the language and problem oriented class, in this class room practical related to the agriculture as well as food processing industry shown to them at the basic levels.

- Analytical skill in terms of maths and science will be developed more and more.
- Focus on the mother tongue as well as English language should be made so that they understood more and more aspect of the science and technology and other areas of discipline.
- Knowledge of the different technology will be given in this time period.

Step 2

In the second stage the education should focus more on the different skill-oriented rather than just number-oriented. Student should learn different technical and scientific skills at this level. Here government can provide more and more skill in terms of food processing industry, poultry farm, fishery industry, dairy industry. So that they can learn that actually how we can work in the actual work environment. Give more and more vocational courses to the students simultenously with the general component of the education.

Step 3

In the third stage government make arrangement for the apprenticehip training in the different skill oriented areas so that they can learn a specific skill for different sector. Here, we have to encourage process related to the research and development in the area of agriculture and food processing and allied activity.

Peripherals Provided for the Sustained and Continuous Development

- Provide knowledge of legal rules and regulation by arranging rural counsellor for the village related problems.
- Provide specialized skill in terms of development of the entrepreneurship and management skill in the area of rural management.
- Provide project based learning related to the disaster management so that they become more and more self-reliant.

- Provide knowledge regarding consumer's rights and corporate responsibility towards the society.
- Provide health related education by arranging different rural medical camps in which students are working for the rural community.
- Provide the different skill for the conservation of the rural natural resources.

Management of the Economically Correct Education

- The management and administration of the education system is in the hands of the state government as well as it is one of voluntary corporate responsibility of corporate world if they are ready to participate in that, they will provide knowledge and financial assistant as and when it is required.
- Day-to-day management done by rural people with the help of the specialized individual in that particular area.
- Developing infrastructure for the rural India is the central government responsibility as well as accountability.
- Develop the feedback forum under the head of the audio visual media corporate so that continuous watch and control will be maintained on the rural development.
- Develop the public forum for the rural people within the rural politics.
- Develop the facility of micro finance for the rural education as well as entrepreneurship.

Conclusion

In short if we want that rural education becomes the weapon for the development and transformation of the rural India and for that we have to develop education system which will provide more and more employment opportunity to the individual in the rural area and which will make them empowered that they can be participator in the process of development of the national growth. Only then we can say that we have really developed economically correct education for the rural India which really makes India shine in real terms at the world level.

REFERENCES

Bhattacharya, A (2010). "Mismanagement of Indian Management Education". *Economic Political Weekly*, June 12-18, Vol. XLV, No. 24.

David, A., Lavinia Gasperini, (2003) "Education for rural development: towards new Policy responses" http://www.rdfs.net/linked-docs/ERP.pdf Retrieved on 08/08/10.

Kevin, Watkins (2007-08). *Human Development Report 2007-2008 Fighting Climate Change: Human Solidarity in a Divided World UNDP*, Replica Press Pvt. Ltd.

Khanna, T. (2008). *Billions of Entrepreneurs: How China and India are reshaping their Futures–and Yours*. Penguin Group.

Kumar and Mitra (2009). "Social and Economical Inequalities: Contemporary Significance of Caste in India Education", *Economic Political Weekly*, December 12-18, Vol. XLIV, No. 50.

Murthy, N.R. (2009). *A Batter India for A Better World*. Penguin Group, New Delhi.

Radhakrishna, R. Ed. (2008). *Indian Development Report 2008*, Indira Gandhi Institute of Development Research, Oxford University Press.

Todaro, P., Smith, C. (2005). *Economic Development*, 8th edition. Pearson Education, Singapore.

Wang, Libing (2006). "Massification of Higher Education in China", *Journal of Educational and Administration*, Vol XX, No. 2, April, pp. 227-245.

10

Attitude of Rural Women Towards Girls' Education

Y.R. Karande, B.M. Thombre, J.V. Mande, D.D. Suradkar and *G.S. Ankush*

Introduction

Education is the most powerful tool for change and can put girls on the path to economic and social empowerment. Education is the process of bringing about desirable changes in the behaviour of an individual. It is the basic requirement for all-round development of personality of an individual. It is rightly said that education is the lifeline of development, let it be spiritual or economical, scientific or technological, national or global. India's ancient culture, civilization and history are a well documented testimony to the great strength of education which catapulted the Indian civilization to its zenith. Education not only imparts knowledge but also trains the mind, body, spirit and ethos, in accordance with the objectives of the society. It is because of these reasons education has always held the most valuable position in the Indian society.

Today, the world has become more dynamic in nature with the rapid changes taking place in every aspect of life. Even though, all over the world, women by and large have been denied equal opportunities for personal growth and development. Although significant gains have been made in the last few years with the increasing number of women entering in workforce. But the struggle to come out of the stereotyped picture still continues.

There are still different areas of discrimination which exist in the Indian society. At the turn of this era, the national attention has been focused on women. The media and education system have also played a vital role in bringing up the status of women. The attempts have yielded some fruits in raising the confidence and self-respect among women.

In spite of all these efforts women are trailing behind the men as far as literacy is concerned. Whereas, it is the fundamental right of equality for all children including girls. The girl's prospects for education are diminishing because of gender discrimination. According to the latest statistics, 65 per cent of 121 million children in the world who are not in schools are girls (Verma, 2006). Two-thirds of the world's population illiterate adults are women. According to the 2001 census, the percentage of female literacy in the country is 54.16 as against male literacy in the country is 75.18 per cent. In Maharashtra state, female literacy is 67.51 per cent as against male literacy is 86.27 per cent. These figures focus upon the magnitude of challenges that we are facing as far as women's education and literacy is concerned. Table 10.1 shows category-wise educational enrollment of girls and boys students in rural areas.

Table 10.1: Category-wise educational enrollment of girls and boys students in rural areas

(In million)

Year	*Primary*			*Middle Upper Primary*			*Secondary/Higher Secondary*		
	Boys	*Girls*	*Total*	*Boys*	*Girls*	*Total*	*Boys*	*Girls*	*Total*
1965-66	25.09	13.06	38.05	4.71	1.19	5.90	1.88	0.33	2.21
1973-74	30.11	16.86	47.04	6.27	2.13	8.40	2.96	0.69	3.65
1978-79	33.14	18.79	51.93	7.91	3.05	10.96	3.26	0.90	4.16
1986-87	39.82	25.98	65.80	12.08	5.64	17.72	5.71	2.08	7.79
1993-94	42.06	30.14	72.47	14.19	7.28	21.47	7.17	3.33	10.50
2002-03*	42.28	38.09	80.37	29.83	24.31	54.14	37.71	28.59	66.30

* Provisional

Source: Selected Educational Statistics 2002-03, Ministry of Human Resource Development, Government of India.

It is evident from the above Table 10.1 that in all stages, boys are enrolled more than girls. However, this difference is higher towards the higher stages.

There cannot be two opinions about the fact that "when a man is educated an individual is educated; when a woman is educated, a family is educated." There seems to be a growing realization of this fact which consequently resulting into increasing trend of educating girls. Her enlightenment will change the face of rural India. (Sandeep Kumar, 2006). Considering, the above fact the present study, therefore, will conduct with the following specific objectives:

1. To study the personal, socio-economic and psychological characteristics of rural women.
2. To know the attitude of the rural women towards girl's education.
3. To delineate relationship between personal, socio-economic and psychological characteristics of rural women and attitude towards girl's education.

Material and Methods

Latur district from the Marathwada region was selected purposively for study because Latur pattern of education is popular throughout the Maharashtra state. From this district Chakur and Ahmedpur talukas were selected purposively. Five villages from each taluka and twelve respondents from each village were selected randomly on the basis of nth number method to constitute the total sample of 120 respondents.

Table 10.2: Number of villages and respondents selected from each village

Sl. No.	*Village*	*Respondents selected for study*	*Percentage (%)*
1.	Belura	12	10
2.	Hadolti	12	10
3.	Jamb	12	10
4.	Telgaon	12	10
5.	Walsangi	12	10
6.	Ganjoor	12	10
7.	Murumbi	12	10
8.	Nandgaon	12	10
9.	Shivankhed	12	10
10.	Sugaon	12	10
Total	**10 villages**	**120**	**100**

One-shot case study design was adopted for the study, Karlinger (1973) stated that ex-post facto approach and one-shot case study design are worthy to apply when the independent variables have already occurred and exhibited their impact. The dependent variable in the study was attitude of rural women towards girl's education. The independent variables included were age, education, size of family, type of family, caste, land holding, occupation, annual income, social participation, sources of information and socio-economic status.

A number of attitude scales have been developed by various researchers to measure the attitude of individuals towards various psychological objects. Though different techniques are available for the construction of attitude scale, Likert's summated rating technique is the most commonly employed one. The same technique was used to construct the attitude scale.

The related items were placed in a random sequence against the rating points, namely agree, undecided, disagree. 3, 2 and 1 score was given to each of the responses respectively for the positive items and 1, 2 and 3 score was given to each of the responses respectively for negative items. The total score of respondents was obtained by summing the weights on all the items.

An interview schedule was designed for the study. Data were collected from the rural women through personal interview. The respondents interviewed generally at homes. The interview schedule was prepared in local language (Marathi) which helped the researcher to collect the information easily and accurately.

Results and Discussion

Personal, Socio-economic and Psychological Characteristics of Rural Women

From Table 10.3 it is observed that majority (55.83%) of the respondents were from young age-group (15 to 35 years), most of the respondents (38.33%) were illiterate and most of them (50.00%) belonged to medium family size, i.e. up to 7 members. Most of the respondents (65%) belonged to nuclear families and 39.16 per cent possessed semi-medium land holding. 46.66 per cent of the respondents had high level of annual income and 43.33 per cent

Table 10.3: Personal, socio-economic and psychological characteristics of rural women

Sl. No.	Characteristics	Frequency	Percentages
1.	**Age**		
	Young	67	55.83
	Middle	38	31.66
	Old	15	12.50
2.	**Education**		
	Illiterate	46	38.33
	Primary	20	16.68
	Secondary	18	15.00
	Higher secondary school	20	16.66
	Junior college	10	8.33
	Graduate	4	3.33
	Post-graduate	2	1.66
3.	**Size of Family**		
	Small	38	31.66
	Medium	60	50.00
	Big	22	18.33
4.	**Type of family**		
	Joint family	42	35.00
	Nucleus family	78	65.00
5.	**Caste**		
	Upper	25	20.83
	Middle	11	9.16
	Lower	84	70.00
6.	**Land Holding**		
	Landless	27	22.55
	Marginal	14	11.66
	Small	27	22.55
	Semi-medium	47	39.16
	Medium	5	4.16
7.	**Occupation**		
	Labour	17	14.16
	Labour + Farming	2	1.66
	Farming	69	57.55
	Business	4	3.33
	Service	6	5.00
	Farming + Business	10	8.33
	Farming + Service	12	10.00
8.	**Annual Income**		
	Below poverty line	20	16.66
	Low	11	9.16
	Medium	33	27.55
	High	56	46.66
9.	**Social participation**		
	Low participation	52	43.33
	Medium participation	50	41.66
	High participation	18	15.00

(Contd.)

Table 10.3: *(Contd.)*

Sl.No.	Characteristics	Frequency	Percentages
10.	**Sources of Information**		
	Low	24	20.00
	Medium	80	66.66
	High	16	13.33
11.	**Socio-economic Status**		
	Lower	6	5.00
	Lower middle	27	22.55
	Middle	46	38.33
	Upper middle	36	30.00
	Upper	5	4.16

of respondents had low level of social participation. Majority (38.33%) of respondents had medium socio-economic status. (Ingle, P.O. and Neeta Dharmadhikari, 1987). About (66.66%) of respondents were making medium use of sources of information. Seventy per cent of respondents belonged to lower caste and about (57.55%) were engaged in farming occupation.

Attitude of Rural Women Towards Girl's Education

Three points quartam scale based on Likert attitude construction procedure having ten statements five having positive meaning and five negative meanings had been interviewed and their responses are given in Table 10.4.

It is crystal clear from Table 10.4 that most of the rural women 96.66 per cent appeared to have favourable attitude with the statement that educated girls are more helpful to their parents than the uneducated girls. It is also noticed that most of the respondents 51.66 per cent have favourable attitude with the statement that there is more difficulty in the marriages of highly educated girls. It was further noticed that majority of the respondents 91.66 per cent were seen to be accepting the idea that educated girls turn into an ideal housewives. It was also noticed that majority of the respondents 66.66 per cent have neutral attitude with the statement that due to education girls become fashionable and lazy. It was also interesting to note that an appreciable percentage of respondents 99.16 per cent have favourable attitude with the statement that education will help the girls to solve their day-to-day problems. It was good finding to note that more than half percentage of respondents 59.16 per

Table 10.4: Attitude of rural women towards girl's education

(N = 120)

Sl. No.	*Statement*	*Favourable*	*Neutral*	*Unfavourable*
1.	Educated girls are more helpful to their parents than uneducated girls	116 (96.66)	3 (2.5)	1 (1)
2.	There is more difficulty in the marriage of highly educated girls	62 (51.66)	13 (10.83)	45 (37.5)
3.	Educated girls will turn into an ideal housewives	110 (91.66)	10 (8.33)	0 (0)
4.	Girls become fashionable and lazy due to education	3 (2.5)	80 (66.66)	37 (30.83)
5.	Education will help the girls to solve their day-to-day problems	119 (99.16)	1 (1)	0 (0)
6.	There is wastage of money for educating the girls	12 (10)	37 (30.83)	71 (59.16)
7.	To educate the girls means to improve the generation to come	114 (95)	6 (5)	0 (0)
8.	There is no necessity of girls education as they have to ultimately served their spouses	40 (33.33)	10 (8.33)	70 (58.33)
9.	Education make the girls self-sufficient	117 (97.5)	1 (1)	2 (1.66)
10.	There is feeling of insecurity for keeping the girls outside for education	74 (61.66)	1 (1)	45 (37.5)

Note: Figures in parentheses indicate percentages.

cent had denied that education of girls is wastage of money. Similarly, significant percentage, i.e. 95 per cent was also observed to be in agreement with the statement like education of girls improved generation to come. Another finding observed majority of respondents 58.33 per cent were seen to be refusing the statement that there is no necessity of girl's education as they have to ultimately serve their spouses. It was remarkable findings to quote that majority of respondents 97.5 per cent seemed to have high regard for education of girls which was reflected in the statement like education makes the girls self-sufficient. It was also observed that majority of respondents 61.66 per cent had favourable attitude with the statement that there is feeling of insecurity for keeping the girls outside for education [Gondhalekar, A.Y. (1975)].

The standard attitude scale based on Likert's technique was specially constructed and used for the study. It was administered to the respondents and results are presented here below as overall distribution of rural women.

Table 10.5: Distribution of the respondents according to their attitude towards girl's education

(N = 120)

Sr. No.	*Favourable*	*Frequency*	*Percentage*
1.	Favourable	79	65.83
2.	Neutral	10	8.33
3.	Unfavourable	31	25.83
	Total	**120**	**100.00**

It is indicated from Table 10.5 that majority of rural women 66 per cent had favourable attitude about girl's education while about 26 per cent have unfavourable attitude. About 8.33 per cent of rural women seem to be undecided on the issue. The mean attitude score of rural women was 23.84.

Relationship between Personal, Socio-economic and Psychological Characteristics of Rural Women and Attitude Towards Girl's Education

One of the objectives of the present study was to delineate relationship between personal, socio-economic and psychological characteristics of rural women and attitude towards girl's education. The data were subjected to correlation and multiple regression analysis.

Correlation Analysis

The coefficient of correlation was worked out to know the relationship of the independent variables with the attitude of rural women towards girl's education. The results are furnished in Table 10.6.

Independent variable, viz. education, land holding, annual income, social participation, socio-economic status, sources of information, occupation had positive and highly significant relationship with the attitude of rural women towards girl's education. While age, size of family had shown highly negative relationship with it.

Table 10.6: Relationship between personal, socio-economic and psychological variables with attitude

Sl. No.	*Independent variables*	*Correlation coefficient (r')*
1.	Age	−0.428**
2.	Education	0.756**
3.	Size of family	−0.302**
4.	Type of family	−0.150^{NS}
5.	Caste	−0.003^{NS}
6.	Land holding	0.228*
7.	Occupation	0.360**
8.	Annual income	0.283**
9.	Social participation	0.386**
10.	Sources of information	0.445**
11.	Socio-economic status	0.252**

* Significant at 5 per cent level
** Significant at 1 per cent level
NS Non-significant

Variables, viz. type of family and caste did not show significant relationship with the attitude of rural women towards girl's education.

Multiple Regression Analysis

Table 10.7: Multiple Regression analysis of independent variables with dependent variable

Sl. No.	*Independent variables*	*Regression coefficient (Bi)*	*Standard Error*	*'t' value*
1.	Age	−0.03694	0.0385	0.959
2.	Education	2.33470	0.3223	7.244**
3.	Size of family	0.13191	002573	0.513
4.	Type of family	−0.95718	0.9046	1.058
5.	Caste	0.24327	0.2978	0.817
6.	Land holding	0025359	0.4179	0.607
7.	Occupation	0.00790	0.2505	0.032
8.	Annual income	−0.00216	0.0051	0.423
9.	Social participation	0.27920	0.4807	0.581
10.	Sources of information	−0.01894	0.1728	0.110
11.	Socio-economic status	0.02669	0.0981	0.272

$R^2 = 0.5927$, F-value = 14.28
** Significant at 1 per cent level of probability

The variable, namely education, was found to be positively significant. The value of R^2 in case of rural women was 0.5927, which indicates that much of the attitude of rural women remained unexplained by the selected variables.

Conclusion

Personal, Socio-economic and Psychological Characteristics of Rural Women

The study indicated that the rural women were of young age, had largely illiterate (38.33%), belonged to lower caste (70.00%), nuclear and medium sized (50.00%) families, and engaged in farming occupation (57.55%). Majority of them had semi-medium land holding (39.16%). They had low level of social participation (43.33%), medium socio-economic status (38.33%), and medium use of sources of information (66.66%). These findings are in line with findings of Thombre *et al.* (1986).

Relationship between Personal, Socio-economic and Psychological Characteristics of Rural Women and Attitude Towards Girl's Education

Formal education, land holding, annual income, social participation, socio-economic status, sources of information, occupation of rural women had positive and highly significant relationship with attitude of rural women towards girl's education indicating that the rural women having higher education, possessing larger sized land holding, more annual income, higher level of social participation, higher socio-economic status, greater exposure to sources of information engaged in farming occupation had favourable attitude towards girl's education.

Age, size of family had negative and significant relationship with attitude of rural women towards girl's education. Results are similar to Chandrasekaran, P. (1988).

While, type of family and caste did not show significant relationship which indicate that the attitude of rural women towards girl's education is not influenced by their type of family and caste.

REFERENCES

Aabha, Gupta. (2002). Education of mother and family climate. Determinants of personality development. *The Ind. J. Soc. Res.,* 47 (1): 1-6.

Ambarao, T. Uplaonkar. (1983). Educational aspiration of rural youth. *Kurukshetra.*: 21-24.

Ashok Kumar, (2006). Educational status of Girl child: A situational analysis in rural India. *Kurukshetra*: 17.

Chandrasekaran, P. (1988). *Attitude of rural women of Tamil Nadu towards the formal.* Education of women. Abstract of Ph.D. (Education) thesis submitted to Madras University, Fourth Survey of Research in Education (1987-88). 1: 139.

Gondhalekar, A.Y. (1975). *Objectives of womens education as perceived by the students and their parents.* Abstract of Ph.D. (Sociology) thesis submitted to SNDT University (M.S.). Third survey of Research in Education (1978-83), pp. 129.

Ingle, P.O. and Neeta Dharmadhikari. (1987). Personal and socio-economic status of Agricultural women labour. *Maha. J. Extn. Edu.* 6: 18.

Kerlinger, F.N. (1973). *Foundation of behavioural research,* pp. 314.

Sandeep Kumar (2006) Education of Girls: Building bridges for future. *Kurukshetra,* November 2006: 15.

Thombre, B.M., Chole, R.R. and Deshmukh, N.D. (1986). Farm women's opinion about girls education. *Maha. J. Extn. Edn.*: 79-83.

11

Making Education Relevant for Rural Transformation

Deota Nilambar Prabhakar

Present Situation of Rural Education

Despite unprecedented growth in world economies and unparalleled improvements in global standards of living over the past few years, poverty and hunger are still realities in several countries. More than 70 per cent of the world's population are rural poors. One of the major inequalities affecting the rural poor is their unequal access to quality education, which is very important for social and economic development. Any attempt to redress the challenges of increasing inequity, poverty and widening human development gaps is possible through access to relevant, equitable and effective education of our rural people. Education for Rural Transformation (ERT) is the only way to reduce the widening human development gaps within and between nations.

Importance of Improving Rural Education

The dynamics of rural transformation in the globalized world has created new educational imperatives that call for a re-evaluation of present educational policies and priorities, and the re-examination of the role of education and learning—formal, non-formal and informal—for rural people from rather new perspectives. India lives in its villages. Rural Transformation is one of the most important factors for the growth of the Indian economy. India is primarily an agriculture-based country. Agriculture contributes nearly one-fifth of the gross domestic product in India. Hence, education is seen as a key instrument for shaping and fulfilling the goal of rural transformation. It should contribute to the well-being of the rural people including food, security, health, and employment, protection of the environment and the management of our natural resources.

Rural transformation faces a key challenge to achieve both poverty reduction and education for all. In order to achieve the Millennium Development Goals, specifically the first two goals—reducing hunger and poverty by half and ensuring universal primary education by 2015, there is a need to change the traditional working modalities and address the needs of rural India. This can be achieved through new multi-sectarian and interdisciplinary alliances and partnerships in education and those working in agriculture and rural development.

Food and Agricultural Organization (FAO) and the International Institute for Educational Planning of UNESCO (2003) emphasized the need for specific modalities to address the demand and supply issues that education faces in rural areas. The report has also envisaged that Education for All (EFA) will never be achieved in areas affected by poverty, high mortality, gender and other forms of discriminations. Sarva Shiksha Abhiyan as a national initiation of Education for All has been addressing the contextual issues of primary education. However, there is a need to have a cohesive approach and concerted efforts to bring significant changes in rural India by bringing out new curricula, and that too, have to be based on Indian culture and ethos.

Making the Curriculum Relevant for Rural Transformation—Some Suggestions

Poverty reduction in villages and rural sectors is possible only through the education which is relevant and universal. But the present education is not at all productive, as such; it is unable to reduce hunger and poverty. Education has to be productive (*Arthakari cha vidya*).

Villages are basically sustained on agriculture and other guilds. Our education is needed to be linked to this aspect rather than merely catering to the bookish and liberal education. It has to be vocational. There is a strong need to change the traditional working modalities which is in the form of common core curriculum, but rather it is made rural-based. These changes have to be based on Indian ethos and culture.

Need of Early Specialization at Secondary Level versus Common Core Curriculum

There is a need to invoke specialization at the earliest stage, i.e. after seventh or eight standard and pupils should be diverted towards productive, bread-winning, creative and socially useful productive courses. Only very few students should be encouraged for bookish, library study. The number of subjects should be restricted to four or five only and they should be on the choice-based method (Choice based credit system). This will sharpen their skills, attitude, aptitude and proficiency by the time they become adult or attain 17-18 years of their age. It will save their time and energy which is otherwise wasted in pursuing other courses—unnecessarily made compulsory and which prove to be the stumbling blocks in their progress. Thus, there has to be considerable freedom and elasticity in the selection procedure or grouping of the subjects.

The explosion of knowledge in recent years and the reformation and reformulation of many concepts in various subjects have highlighted the inadequacy of existing school programmes and brought about a mounting pressure for a radical reform of school curriculums so that it can be based on the needs of the rural areas.

Various commissions are recommending for the reconstruction of the general courses at the various levels, but specialization in courses is often seemed to be missing and neglected. Today's education makes a pupil "master of all and jack of none". He, therefore, is put in very shameful, pitiable and unproductive and depressed condition, as his content mastery remains shallow though to some extent, wide enough instead of being deep and narrow. Thus, till the pupils pass 10th or 12th, he rarely shows any kind of skill or scholarship properly developed up to a satisfactory level.

It is good that S.S.C. Boards are now brooding over this issue sincerely. Moreover, if possible entire schooling has to be given in child's mother-tongue/regional language in rural areas which will make their teaching-learning burdenless and stress-free.

Endorsement from Bhagwad Gita

This model is already endorsed and recommended in our Indian culture and literature. This is also suitable to our caste-system which was based on the doctrines of *Bhagwad Gita* and *Manu Smriti*—across the country, which is based on the principles of genetics, inborn-trait approach, inclinations and innate potentialities and the role of education in this case has to be simply to develop those potentialities to their fullest capacities.

The history of education shows that the main grounds on which subjects have been included in the curriculum is utility. In ancient times in India, there was a trifocal system of education. The priestly class studied the sacred books, the fighting class studied polities and the use of arms and the other classes studied arts and crafts. They were mostly mercantile community and service oriented people. All had their own curricula and specialization, which they have insisted from the childhood itself—so that till a child becomes an adolescent/adult, he becomes almost proficient and skilful in his area of specialization and expertise and used to attain perfection and excellence.

Thus one can see that the professional and vocational education was linked to the duties of the four castes ordained according to the innate-inborn nature without emphasizing on the evils of casteism.

Thus, according to Lord Krishna in *Bhagvad Gita*, Ch. 18th Verses 41 to 44—different education curriculum linked to different castes is as follows:

1. BRAHMANA KSHATRIYA VISHAAM
   SHOODRAANAAM CHA PARANTAPA/
   KARMAANI PRAVIBHAKTAANI
   SVABHAAVPRABHAVAIR GUNAIHI //
   Of Brahmins and Kshatriyas and Vaishyas and also Shudras, i.e. service class—the duties are divided according to the qualities born of nature.
2. SHAMO DAMAS TAPAS CHAUCHAM

KSHANTIRAARJAVAM/
EVACHA DNYANAM VIDNYAANAM AASTIKYAM BRAHAMA KARMA SWABHAAVAJAM //
Serenity, self-restraint, austerity, purity, forgiveness and also unrightness, knowledge, wisdom, faith—these are the duties of the Brahmanas, born of nature, i.e. the curriculum meant for the Brahmins should be such that it should foster such values in them.

3. SHAURYAM TEJO DHRUTIR DAAKSHYAM YUDHHE CHAAPYAPALAAYANAM /
DAANM EESHWARABHAAVASCHA KSHAATRAM KARMA SWABHAAVAJAM //
Bravery, boldness, fortitude, promptness, not flying from battle, generosity and lordliness are the duties of Kshatriyas, born of nature.

4. KRUSHI GAURAKHYA VAANIJYAM VAISHYA KARMA SWABHAAVAJAM /
PARICHARYAATMAKAM KARMA SHOODRASYAAPI SWABHAAVAJAM //
Ploughing, cattle-rearing, trades are the duties of the vaishyas, born of nature. And of the nature of service is the duty of the shudras—(philanthropic, missionary class, service-oriented people)—born of nature.

Summing up

If educational curriculum is thus remolded and reshuffled, it will lead to success. That is what is guaranteed by Lord Krishna when He says:

> SWE SWE KARMANYABHIRATAH SAMSIDHHIM LABHATE NARAH /
> SWAKARMA NIRATAH SIDHHIM... vv45 /ch.18 *Gita*.
> Devoted each to his own duty, man attains perfection, i.e. Qualitative excellence.

Thus, according to ancient scriptures......Curriculum at school level, especially in rural areas should include subjects such as value-education, ploughing, cattle-rearing, trade and commerce, which are mostly family trades and agriculture, horticulture, food-preservation, military, armed force-training, defence training, and other professions which are service-oriented ones like pottery, coblary, first-aid treatment, nursing, sanitary, etc.

If this kind of reformulation in curriculum is made, then only total transformation of the rural will take place on positive side and they will become economically independent and viable, more peaceful and prosperous.

REFERENCES

Alladi Mahadeva Shastri (1979), *The Bhagwad Gita with Sri Shankaracharya's commentary*, Samata Books, Madras.

Marathe, R.M. (1953), *Principles of Education*, D.N. Moghe, School and College Book Stall, Kolhapur.

National Policy on Education, 1986.

National Curriculum Framework, 2005.

12

Education for Rural Development and Its Present Status

Pramila Gururajan

Introduction

Education is the first and foremost a human right as proclaimed in Article 26 of Universal Declaration of Human Rights. It is also the key to building up skills and capacities in all domains necessary to techno-economic development. According to Chaube (2002), "Education makes man flexible, to change and adjust with the new situations." Naturalists are of the opinion that, "Education is seen from the process of adjustment to environment, it aims at enabling the individual to be in harmony with and well adapted to his surroundings."

The NCF-2005 observes that our country engages nearly 55 lakh teachers spread over around 10 lakh schools to educate about 2025 lakh children. At least 50 per cent of our children who appear at the school leaving examinations pass out of the secondary school system. Despite these trends, 37 per cent people of India lack literary skills, about 53 per cent children drop-out at elementary stage and over 75 per cent of our rural schools are multi-grade.

Mahatama Gandhi had visualized education as a means of awakening the nation's conscience to injustice, violence and inequality entrenched in the social order. *Nai Talim* emphasized self-reliance and dignity of the individual which would form the basis of social relations.

India is a country of villages and about 50 per cent of the

villages have very poor socio-economic conditions. Since the dawn of independence, concerted efforts have been made to ameliorate the living standard of rural masses. So, rural development is an integrated concept of growth and poverty elimination has been of paramount concern in all the consequent five year plans. Rural Development (RD) programmes comprise following:

- Provision of basic infrastructure facilities in the rural areas, e.g. schools, health facilities, roads, drinking water, electrification, etc.
- Improving agricultural productivity in the rural areas.
- Provision of social services like health and education for socio-economic development.
- Implementing schemes for the promotion of rural industry increasing agriculture productivity, providing rural employment, etc.
- Implementing schemes for the promotion of rural industry increasing agriculture productivity, providing rural employment, etc.

The NCF-2005 observes that while urban middle class children are stressed from the need to perform extremely well, rural children are not sure about whether their preparation is adequate even to succeed in the examination. Learning achievement of rural children is low compared to urban children at all stages of school education. A study conducted by Sharma, S. (DPEP Calling March 2000) on Achievement Levels of Urban and Rural Children reveals that achievement levels of rural primary school children, both boys and girls, are lower than urban children.

Urbanisation in India

Currently about 30 per cent of India's population is in urban areas, up from 17 per cent in 1951 to 23 per cent in 1981. 70 per cent of current urban population live in about 400 towns of above 100,000 population size. Such towns numbered 76 and 218 in 1951 and 1981, accounting for 45 per cent and 60 per cent of urban population. Towns less than 100,000 population increased from 2767 in 1951 to 3987 in 2001 but their share in India's population has actually declined. Urban growth is mainly through natural increase, boundary changes or a real reclassification. Rural-urban migration has accounted for less than 30 per cent of urban population increase since 1981, and less than 20 per cent of the rural natural increase. India's rural population is now about 830 million, living in about 600,000 villages. In 2001, 54 per cent of the rural population lived in the 17 per cent of villages with more than 2000 population.

- *Rural-Urban Disparities are large:* 55 per cent of rural females and 36 per cent of rural males are illiterate, as compared to 30 per cent and 19 per cent in urban. Infant mortality is 61 in rural against 37 in urban. 46 per cent of rural children are underweight and 41 per cent of rural women have low BMI, against 33 per cent and 25 per cent in urban areas. Only 50 per cent of rural people have *pucca* houses and 60 per cent electricity, compared to over 90 per cent in urban. 78 per cent of rural households still use firewood for cooking. Less than 10 per cent of rural households own mechanised transport as compared to over 30 per cent in urban.

Responding to Rural Diversity

Rural people and rural areas are not homogenous in a country. Converting national policies and priorities of education into effective components of rural transformation will mean adopting and adjusting to specific rural circumstances. The diversities can be listed as follows:

- Geographical and ecological differences—remoteness and relative inaccessibility of areas like Andaman and Nicobar Islands, some hilly areas, and their ecological features narrow the possibilities of economic development, which is also associated with educational underdevelopment; many rural poor live in marginal and degraded lands, where vulnerability and poverty incidence and intensity are greater;
- Ethnic, cultural and linguistic differences often put groups of people in a minority status and subject educational and other forms of disparity. We should compensate for

historical discrimination as well as to recognize the value of specific cultural and linguistic identities in education programmes;

- Gender disparity, generally boys are considered more important than girls and opportunities are unequal even salary-wise difference for the same work women are paid less than man;
- Diversity in sources of income and access to assets—poor rural people typically diversify their sources of income as a coping income mechanism;
- Poverty often associated with other forms of disadvantage. Education plays important role in helping the victims and overcome the multiple layer of discrimination and disparity to which they are subjected;
- Urban rural gap;
- Persistent gender gap against girls;
- Relative lack of emphasis on alternative, non-formal education in the place of formal education; and
- Less participation of communities and local leadership in management and delivery of education.

Equity, Quality and Efficiency

Rural people do not get access to high quality education, information and communication technology. Access to high quality has a vital role in fulfilling other components of the vision for humanity's future. There should be equitable access to education and it should be of acceptable quality. Education should link to anti-poverty participatory and accountable system.

Class Struggle and Rural Transformation in West Bengal

The political debate on West Bengal's rural transformation is not new. But after Singur and Nandigram, it got a new lease of life. Though criticism of the Left Front Government's industrial policy has been central to the political contestation within the Left democratic movement, for *anti-communists* in general both on the Left and the Right, this became an opportunity to celebrate the mish-mash of 'people's participation' and 'civil society' as the slogan and locus of resistance and change. Neo populism and neo liberalism readily danced the *'tandava'* as Medha Patkar and Mamata Banerjee stood shoulder to shoulder with Amar Singh. The proponents of 'civil society' (claiming to be a particularistic *'Sushil Samaj'*) reflected these *United Colours* even as it celebrated the 'monolithic rural'; and denial of the importance of 'Operation Barga' in changing the social and political structure of West Bengal was legitimized by the mainstream media.

Some members of the intelligentsia bemoaned the historical 'lack of democracy' under the Left Government so much so that a few 'Left' intellectuals wrote a letter in *Anandabazar Patrika* urging the imposition of 'Emergency' in West Bengal. The 1960s and 1970s in West Bengal had obviously become a distant memory. But more importantly, the retreat from class was central to this transition.

A study by Sudipta Bhattacharyya, which was done in 2005, delves into the question of rural transformation in West Bengal and the sense in which it had historically opened up an 'alternative path' based on class struggle. Based on primary field survey and secondary sources of information, this study analyses the West Bengal experience of participatory rural transformation as a direct fall out of the changing class structure of rural society and the rise in class-consciousness among the rural poor.

It documents the political achievements of the West Bengal under the Left Front government as nothing but agriculture based development led by direct class action and the interventionist state building on class conscious peasant movements in Bengal as opposed to idealized homogenous rural communities. While this class struggle was central to the Panchayati Raj System emerging as a system of democratic empowerment, the paper also critically points to the limits and the failures as of now of the 'unfinished agenda'.

The Need of E-Panchayat as a Road to Rural Transformation

The change or lack of change has not been because governments have spared efforts. Millions of rupees have been doled out or otherwise spent on developmental projects over the years. As once famously quoted by Rajiv Gandhi—"only 15 paise of every rupee spent ever reached the poor for whom it was meant".

Apart from the sheer size and variable composition of the country that proved daunting, lack of transparency and administrative inefficiencies have taken their toll. It is in this context that one should assess the importance of the 73rd amendment of the Constitution of India.

The 73rd Amendment of the Constitution of India is a watershed development that could genuinely impact the role of Panchayati Raj Institutions in self-governance. Panchayati Raj Institutions have been vested with powers and authority to enable them to function as institutions of self-governance that can take decisions regarding:

- Preparation of plans for economic development and social justice.
- Decision-making powers relating to the wide ranging subjects such as Agriculture, Land.

Improvement, Minor Irrigation, Fisheries, Social Forestry, Rural Industries, Drinking Water, Health and Sanitation, etc.

The amendment not only clears the way for a third tier of the executive, it also provides for the financial resources that could breathe life into the idea of local level implementation of citizens' needs. The amendment also provides for the representation of minority and marginalised groups.

The World Bank in its summation of the Millennium Development Goals (MDGs) states—'Infrastructure is an integral part of the development of any country. It is about providing basic services—water, sanitation, energy, roads and access to modern information communications technology.' Today, in a climate that enjoys both political will and financial support of the government, technology infrastructure forms the core of the success of any e-Panchayat effort. The importance of computers and communication infrastructure lies in the fact that it enables delivery of services even to the remotest village. Other than the simple delivery of services from self-governing bodies, it changes the way these bodies function.

Rethinking Education for Rural Transformation

Goals set globally by any individual states for education and development in the 21st century cannot be realized without giving special attention to the situation of rural population in developing countries like India. Breakdown of numbers for rural areas on education indicators are often not reported—a sign of neglect of the problem. But it can safely assumed that non-attendance in school, early drop-out of students, inexperienced teachers, their boring teaching methods, poverty and gender inequality in education are disproportionately high in rural areas—paralleling concentration of poverty in villages. Urban-rural disparity in educational investments and in the quality of teaching and learning is widespread and persistent.

The Rural Poverty Report 2001, produced by the International Fund for Agricultural Development (IFAD), makes a plea for getting the priorities right: Most of the world's poor are rural and will be so for several decades. Poverty and hunger have fallen massively, mainly due to rural and agricultural development, especially during 1975-1990. Rural poverty reduction deserves much greater emphasis.

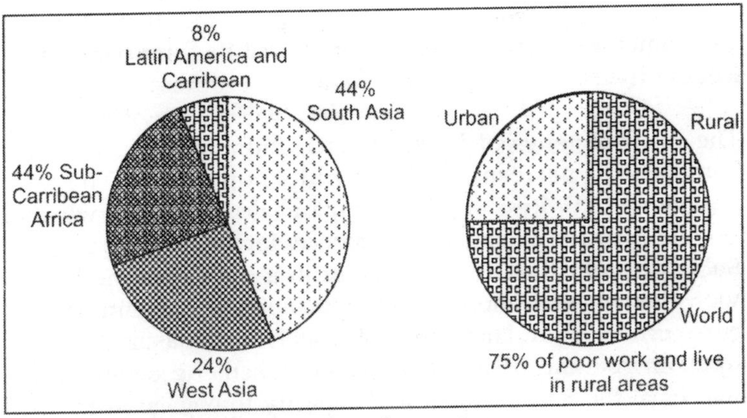

Fig. 12.1: Global distribution of rural poverty
Source: FIAD, Rural Poverty Report 2001, p. 16.

Separate educational policies and programmes for rural areas are not necessarily the answer. Rural areas are diverse and are in the state of transition. It is essential to turn the continuing and inevitable transition of rural areas, often with adverse consequence of rural economy, environment and people's life, into an active and positive process of transformation of rural communities. Educational programmes have to become a vital part of this transformation through committed partnerships of the government, communities, business, and civil society as a whole.

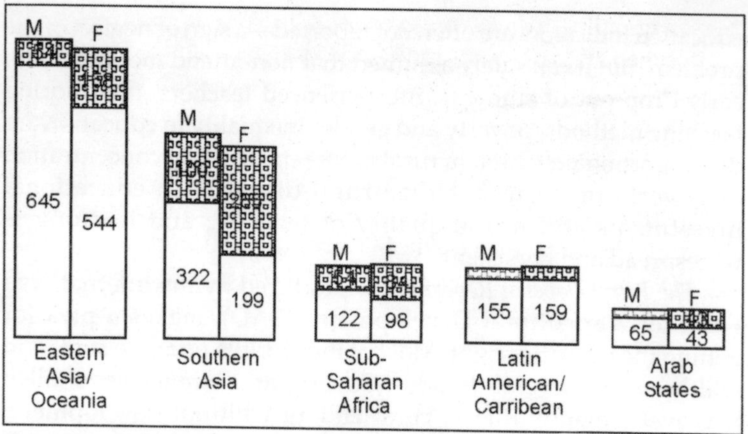

Fig. 12.2: Estimated number (millions) of literate and illiterate males and females aged 15 and over

Source: UNESCO, World Education Report 2000, Fig. 2.2.

The Concept of Rural Transformation and Its Connection with Education

The rural societies of Brazil, China, India and South Africa comprise 25 per cent of the world's population. They are undergoing a process of change unparalleled in history, whether in scale, speed or potential consequences for humanity as a whole. Such transformation is taking place in a context that is loaded with fundamental uncertainties: climate change; the impacts of growing scarcity of land and fresh water; the triple impact of the food, energy, and financial crises; and whether the human race will have the wisdom, will and capacity to engage in national and international collective action to avert disaster. Rural transformation is about human development and is not limited to the development of things.

This rapid change in this context is creating conditions of enormous risk and vulnerability for rural people. At the same time whole new opportunities are emerging, linked for example to renewable energy, provision of environmental services, or food production. The process of change is made ever more complex for the current generation by the fact that it needs to deal with the heavy weight of many historical inheritances: poverty, inequality and injustice; dual agrarian structures; lack of rights and social marginalization of large groups in the rural population, including women and tribal and indigenous peoples; lack of access to health, education and other basic services; and insufficient private and public investment.

But despite this heavy inheritance, our hope for ultimate success is based on the evidence of the impressive achievements in the emerging economies. While outcomes have not been uniform between and within countries, hundreds of millions have been lifted out of poverty, food production has increased many times over since the famines of the late 1950s and early 1960s, natural resources and ecosystems can no longer be destroyed in obscurity and with impunity, hundreds of thousands of small and medium firms have been created and are contributing to the economy of our planet, cell phones have reached almost every village, many more young women and men are going to school when compared with their parents' generation, governments are more accountable to citizens than ever before, and civil societies are more active and vibrant than ever. What the rural societies of the emerging countries have done in the last generation, is an achievement that has not been registered by any other nation in a similar period of time and in such a scale.

The solutions to the problems of poverty and deprivation in rural areas and their spread out in urban areas do not lie in preventing urbanization and keeping the rural confined to rural areas. According to Norman (1998), "Changes in both rural and urban areas are important, marked by movement of people, demographic transition, and new economic pressure and opportunities. There should be quality schools, trained teachers, good school environment with all basic facilities and opportunity to continue higher education in their own rural areas. The term rural transformation seeks to convey a vision of positive process of change and development of rural communities in the context of national change in which education is the key instrument for shaping and fulfilling the goal of rural transformation. According to Aggarwal (2008), "Education in all forms and at all levels, as the means of equipping people with skills and knowledge and enhancing their capacities, clearly will be a key element. All major components of educational system—from basic education, literacy and continuing education, vocational and technical education." Tertiary, professional and vocational education should be reoriented to serve the needs of rural transformation. National objectives cannot be fulfilled without considering rural transformation. To make education the vehicle for rural transformation calls for looking at policies and priorities for education in a new perspective. Qualities and relevance of educational activities should be checked. The rapidly changing rural scene and the dynamics of rural-urban interaction require flexibility and adjustment in educational programmes not often found in the conventional formal system.

Rural Development Activities in India

Aga Khan Development Network (AKDN)

AKDN's rural development efforts started in the early 1980s when the Aga Khan Rural Support Programme (AKRSP) was established in Gujarat. Rural development programmes seek to contribute to rural poverty reduction through community involvement and empowerment that leads to the efficient management and improved productivity of natural resources. Today, over 400,000 beneficiaries across 900 villages in four states (Gujarat, Madhya Pradesh, Maharashtra and Rajasthan) have organized themselves into more than 1400 village-level institutions.

Firmly committed to reducing rural poverty in the semi-arid region of India, the Aga Khan Development Network (AKDN) and its partners are working to improve rural livelihoods in select and environmentally degraded areas in the states of Andhra Pradesh, Gujarat, Madhya Pradesh and Rajasthan.

These states are characterized by erratic rainfall, depleting or contaminated groundwater, poor soil conditions and prone to natural calamities, primarily affecting agricultural incomes, still the mainstay of India's predominantly rural economy.

The profile of livelihoods in India, especially in these states shows that agriculture and animal husbandry still remain the main sources of livelihood for rural communities, though there is a significant shift to non-farm sectors such as mining and quarrying, construction and manufacturing during periods of drought. The ultimate goal is for communities to have the confidence to make informed choices from a range of appropriate options that leads to sustainable and equitable development.

AKDN's rural development programmes in India include community federations that have been promoted by the Aga Khan Rural Support Programme (India). Increasingly, these federations are taking over the roles and responsibilities of AKRSP(I) in promoting and strengthening community institutions at the village level. Support for watershed development activities by rural beneficiaries has given rise to savings amongst beneficiaries of 28.2 million rupees (US$ 622,222), increased amounts of water for drinking and irrigation, higher agricultural productivity, greater capability to cope with drought and lower payments to moneylenders. Community-based irrigation management, efficient water resource management and joint forest management approaches have been successfully piloted. A 1995-2000 impact study undertaken in certain areas showed beneficiaries' incomes increased between 40 and 80 per cent, while expenditure on food increased by 85 per cent. Female literacy levels rose by 10 per cent while distress migration declined from 80 per cent to 35 per cent and distress migration declined from 150 to 90 days per year.

Association for Rural Advancement Through Voluntary Action and Local Involvement (ARAVALI)

ARAVALI was initiated as a result of the joint effort of the Government of Rajasthan and a few leading voluntary agencies in 1994 to promote innovations in development and act as a interface between the government and the voluntary organizations. Aravali began formal operations in 1997.

ARAVALI's mandate is to ensure that benefits of development reach resource or means poor communities in Rajasthan and to enable this to happen in a structured manner, it is necessary that the government and non-profit organizations working in the area of rural livelihoods, pool their strengths and become partners.

Within this context ARAVALI intends to ensure that there are an increased number of effective voluntary organizations working closely with the rural poor in every district of Rajasthan and that an enabling environment is developed within which the government and these organizations can form effective partnerships. ARAVALI's work area includes almost all of Rajasthan. It is currently working intensively with around 20 organizations all over the state and has constant contact with another 70 organizations through its information exchange programmes.

ARAVALI broadly sees the following roles for itself:

- Promotion of development innovations and their upscaling,
- Networking and liaison between and among GOs, NGOs, Research bodies and private sector,
- Capacity Building,
- Promotion of Collaborative Initiatives, and
- Policy and Strategic Research.

Development Support Centre (DSC)

Development Support Centre (DSC) is a resource organisation that provides knowledge based support to Non-Governmental Organizations (NGOs), government agencies and other stakeholders in the area of natural resource management.

Established in 1994 in the state of Gujarat, DSC provides a variety of services that aim to improve rural livelihoods through participatory management of natural resources such as land and water on which rural population directly depend upon.

DSC's present focus is on four thematic areas:

- Watershed Development,
- Participatory Irrigation Management,
- Agricultural Productivity Enhancement, and
- Joint Forest Management.

In the above thematic areas DSC offers the following portfolio of services:

- Capacity Building/Training of NGOs, CBOs and Government functionaries,
- Field Support Services,
- Policy Advocacy,
- Communication Services,
- Research and Monitoring Services, and
- Networking.

Mahila Abhivruddhi Society, Andhra Pradesh

Mahila Abhivruddhi Society, Andhra Pradesh (APMAS) was set up to meet the increasing need voiced in various forums to bring a quality mode to the growing self help group movement in Andhra Pradesh. APMAS, a state level institution, supports the women's self-help movement and promotes sustainable livelihoods. APMAS' core activities are:

- Quality Assessment;
- Quality Enhancement;
- Livelihood Promotion;
- Research and Advocacy.

Registered as a public society, APMAS started functioning from July 2001 and represents a partnership between public-private institutions like the Government of Andhra Pradesh, banks, representatives of civil society organizations and SHGs.

Rural Development and Panchayati Raj Department Policy Note 2010-11

Perarignar Anna's vision is being translated into reality in Tamil Nadu under the dynamic leadership of our Honourable Chief Minister, Kalaignar M. Karunanidhi. Never before in the history of the State has so much been done for the rural poor in so many different ways as in the past four years. By virtue of the Anaithu Grama Anna Marumalarchi Thittam (AGAMT), every Village Panchayat of Tamil Nadu will have its own library, playground, village pond, and burial ground-cum-cremation shed together with drinking water systems, streetlights and cement concrete streets in every hamlet, by 2011. Under the Mahatma Gandhi National Rural Employment Guarantee Scheme (MGNREGS), a sum of Rs. 3,352.58 crore has been disbursed as wages till 31 March, 2010 to the rural poor, among whom 56 per cent are Scheduled Castes and 76 per cent are women. *Tamil Nadu has won accolades as one of the best-performing States in this Scheme from the Honourable Supreme Court of India.* As regards rural roads, the total length of black-topped roads has gone up from about 29,280 kilometres in 2006 to about 54,620 kilometres in 2010. The women's Self-Help

Groups movement has been given a fillip as may be seen from the fact that the total Bank Credit disbursed to SHGs during the past 4 years was Rs. 6,364 crore as against a sum of only Rs. 1,765 crore disbursed to SHGs during the 17 years from 1989 to 2006. The Kalaignar Veettu Vasathi Thittam launched by the Honourable Chief Minister on 3 March, 2010 is by far the biggest State-funded Scheme and aims at replacing all the huts in rural Tamil Nadu with permanent concrete houses over a six year period from 2010-11 to 2015-16, with 3 lakh huts being taken up for replacement during 2010-11 at a cost of Rs. 1,800 crore. In short, there has been a major transformation of the rural landscape in Tamil Nadu during the past four years.

Socio-Economic Factors Affecting Rural Livelihoods

The poor have meagre holdings or access to land, little or no capital and off-farm employment is seasonal. It is almost impossible for farmers to secure credit and loans needed to purchase agricultural inputs except at prohibitive rates from private moneylenders leading to risk-prone farming. Markets are under-developed or difficult to access. Extension services are few and far between, and development initiatives aimed specifically at their needs is sparse.

Few employment opportunities and low levels of education and skill result in low cash incomes. This in turn affects the ability to purchase basic needs (such as medicines, education for children, etc.). Women and children in particular are the hardest hit especially when access to safe and adequate sources of water are low, resulting in high vulnerability in terms of health.

Women are also more affected by underemployment.

The relevance of this is all too clear when one realizes that 29 per cent of India's population still live below the poverty line, earning less than US$ 1 per day. A comparison with other countries in South Asia reveals that 33 per cent of Pakistan's population is below the poverty line while it is 34 per cent for Bangladesh, 42 per cent for Nepal and 25 per cent for Sri Lanka.

Promoting Self-Reliance

A central strategy of the rural livelihoods approach is to put people at the centre of development, thereby increasing the effectiveness of development assistance and therefore, improving performance in poverty reduction. Involving the poor results in local empowerment, which in turn leads to opportunities for local leadership, including that of women, to emerge. These leaders play a critical role in bringing about and sustaining development and consequently social change such as pluralism, public participation and democratic principles. Village institutions form the basis of community organization and function through 'Village Development Committees,' comprising representatives of all communities in the village (including at least 30 per cent women's representation). These Committees develop village development plans and work closely with the Panchayat (the lowest unit of the government that functions at the village level).

Other community organizations such as farmers' federations and women's self-help groups also facilitate the process of community driven development. These institutions work best if they have some independent means of sustaining themselves which is usually enabled by introducing them to micro-credit schemes. For example, a woman's federation in Bharuch district in Gujarat state recently accessed a loan-based scheme for animal husbandry. Likewise, federations of farmers groups have considerably reduced agriculture input costs (seeds, fertilizers and pesticides) through bulk purchases based on demand from member institutions, simultaneously ensuring the quality of inputs supplied. These organisations have also contributed to improved cropping techniques, rational use of fertilisers and the adoption of appropriate low-cost technologies.

Communities eventually go on to form "apex institutions" (federations of various community institutions) at the block (a unit of a district) and "taluka" (a unit of a block) level. These institutions also act as forums where regional issues are discussed and solutions formulated. These institutions also dialogue with the government and other agencies (including banks) to get access to and benefit from various schemes.

The federations also serve as agriculture extension agents, and transfer information from agriculture institutes related to cropping practices, thereby ensuring that information reaches farmers in remote areas. Collective marketing of agricultural produce, and enabling member institutions to sell their produce at the best price possible is another important activity.

Farmers' federations and the women's federations have also led social campaigns in the regions such as reducing unnecessary expenditure on social customs, promoting the education of girls, anti-liquor campaigns, and the promotion of organic farming. Mass awareness campaigns by women's groups in Surendranagar in Gujarat for example, have led to a reduction in wasteful and extravagant expenditure on weddings and on social customs such as 'funeral feasts.'

Skills Development

In addition to institution building, programme activities also include human resource development including skills development to build up the skills base of villagers, especially women. For example, in the Netrang programme area of Bharuch district, women have been trained to repair and maintain hand-pumps. In another area women have been trained as masons. Communities receive organization and financial management training to support the effectiveness and sustainability of village-level institutions, and key resource people are provided with technical skills to plan, implement and maintain the development activities. The ultimate goal is for people in the participating communities to have the access, confidence and competence to make informed choices from a range of appropriate development options.

In 2001 alone, over 300 training programmes benefited almost 6000 villagers, 64 per cent of which were women. These were essentially to increase awareness about savings and credit programmes, provide exposure to 'model' villages and orient rural communities to the principles of natural resources management. In addition, over 50 NGOs and 400 government staff have also been trained in various participatory processes.

Creating Rural Assets

Institutional structures are created at the village level through which the rural poor can prioritize their needs and decide how best to manage common resources. Communities build personal and community capital through efficient management of their natural resource base such as water storage and enhanced water use efficiency, irrigation systems, soil conservation or forestry. These efforts include the construction of small scale infrastructure, such as check-dams, irrigation canals and water harvesting structures or agricultural storage facilities.

Over 400 structures have been constructed for harvesting and storage of rainwater that is directly lifted for irrigation, or recharging the groundwater aquifers for more rational extraction through wells. These have led to an additional 4000 hectares of irrigated croplands in the programme areas, which is being further expanded through the adoption of water saving devices such as drip irrigation and sprinklers.

Income growth is promoted by increasing agricultural productivity through improved farming methods such as using drip-irrigation, provision of better seeds, creation and improvement of markets, land development, micro-credit, increasing off-farm incomes and supporting enterprise development. Local capital is mobilized by promoting savings and developing financial services to enable broad access to credit. Programmes are designed to have a combined effect so as to create a critical mass of economic activities that raise living standards.

In Surendranagar area in Gujarat for example, it was found that a severely degraded natural environment would not allow rural communities to rear cattle and, therefore, the only viable option was to rear goats. The rural development programme stepped in to help create a viable market for goat milk in the area and helped the community to get the government to set up a cheese making plant. In another water scarce area, a women's federation lobbied with the government to buy them a water tanker which they now use to sell safe drinking water to local communities practically at their doorsteps and at fixed and mutually agree to prices. This has considerably reduced water scarcity in the area by providing households assured water supply and also saves women the time they earlier spent on collecting water.

Skills Development

In addition to institution building, programme activities also include human resource development including skills development to build up the skills base of villagers, especially women. For example, in the Netrang programme area of Bharuch district, women have been trained to repair and maintain hand-pumps. In another area women have been trained as masons. Communities receive organization and financial management training to support the effectiveness and sustainability of village-level institutions, and key resource people are provided with technical skills to plan, implement and maintain the development activities. The ultimate goal is for people in the participating communities to have the access, confidence and competence to make informed choices from a range of appropriate development options.

In 2001 alone, over 300 training programmes benefited almost 6000 villagers, 64 per cent of which were women. These were essentially to increase awareness about savings and credit programmes, provide exposure to 'model' villages and orient rural communities to the principles of natural resources management. In addition, over 50 NGOs and 400 government staff have also been trained in various participatory processes.

Benefits and Impact on Quality of Life

Assets thus created often result in more than just increased income generation. AKDN's rural development programmes have benefited over 300,000 households in over 1,000 villages in western and central India since 1983. Development activities have ensured more water for drinking and irrigation, higher agricultural productivity and rural incomes (including household savings), greater resilience to droughts and the ability to manage the natural resource base better.

Vinayak Reddy (2005) says, "With over 10,000 households now accessing assured sources of safe drinking water, women have benefited significantly. Since they no longer have to walk long distances to collect water, the time saved can now be spent with family or education of their children." Alternatively, they have more time for income generation activities. Health improvements due to improved diets and access to safe drinking water also lead to a reduction in the costs of medicines and trips to the doctor. Similarly, the number of days of illness has been reduced by 50 per cent (down to 15 days per year, as compared to about 30 days per year earlier).

Simultaneously, literacy levels have risen by 10 per cent (8% in the case of women). Growing gender sensitivity and changing gender equations are also evident from a phenomena that 350 per cent increase in the expenditure incurred on medicines for women. School attendance levels show an improvement, especially in the case of girls who now no longer have to accompany their mothers at dawn to collect water.

Impact studies conducted in some areas reveal an average increase of beneficiary incomes by about 60 per cent, going up to 80 per cent in some cases. More savings and increased access to credit reduces the dependence of the poor on local moneylenders. Even the landless benefit from increased demand for farm labour when improved agricultural practices results in two or three crops instead of just one every year, leading to, among other things, a reduction in migration. In 147 villages in four states, savings amongst beneficiaries was estimated to be approximately US$ 0.6 million (Rs. 28 million approximately).

As rural employment has improved, stress-migration levels have shown a marked reduction (down to 35% from 80% earlier). Even the duration of migration has reduced to 90 days per year (down from 150 days a year earlier).

Women's empowerment has also led to them participating in the local political process. In recent local village level elections in a programme area, 52 elected members (including 15 women) out of a total of 179 (approximately 30%) who were elected belonged to village institutions established by AKDN's rural development programmes.

Sustainability and Partnerships

Long-term commitment is the key creating sustainable impact. Consequently, rural development programmes in India have now run 20 years and helped create replicable models that can be quickly adapted to a variety of contexts; as well as long-term relationships with donor agencies and peer organizations for the mobilization of funds, human resources and expertise.

Bhargava (2007) says "In terms of organizational elements, programmes are usually area-based programmes that serve a defined population, are implemented over a long time frame and at a significant scale and are characterized by comparatively thorough coverage of all of the population within their target area."

Ensuring sustainable impact requires consistent efforts over considerable time periods. In the case of rural development programmes, this has meant at least ten years of concerted efforts at the grassroots level before results and subsequent impact on the quality of life of the poor is visible for all to see.

The role of Rural Non-Farm Sector (RNFS) is crucial both in generating productive employment and alleviating poverty in rural areas because of the limited absorptive capacity of the urban sector and near saturation of the agricultural sector in further absorption of workers. Policy workers are increasingly recognising the importance of RNFS in providing sustainable livelihoods to a large number of people in rural areas.

However, in spite of a lot of research that has been carried out, our understanding of the RNFS, particularly its role in the broader development process, is relatively poor and does not provide adequate insights to policy-makers grappling with the enormous diversity of the sector. There is, thus, an urgent need to address the specific requirements of the RNFS so that these can be better integrated into policies and strategies at various levels in order to affect poverty reduction and ensure growth with equity.

The creation of rural communities that is resilient, proactive, knowledgeable and possess noble ethical and moral values. An enhancement process of Rural Transformation Movement—inculcating the dynamism element which becomes the vital part in community empowerment and rural leadership process.

Recent Development in Rural Transformation

In Wi-Fi classrooms, Bangalore's poor catch up
V Shoba
The Indian Express Group
Tags: Indus International School, Wi-Fi
Posted: Sun Aug 08 2010, 03:19 hrs
Updated: Sun Aug 08 2010, 09:08 hrs
Bangalore:

While a city school fears poor children will be detrimental to classmates, another starts an IB school for BPL kids, India's first.

Behind the snazzy Greco-Roman blocks of Indus International School, past its riding club and indoor sports stadium, is a clutch of humble buildings, spruced up with Chittara and Yakshagana art, that don't seem to belong. But step inside and the story is all about belonging.

These classrooms are part of India's first international baccalaureate (IB) school for children from below-poverty-line families in the neighbourhood, which shares not just the sprawling Sarjapura campus of the $35-per-child-per-day international school, but also its curriculum—up to class V—at a nominal fee of 7 cents per child per day.

In the Wi-Fi classrooms of the community school that overlooks a pond, well-groomed children in green uniforms type on their Intel Classmate laptops and speak among themselves in whispers—Kannada, Telugu, Tamil, Urdu, and of late, a smattering of English.

REFERENCES

Aggarwal, J.C. (2008), *Educational Reforms in India for the 21st Century.* Shipra Publications: Delhi.

Bhargava, H. and Kumar, D. (2007). *Rural Transformation: Socio-Economic Issues.* Publisher: ICFAI.

Chaube, K. (2002). *Environmental Development.* Centre for Scientific Research, pp. 75-76.

Norman Uphoff, Milton J. Esman, and Anirudh Krishna (1998), *Reasons for Success: Learning from Instructive Experiences in Rural development,* New Delhi, Vikas Publications.

Sharma, S. (2000), Achievement Levels Urban and Rural Children. *Indian Education.* Volume XXXV, Number 2, August.

The Indian Express, Baroda August 8 Issue.

Vinayak, Reddy A. and Bhaskar Rao, G. (2005) *Transformation in India: The Impact of Globalisation.* New Century.

WEBLIOGRAPHY

1. http://india.gov.in/sectors/rural/definition_state.php - 19k.
2. http://en.wikipedia.org/wiki/Rural_Development_Foundation,_I.-29k.
3. http://www.indiarural.org/projects_education.htm - 18k.
4. http://www.akdn.org/india_rural.asp - 51k.

5. http://www.akdn.org/india_rural.asp - 51k.
6. http://www.ruraltransformation.in/New_Delhi_Declaration_on_the_Rural_ Transformation_of_Emerging_Economies.pdf.
7. unesdoc.unesco.org/images/0013/001359/135913eo.pdf.
8. http://www.tn.gov.in/policynotes/pdf/rural_development.pdf.

13

Key Approaches of Education for Rural Transformation

Priyanka Kacker

Introduction

India is a vast democratic country with diversified culture, languages, religions etc. However, we all are facing similar problem irrespective of our religion, languages and culture, to start with Rural Transformation (RT). Rural development doesn't mean urbanisation of rural areas. It does not consist of creation of *pucca* buildings, metalled roads, electrified houses, TV and video sets in houses. In fact, some of these symptoms of development are noticeable in some villages and yet they cannot be called developed, e.g., Kuwait, Sudan, with very high per capita income, cannot be called a 'Developed' country.

The real crust of development is that people living in the rural areas, develop the capability of live well—a life pattern which keeps them in good health, have adequate means to eat, to clothe, a reasonable shelter to live and access to various requisites to life which modern science and technology has made it possible to have, to enjoy life. This does not mean copying urban style of life but one evolved in the socio-eco-cultural milieu which they have inherited. Therefore, content of rural development will vary from area to area.

Pumping in some symptoms of development from outside, lead to sustainable development that is why, perhaps, many of the measures undertaken by outside agencies have failed to create the desired impact on rural development (S.K. Naik, 1993).

Rural Transformation involves creating wealth, employment, good health services, water, roads, sanitation, education, etc. for the betterment of the rural people.

In many empirical studies, throughout the world, it is found that there is correlation between literacy and development. So for rural transformation education is very important. Today after 64 years of Independence, we have more than 336 crore adults; who do not know reading and writing. Some of the reasons for this are apparent. To mention some, many children live in unhealthy, unhygienic, crowded conditions, amidst deep social tension and backwardness due to poverty. The caste system, untouchability, orthodoxy and many other social evils and the privileged class had kept the underprivileged illiterates, indeed, shamefully low during the last decade of the 20th century.

As a result of this, out of every hundred children, even if they join the school, seventy five children drop-out before they reach 8th standard or complete primary education and they remain virtually illiterate thereafter.

As per the estimates by the UNESCO, the illiteracy for the age-group 15 and over, it is estimated that in 1990, India had 280 million adult illiterates in the age-group 15 and over which form 51.7 per cent of the corresponding population.

According to these estimates, India has the highest number of illiterates in world constituting 29.1 per cent of the total, estimates of 962.6 million illiterates of the world. These projections also indicate that India and China taken together contain 502 million illiterates and it comes to 52 per cent of the world's total illiterates.

So, for rural transformation education is one of the most important aspects which are being discussed in this chapter.

For rural transformation we first need to do detailed and extensive surveys to find out the area which requires transformation at the most and require attention immediately. For the surveys, students from Education, Psychology, Social Work and other related branches can be chosen for the purpose of surveys and then some intervention through out the country can be done as part of their dissertation and Ph.D. research work. Students can be sent to different regions for surveying and on the basis of results of the survey intervention plan can be prepared which the student with the help of some NGOs or organisation can implement as part of their Ph.D. thesis, e.g. Adult education, Training programmes for rural teachers, etc.

On the basis of the results of the survey we can take some preliminary steps for Education for Rural Transformation (ERT). Rural transformation requires three very important aspects that are:

- Heavy investments are needed for inclusive, sustainable and diversified rural development to occur;
- Need for the right governance systems, institutions; and
- Policy processes and improving the efficiency and effectiveness of public policy and programmes (Report, New Delhi, 16 April, 2010).

However, these things require time and huge funds and we require immediate action, i.e. some preliminary steps; so that when we fulfil the above three important requirements at that time we will be well prepared to use our resources as our planning for Rural Transformation is already done. The initial steps for ERT are discussed below:

Same Curriculum Throughout the Country

Same syllabus, same subject contents, same examination pattern and almost same teaching style throughout the country. The curriculum time-table should also be same. Curriculum time-table means monthly syllabus to be taught in one month should be the same in all the states and in all the schools. The reason is, in mid-session if a student want to shift from rural to urban school then the student will not have any problem related to studies. The child can adjust well with the curriculum.

Different boards of education should have same curriculum and should follow the same pattern of questions, date and time of examination. The question paper should be prepared by Central examination body and distributed equally. They can have different sets of paper for different regions. This should be done only for convenience sake.

Exchange of Students and Teachers

Teachers who are posted in urban areas, at least for few months/ years they should be posted to rural areas in order to teach the students of rural areas in the same manner which they follow in urban areas. Same process can be followed by sending rural students to urban schools in order to learn the course content so that they can reach the level of students of urban areas. Similar kind of exchange programme can be done for foreign countries also.

Grade Examination at Every Level

There should be uniform grade of examination at primary, junior secondary, senior secondary and higher secondary levels. This will give an idea to the students of rural areas, the standard of urban areas and accordingly they can improve themselves with the help their teachers. By doing grade examination students of both areas will prepare for common syllabus, this will create equality in rural and urban standards or we can say that this will decrease the curriculum gap between the rural and urban areas.

Technical and Vocational Education

Teachers: Educational/vocational training can be provided to teacher to gain professional skills and since it will be a National or International training programme every year or every six months, it will help in developing common skills in all teachers. The training programme will be organised by school or University concerned or a governing education body.

Underprivileged Children: Technical and vocational education and training can be provided to underprivileged students of rural areas. The training can be given in urban as well as rural areas. Places where technical and vocational educations are not available for that urban technical education/vocational institutes should be empowered to establish such educational and vocational institution in rural areas. This will also stop migration of rural students to urban areas and they will be self-sufficient at their village level.

Non-Campus Distance Education

People who want to study but because of some reason like financial crisis, distance, job etc. they are not able to join regular classes can get enrolled themselves for such education programmes and can learn staying at home. Non-campus distance programme for those also whose syllabus is different from other universities and after completion of graduation they want to join other university. So they can parallel study the course which other universities are teaching while studying the current syllabus of their own university. This will help the student to adjust better when he/she join the university which he/she wished to join.

Adult Education

From the beginning of Five Year Plans, the Government of India gave importance to Adult education. It has been launched a country-wide programme of adult literacy drive as a part of social education in 1950 under the Community development programme. Its success was limited because of many socio-economic reasons. There was less motivation for adults towards the programme and local resources and voluntary organisations did not involved fully.

For this first the NGOs or the organisations involved in the Adult Education plan must be feel enthusiastic for their work and Education counsellors should provide a motivational incentives whenever required to the adult people, so that their level of motivation do not go down. For example, Person with good performance will get job or will get vocational training or can work as supervisor etc. in the industry established in village.

Stop Migration

Individuals rationally decide to migrate because they are attracted by the bright lights of the city which promise, in the long-term, to offer better economic opportunities than the countryside. The structuralist approach to migration, on the other hand, tends to portray migrants as victims rather than rational decision-makers, since movement is determined by macro social, historical and dialectic processes such as the socio-spatial restructuring of production at the national and global levels. Push-pull factors are seen as a process of polarization with respect to access to resources, and migration as one of the new options available to the most vulnerable population strata.

Gender and generation also play a crucial role in migration, decision-making and selectivity (Chant, 1992). For example, women (either mothers or daughters) are more likely to feel responsible for the well-being of other household members then their male counterparts and this may be an important factor in migration decisions especially when women's employment opportunities in home environments are limited. Migrations can also provide an escape from social and family constraints and give women a level of independence they may not easily have access to in their home areas (Gadio and Rakowski, 1995). Young men with restricted access to family land waged work may also decide to move. While in all cases the impacts on areas of out-migration may be significant (in terms, for example, of labour availability, remittances, household organisations and agricultural production systems), they are also likely to vary depending on who moves and who stays. To stop such migrations from rural to urban areas we can start giving non-agricultural educational and vocational training to people of rural areas due to which they can start their own business in their village only. Non-agricultural rural activities include non-farm activities, which are carried out in the farm but are not related to crop production (such as furniture and brick making or beer-brewing, which are sold in both rural and urban markets) and off-farm activities, which are carried out away from the farm, and thus involve a special dimension, often revolving around urban centres (Cecilia Tacoli, 1998).

Drop-outs from Primary Schools

There is a large rate of drop-outs from primary schools even in States where primary education is free and supposedly compulsory. The root problem is the mass poverty in rural areas. In that situation a child becomes a helper in economic activities from young age. Tending to cattle, fetching firewood or water and helping parents in their field work are commonly seen in rural households.

For this NGOs and Government can give scholarships to those, whose children are coming regularly and scoring good marks in exams. This will motivate the parents to send their children to schools and also there will be some financial help.

Gender Differences

The literacy gap between males and females should be reduced so that there will be a sense of equality in terms of education in society. A study conducted by the Centre for Science and Environment (CSE), Delhi in Himalayan village Chamoli, UP unfolds that women spend 59 per cent, children 36 per cent and men 15 per cent work hours every year confirming back breaking work load on rural womenfolk. These are perhaps the alarming indicators about the Indian rural women, whose work is filled with drudgery and hardship-leading to feminization of poverty, thus, in real sense excluding them from full participation in development efforts to eliminate poverty. Though rural women produce upto 80 per cent of food in the developing countries, yet, studies include they have little to only a fraction of farm land, and access to just 10 per cent of credit and 5 per cent of extension advice (S.K. Agrawal, 2005).

For this women from villages should be given educational and vocational training. Also they will be given job opportunity in their village so that they can take care of their family, children and can earn money too. For example, small scale business, dairy products, handicrafts, etc. They can also become the broker or the agent who can help their village women to sell their products to different parts of the world so that they will get money for their hard work.

Incentives to the Farmers

Make a Policy which says that, those who will complete their formal education or those who have done their matriculation and cleared the examination will get some per cent reduction in their loans or will get seeds and fertilizers at much subsidised rates. Those whose children are studying technical or vocational or teaching field and working for the development of village they will get seeds and fertilizers free of cost or at very subsidized rates etc.

Agricultural Education

Greater stress has to be given on the Agricultural colleges to bring about an integrated approach to education, research and extension. Provide training to the farmers. Demonstrate and train farmers about the improved agricultural facilities and organise village cooperatives and Panchayats. The programme will include Cattle development, High Yielding Varieties (HYVs) programmes, Agro-area etc. Young students must be trained about the importance of land and the rivers, flora and fauna of the countryside.

Though there are 73 Agricultural colleges with annual admission strength of about 10,000 as compared to 18 Agricultural colleges with strength of about 1,000 in 1951. 8 Agricultural Engineering colleges have been set-up in different parts of the country with a total annual admission strength of about 250 students. There are Veterinary Colleges, Fisheries Colleges, rural oriented Home Science Colleges and Forest Colleges. But for higher economic returns from agriculture, technical educational programme is essential. We need to restructure our educational curricula and course to meet these basic requirements of the country. We need to increase the number of such colleges and number of seats so that more number of students can be benefited from these colleges. Also for this we need to motivate farmers and their children to get enrolled in such educational/vocational programmes as they are the future of our Country's Rural Transformation.

Colleges in rural areas can have reservation for only rural students. They will be given job opportunity to work in the rural areas, so that they have interest in developing their own village. Infrastructure and funding can be provided by State government and Private agencies. The main focus of these colleges will be research and development in the field of agriculture, e.g. preparing good and healthy seeds, organic fertilizers and manures, etc.

Use of Technologies

Training for how to use computers and internet: There are so many areas within India where internet connection and computers are available but people do not know how to use these technologies. Training must be provided to people living in rural areas so that they can utilize internet and computers for the purpose of learning and also for doing work related to their job or business. For example, sending designs of handloom sarees to designers and buyers located in different parts of the world, to learn different ways of domestic animal farming with the help of translated version of videos available on internet, seed technology, biotechnology, etc. For this purpose, if the people are not comfortable with the language, then a person from the village can be chosen who knows English language better and that person can explain these techniques in their local language. For this the person will be paid by NGO or State government.

E-Resource facilities: Electronic books, journals, articles, and magazines should be available on internet in different languages so that the areas where there is no library or no source of information, the people of that area can surf internet to get information.

Information and Communication Technologies (ICTs): ICT facilities can be used for rural transformation. Same syllabus, same subject, same content can be accessed by everybody including children and teachers so that the pattern of education can be maintained and if students want to come to the urban areas; they will be already aware with contents of the subject. For this, syllabus will be displayed on internet; the contents will be prepared and explained in detail in a particular format by different Professors and Teachers of Universities and Schools.

Also the content will be in three languages—English, Hindi and local language so that it will be accessible by all.

The clever deployment of ICT for creating connectivity in thousands of colleges and hundreds of universities is, therefore, not a luxury but a necessity. This would bring in free flow of information, which would give access to various good elements of teaching and learning at places of eminence, which would enhance the academic ambience at far places across the country. Much more than that, it would expose vast number of youths in rural, semi-urban and urban areas to best teachers and best of academic infrastructure in India and abroad. This is not only cost effective approach but would reduce migration of students to cosmopolitan cities. This would also have impact on research in universities. The information and communication connectivity would help to propagate concept of digital repository of research material thus making it possible to have an access to wider breadth of 'knowledge' at low cost (Sita Ram Sharma, 2006).

ICTs can work as a useful tool of learning and expression. The common problem is expanding access to ICTs and developing their use to enhance basic education. The Dakar framework for Action articulates the dilemma that their increasing use 'may tend to increase disparities, weaken social bonds and threaten cultural cohesion'. This dilemma applies also to the promotion of literacy and context-sensitive Education for Sustainable Development, and includes the question of how use ICTs relates to traditional learning tools (paper and pen, chalk and talk, for example). This is an area where common cause should be made by advocating strongly for local input into how ICTs should be used.

To resolve this issue we can in advance make sure that the all contents are explained by the teachers before students can surf the net and get information. Also ICT contents can be explained by the teachers using Chalk-Talk-Interaction. Teachers can motivate students to give more examples related to the content and to prepare street plays, flash cards, skits and many other things based on the contents of ICTs which will be the part of their examination procedure. Also there will be paper-pen examinations which will be subjective in nature and students have to write answers in detailed based on what they have studied as part of their syllabus throughout the year.

Health Education

The issues of development, environment and health are closely entwined, reflecting the complex links between the social, economic, ecological and political factors that determine standards of living and other aspects of social wellbeing that influence human health. A healthy population and safe environments are important pre-conditions for sustainable development. However, the education of many children and young people around the world is compromised by conditions and behaviours that undermine the physical and emotional well-being that makes learning possible. Hunger, malnutrition, malaria, polio and intestinal infections, drug and alcohol abuse, violence and injury, unplanned pregnancy, HIV/AIDS and other sexually transmitted infections are just some of the problems that have enormous implications for health (UNESCO).

Health education activities should be organized at different parts of the States where people are not aware of their health conditions and causes of it. This can be done by Health practitioners, Psychologists, Social workers, AIDS counsellors etc.

Physical Education

For better health and for better well-being physical education is very important. For this course is being run in 7 universities and 22 colleges spread over 13 states in the country, where UGC is providing assistance to these institutions for approved items of expenditure like salary of the staff, books and journals, equipment and laboratory building. But there are still many activities that can be done to provide physical education.

In many parts of the country people have capability and skills to show good performance related to any kind of sports like tracking (desert, Forest), Cycle Safari on plain, Mountainous terrain/rocky terrain, water sports, skiing, malkham, boxing, etc. Such extraordinary people must get proper training and must get proper motivation so that they can prepare themselves for National and International game, tournaments and can make country, their parents and village proud. For this they must get proper Boarding and Lodging, Honorarium, TA/DA, Equipments, etc. This will not only promote Indian games but also help people to shine and earn money.

Human Rights Education

Most of the people are not aware of their rights whether the individual is from urban or rural areas. Human rights education should be provided by social workers, students of law, teachers, etc. so that people who are not aware of their rights can use their rights to progress and to stand confidently on their feet to achieve their goals without being cheated.

Internships

Internship can be introduced as part of curriculum of the B.Ed. and M.Ed. students. As part of B.Ed. and M.Ed. internship students can be sent to Municipality schools or the schools having poor academic performance, for teaching and educating the children. At the end of the year based on the school children's performance grades can be given to B.Ed. and M.Ed. students. This will serve two purposes: improvement in teaching style of Municipality school and Training of B.Ed. and M.Ed. students to deal with worst teaching systems and how to improve it.

Children University

In Gujarat the first Children University of India has been opened recently. The motto of this University is diverse yet much focused. It will work in the field of research, education and training, and some extensive services. The University with the help of trained and experienced teachers, consultants, will provide education and training to the students of B.Ed. and M.Ed. Then these trained students will provide training to other teachers located in different rural and urban areas. The training and education will also be provided to special/disabled children. Education related to health, vocational, physical, etc. will also be provided. Also trained psychologists will help in diagnosing children with difficulty in learning and based on that proper intervention plan will be prepared to help those children.

We should encourage such University to grow and spread its network not only in Gujarat but also in different parts of the country where transformation is required urgently and needs more attention. We can get associated with the Children University and help them reach to achieve their goals. This will help in better and much faster rural transformation.

Assessment

Time to time assessment should be done to find out whether the planned strategy is working effectively or not. For this a governing body can be made who will do this assessment part every 6 months or 1 year. Also psychological assessment should be done by a team of psychologists in order to find out, if there is any difference in quality of life and well-being of people or not. This will help in deciding whether the strategies are working properly or not. Time to time psychological assessment will also help in finding the motivational level of the governing body and the rural people so that, if there is any problem, proper intervention can be given to both members of the governing body and rural people. This will help in maintaining the motivation of the system and goal achievement.

Role of Media

Media can play a very important role in Education for Rural Transformation by making people aware of different policies, their rights, and importance of education. If this awareness is spread like a fire then Education for Rural Transformation will become much easier that we cannot think of.

Unity

The above mentioned points can only be achieved if all of us understand our responsibilities and duties. Its our responsibility and duty to teach others. It does not matter from which discipline we belong. Anyone can help in Education for Rural Transformation and ultimately the rural transformation. Whether, we are from education, law, psychology, social work, health, medicine, political science, etc. we all can give our favours to the society to improve it. And for this we have to work together as a team.

Conclusion

Education for Rural Transformation is very important. Though funds, right governance, efficiency and effectiveness of policies are very important but still as an educator, psychologist and social worker, we can do many things for rural transformation. If these key approaches like educational/vocational training, information about and use of latest technologies, physical, health education, etc. are being followed and provided effectively then we can achieve our goal that is Rural Transformation.

REFERENCES

Agrawal, S.K., (2005), "Rural Transformation through Decentralized Technologies: Empowerment and Participatory Systems Management Approach for Sustainable Livelihoods", *Journal of Rural Technologies*, Vol. 2, No.2, July.

International Conference on the Dynamics of Rural Transformation in Engineering Economies, New Delhi, India, April 16, 2010. www.ruraltransformaion.in.

Sharma, S.R. (2006), *University Grants Commission, Role in Development and Growth of Higher Education*, Mangal Deep Publications, Jaipur.

Tacoli Cecilia, (1998), "Rural-urban interactions: A guide to the literature", *Environment and Urbanization*, Vol. 10, No.1, April.

United Nations Decade of Education for Sustainable Development, (2008), http://www.unesco.org/education/tlsf

14

Spawning Micro Education for Rural India

Rishi Raj Balwaria and *Pratibha Gupta*

Introduction

As quoted by Mahatma Gandhi, "India lives in its villages". Even today around 65 per cent of the State's population is living in rural areas. People in rural areas don't have the same quality of life as is enjoyed by people living in suburban and urban areas whereas the Constitution of India focuses on the Union of India to be a sovereign, socialist, secular, democratic republic, assuring its citizens of justice, equality, and liberty. The Government programmes like Universalisation of Elementary Education (UEE) and its related programmes like Sarva Shiksha Abhiyan gave emphasis on Education for All. Even after more than 60 years of independence of our democratic India still we are not completely independent.

We observe disparities between urban and rural areas. Including other sectors, education sector too, in the rural areas are underprivileged. Lack of quality education/poor quality schools leads to cascade effects of poverty, unemployment, poor and inadequate infrastructure in rural areas on urban centres causing slums and consequential social and economic tensions manifesting in economic deprivation and urban poverty leading to other economical and social problems.

Insight of the PROBE Report for Rural Education

As noticed by the PROBE Report, 1999 the poor quality of rural schools diminishes their attractiveness and the benefits of schooling. The PROBE report showed that Public Schools in rural India were woefully inadequate in respect of physical infrastructure, with 82 per cent of schools needing repair. Books are often unavailable, and teacher absenteeism tends to be high. This study of primary schools found that 19 per cent of teachers were absent on any given day, and 23 per cent were absent in rural schools in India. Teachers present are unprepared and poorly paid, and violence and harassment are common. Many children did not like school because they were mistreated or discriminated against, and fear of violence in schools leads children to drop-out. From the report it easily observed that we need to improve our education system, which lacks investment in schools and teachers and a results of this leads to low quality of schooling means little learning and low educational attainment reduces the possibilities for employment. And this will require a wider vision for developing the opportunities for the Quality Rural Education. This vision can be made possible through Micro education.

Need for Micro Education

In our country people have adapted information and communication technology and have alternative solution of the problem. But on the other hand they do not have enough money and other advanced resources for their life. Another reason would be we are so different in culturally, demographically, sociologically, and economically, accordingly our needs are different. We need different solution for the different regions and the most acute problem exists in our rural areas.

The rural India is changing rapidly, and young people need to be prepared to rise to the new opportunities. Agriculture is also changing, with new technologies, products, markets, and business environments. And many rural people will need to become engaged in non-farm activities or migrate to urban areas. To seize these opportunities, all will need skills that differ from those of their parents—but education and training systems are not ready to face the challenge. When their needs are changed, and they are looking for others to seek help, and start migrating from their origin they loose their spirit and originality. To overcome this situation micro education can be a ray of hope to them.

Rural people mostly depend on agriculture, seasonal occupations and in small-scale industry. Therefore, they have to depend on many factors and have continuous worry of the future. Their children are also working in one or the other form to help the family members. For them it is difficult to go to schools for continuous six hours a day. Looking at the situation we need to develop a model for the rural India that provide them benefits for them in terms of economical needs, better quality life, vision for futuristic society. The presenter would like to suggest a solution for the transformation of rural India by introducing Micro Education.

We all observe market and we know the fact that rural people earn in daily or weekly wages. Accordingly they consume most products such as shampoo, biscuits, tooth powder, etc in micro units. When the businessmen are so much aware about the market why not the government people/NGOs and others have not getting the ideas to develop micro education for the rural class of our country. There has to be the beginning of education focused on specialized topics "micro-education" which engages small numbers of people in the teaching-learning process there are a number of opportunities and challenges embedded in these efforts. Micro education for the betterment and development of the rural education needs to be explored in more detail and a lot of questions need to be asked to oneself about how to design these various approaches, when to use these designs and what success can be achieved with these efforts. That helps them to get education as per their requirement.

Meaning of Micro Education

The literal meaning has very small scope for the transformation of rural India, we need wider perspective and scope. In the wider term micro education would deal with spreading awareness about gender education, importance of education, need and awareness about environmental education, professional skills for 21st century skills, content for school children, providing bit by bit information through technology. For example, it would be through T.V. Advertisements, mobile Caller tunes, Radio announcements, educational advertisement on electronic display boards and LCD display already present at Railway Platforms.

Micro Education a Collective Approach

It would be a mandatory requirement for all the state as well as Central Government to share some part of its profit money in development of rural India. We cannot blame on others, it will only be possible by making common efforts by all the people of the country. The economic prosperity and good quality of any nation depends upon the development of human resources of that nation.

The significant fact in the development of manpower resource refers to the competencies and the level on which these competencies are imparted that largely depend on the way one tries to develop these competencies with the available resources. Therefore, for this purpose we need to acquire requisite competencies in the rural students. All the students now need to become self-acting, self-confident, and creative and by themselves they would become "managers of their own future" and for achieving this objective the country and states need to take the initiative. States like Rajasthan take care that the rural students get free textbooks from the Secondary Education Boards of Rajasthan. It is a good initiative by the government and would be extend in other states in rural areas.

For example, if we compare the public and private banking, public banks are situated in urban and rural areas but private banks are mostly in urban areas so that they can earn more money. Likewise other areas are like Internet and information technology. Government may make compulsion at the starting stage that minimum one-fourth of our assets will come from rural areas otherwise they will be penalised. The profit making organizations should start contributing directly/indirectly to the development of education in rural India. Development of the common platform to take care of rural India should be made compulsory as per their size and volume of market asset. This will help them in getting educational loans and start small business which will improve there life style and standard.

Suggestions for Implementing Micro Education

As rural India is deprived of money and other resources we should develop an easy access network for them for the agricultural loans, educational loans and for other requirements once they learn they would observe in the same programme for expanding the programme in other regions. Below are some of the contemporary thoughts as an initiation towards micro education:

1. ***Awareness programmes:*** Educational and general awareness programmes through Puppets shows, Bhavai, and other folk based programmes can be developed for the rural India.
2. ***Open air/Field classroom:*** Our own older people, retired people, retired teachers should take initiative to provide education when they are free from field work, or taking rest in the open air.
3. ***Education through regional languages:*** In the present days the modes of transacting education in rural schools is not change. As a result we observe a high dropout rate in rural areas. The reason would be facing difficulty in learning and retaining through different language. As NCF 2005, emphasized that the medium of education for educating rural areas should be through regional languages.
4. ***Free Education at any place and at any time:*** When our major aim is to provide education for all. We need to make free education and common platform that rural people get education at any place and at any time. LCDs can be displayed at the common places where all the rural people assemble for usual gathering. For Example, they usually assemble for collecting water for their daily usages. It will spread awareness conversation for the rural people.
5. ***Paying money to students for coming to schools:*** For the first 1 to 3 years government, NGOs or any interested volunteer organization would show interest in paying the money. It helps in improving the economical status and develops a positive response for receiving education.
6. ***Educational Caller Tune for rural people:*** Use of mobile is very common among rural people. Whenever, they call to the other mobile they must listen the educational conversation. To spread educational awareness and information mobile companies should provide free Educational caller tunes for rural people.
7. ***"Sandwich" Programmes:*** These programmes should have

specific objectives and for those who already have education up to primary level. Programmes are the combination of local training with access to urban or well developed rural areas. This ensures the optimum utilization of the knowledge-based resources, research methods, and exposure to a wider range of modern technologies. Helping them in gaining better employment opportunities, leading towards quality life.

Conclusion

The rural India is changing rapidly, and youth of present society and a futuristic citizen of democratic India need to be prepared to rise to the new opportunities. Educational sector, agriculture sector etc., are changing, with new technologies, products, markets, and business environments. To seize the upcoming opportunities, all we need is to develop needful skills. This will help them to get education as per their requirement and also to train them for the 21st century skills and for the better life. What we need and what we all are doing, we need to introspect ourselves whether we are moving towards the right vision or not—the vision of micro education.

REFERENCES

Carmichael, D., (1980). "The Challenge of Rural Education." *Baylor Educator* 5: 21-25.

Dunne, F., (1981). "Is There Such a Thing as Rural Education? A Portrait of the Small Rural School." *The Small School Forum* 2: 2-4.

Dunne, F., William S., and Carlsen, (1981). *Small Rural Schools in the United States: A Statistical Profile*. Washington, DC: National Rural Center, ED 206-436.

Education Writers Association, (1989). Wolves at the schoolhouse door: An investigation of the condition of public school buildings. Washington, DC: Education Writers Association. *Retrieved from http://www.ericdigests.org/pre-9215/*capital.htm

Hobart, L., (2010). "Hollowing Out the Middle: The Rural Brain Drain and What It Means for America". *Journal of Research in Rural Education*. 25(3).

NCF, (2005). NCERT, Government of India, New Delhi. Retrieved from http://www.ncert.nic.in

Probe Report, (1999). *Retrieved from* www.siteresources.worldbank.org

15

Girls Education

A Challenge for Rural Transformation in India

Swaleha Sindhi

Introduction

Socialization of the girl child in India seems to have followed a set pattern where she has been trapped and moulded by deep-rooted combined cultures of patriarchy and hierarchy. Women as such can be dubbed as a population at risk because of their limited access to resources and opportunities and their systematic exclusion from the position of decision-making. What is more important is that the process of exclusion tends to start at the grass-roots, the family level. Herein a girl child is subjected to kind of languages and practices, which patronize exclusion of various natures at variety of levels. What could be more heinous than killing female fetus and infants? The decade of 1990s has seen female feticide and infanticides, the most horrendous of gender crimes, increasing steeply. It is the violation of the most basic human rights, the right to be born.

The growth of biomedical technology has tended to add rather than solving the problem. The blatant misuse of technology has resulted in girls gradually becoming an endangered genre. Women are increasingly been found "missing", the phenomenon identified by Sen (1992, 1) and received a great deal of attention in policy circle. The model estimates the number of women there would be without any female disadvantage in survival, given the actual life expectancy and the fertility rates. The estimation suggests a staggering figure of 37 million missing women in India in more than 100 million worldwide. Indian data present the age specific mortality for females consistently higher than that of males until the fourth decade. This has been only partly explained based on excess mortality at childbearing age due to maternal mortality. The explanation for female disadvantage in survival in infancy and childhood has been variously described. Apart from female infanticide, the extra mortality has been attributed to the comparative neglect of female health and nutrition, especially during childhood. Considerable direct evidence exists of neglect of female children in terms of health care, admission to hospitals, and even feeding.

The debatable question here is—What causes the relative neglect of females and what can change it? Studies have confirmed that apart from traditional culture and values, the identification of economic coefficient in social standing may prove vital. For example, educated women have better access in labour market. Increased participation in labour market brings about increased income. Female income contributes to the prosperity of family more visibly and thereby helps in reducing inter-household disparity and poverty. Being less dependent on others, this also brings about more voice in decision-making. Social status tends to improve. Women with higher social status are likely to be more sensitive to female child's need and aspiration. Therefore, education brings economic liberation, which in turn facilitates social liberation. Further, women's economic rights in terms of land ownership and inheritance may be important. The positive aspect is that a good mix of public policy can influence all these. Meaning thereby, there are chances that the missing women can be rescued.

Government Programme for Rural Girls

The Mahila Samakhya Programme was launched in 1988 in pursuance of the goals of the New Education Policy (1986) and the Programme of Action as a concrete programme for the education and empowerment of women in rural areas, particularly of women from socially and economically marginalized groups. The policy framework, provision of educational opportunities for women and girls has been an important part of the national endeavour in the field of education since independence. Though these endeavours did yield significant results, gender disparities persist, more so in rural areas and among disadvantaged communities. The National Policy on Education (NPE, 1986) as revised in 1992 was landmark in the field of policy on women's education in that it recognized the need to redress traditional gender imbalances in educational access and achievement.

The NPE also recognized that enhancing infrastructure alone would not redress the problem. It recognized that "the empowerment of women is possibly the most critical precondition for the participation of girls and women in the educational process."

The Programme of Action (POA, 1992), in the section "Education for Women's Equality" (Chapter-XII, pages 105-107), focuses on empowerment of women as the critical precondition for their participation in the education process. The POA states that education can be an effective tool for women's empowerment, the parameters of which are:

- enhance self-esteem and self-confidence of women;
- building a positive image of women by recognizing their contribution to the society, polity and the economy;
- developing ability to think critically;
- fostering decision-making and action through collective processes;
- enable women to make informed choices in areas like education, employment and health (especially reproductive health);
- ensuring equal participation in developmental processes;
- providing information, knowledge and skill for economic independence; and
- enhancing access to legal literacy and information relating to their rights and entitlements in society with a view to enhance their participation on an equal footing in all areas.

In the Mahila Samakhya Programme, therefore, the empowerment of women is seen as a critical precondition for the participation of women and girls in the education process. The principal strategy identified for ensuring participation is through mobilizing and organizing them into *sanghas* (collectives). It was decided that the best way to achieve this would be to follow a strategy where the programme would not lay down either targets to be achieved or specific agenda to be followed but would take its programmatic cues from the women in the Sanghas.

The predominant composition of the Mahila Sanghas is SC/ST women, women belonging to landless and marginalized families, who are engaged in wage labour. This is the very group that is most alienated from educational and other Government programmes and processes. Reaching them has been a difficult but exhilarating process.

In spite of Government's constant effort to improve the rural women's condition through different programmes and policies it is still a challenge for the government and the NGOs to improve the conditions of the rural girl education and to improve the socio-economic conditions of the rural women. In rural India there still are some major problems that needs attention of the nation, the reasons for such problems are as follows:

Gender Inequality in Access to Education

Education seems to be the key factor, which only can initiate a chain of advantages to females. However, the access to education is differently perceived for male and female. Key indicators such as literacy, enrollment and years spent in school explain the situation in the access to education and each of these indicators reveal that the level of female education in India is still low and lagging far behind their male counterpart.

Literacy

Literacy is undeniably the most fundamental of all goals adopted all across the world and rightly so in India. The ability to read and right is unquestionably the gateway to all social transformation and hence almost a basic human right. Yet, statistics suggest that women are lagging far behind men in this respect. The Census of India 2001 figure suggests that literacy rate in India has gone up by about 13 per cent point over the last decade, from 52.21 per cent in 1991 to 64.84 per cent in 2001. Yet, the female literacy still stands at 54.16 per cent in comparison to an impressive figure of 75.85 per cent male literacy. The male-female gap in literacy rate is still more than 20 per cent point, which kept on increasing till 1991 and declined marginally by about 3 per cent point over 1991 to 2001.

Table 15.1: Literacy rates in India (1951-2001)

Census Year	*Persons*	*Males*	*Females*	*Male-Female gap in iteracy rate (in %)*
1951	18.33	27.16	8.86	18.30
1961	28.30	40.40	15.35	25.05
1971	34.45	45.96	21.97	23.98
1981	43.57	56.38	29.76	26.62
1991	52.21	64.13	39.29	24.84
2001	64.84	75.85	54.16	21.69

Source: Census of India 2001.

The population trend since 1981 suggests that a decadal addition of about 26-27 per cent has been seen in the age-group 7 years and over. However, the literacy situation of adults in 15 to 35 age-group could not pick up much. Despite improvements in adult literacy, the fact remains that as many as 121 million Indians in the age-group 15-35 are illiterate and nearly two-third of them are women. The recently brought out NSSO's 60th round survey on employment and unemployment (January-June 2004) provides no less glaring picture of the differential in male-female literacy in the country. The survey reports that while male literacy was 62 per cent and 80 per cent in rural and urban areas, respectively, the females corresponding rates were 43 per cent and 68 per cent.

Primary School Enrollment

Low adult literacy rates for women are a reflection of past underinvestment in the education of women and thus do not necessarily capture the recent progress. It is imperative here to look at the way the difference between school enrollment rates for boys and girls have changed over time, especially the primary school enrollment.

Table 15.2: Growth in enrollment, 1950 to 2001

(in millions)

Primary

Year	Boys	Girls	Total	% Girls
1951	13.8	5.4	19.2	28.13
1961	23.6	11.4	35.0	32.57
1971	35.7	21.3	57.0	37.37
1981	45.3	28.5	73.8	38.62
1991	57.0	40.4	97.4	41.48
2001	64.0	49.8	113.8	43.76

Secondary

Year	Boys	Girls	Total	% Girls
1951	1.3	0.2	1.5	13.33
1961	2.7	0.7	3.4	20.59
1971	5.7	1.9	7.6	25.00
1981	7.6	3.4	11.0	30.91
1991	12.8	6.3	19.1	32.98
2001	16.9	10.7	27.6	38.77

Source: Survey on Employment and Unemployment, January-June 2004.

It is evident that there has been a steady growth in enrollment of children at all stages over time, including an impressive growth during 1990s in primary stage (6-11 years age). However, still the percentage of girl's enrollment *vis-à-vis* boys has been in the range of 38–44 per cent at all levels. The problem is not only confined to low enrollments, the girl's school attendance has also been found incredibly low. Rural girls belong to disadvantaged groups as if SC and ST present the worst scenario with a 49.9 per cent and 55.9 per cent respectively having dropped out. As revealed girl dropout ratio has tended to increase with the enhancement in the level of education. At the primary level, girls drop-out rates of 42 per cent is far less than that of 58 per cent at upper primary and a staggering 71.5 per cent in higher classes. This clearly outlines the pattern of gender inequality in access to education, which seems to be deepening as we move from lower to higher educational attainment and from urban to rural and to disadvantaged group in the society.

Why Women Remain Undereducated?

What explains the gender differentials in educational attainment?

What makes women to remain outside the preview of change? Studies have tried to answer these questions on various planes. Economic benefits of education and the costs involved in undertaking such educational attainment have been perceived differently for men and women. Parents who bear the private costs of investing in schooling for girls and women fail to receive the full benefits of their investment. This is largely true because much of the payoff in educating women is broadly social in nature rather than economic. This endures the gender differentials.

Economic Costs and Benefits

Parents and guardians perception of current costs of education and future benefits there from determine the size of investment to be made. This influences the decision whether girl child should continue taking education or not. There are net benefits still exists in keeping children out of school and this helps promoting drop-outs. The costs include direct financial costs, indirect or opportunity costs, and non-pecuniary costs that are borne privately by the parents or the student. The benefits include returns both to the family (in higher returns to family in terms of share in children's income) and to society (in term of improved quality of life and discipline).

However, it is rather difficult to capture these costs and benefits in concrete quantified terms and hence there has been lack of concerted attempt to quantify these aspects. Costs are often measured in terms of distance to school and other direct costs involved such as fee paid, books bought, dressed made, etc. The costs are also perceived based on availability of school. Attempt has been made to estimate the opportunity costs of schooling on enrollment or attainment. Compared to costs estimation, benefits have been difficult to measure. Expected earnings in the labour market popularly measure improved productivities. Conceptual issues in measuring costs and benefits apart, the very perception of it tends to differ in the minds of parents for boys and girls children. These perceptions affect the willingness of parent's to invest in educating their daughters. At times, the favour to son is made not only in education but also in allocation of food at mealtime, distribution of inheritance and even the language used. Such behaviour of parents may not always be taken as discriminatory but a rational response to constraints imposed by poverty and the expected returns determined by labour market. Investment in female education takes a long drive only when the perception of benefits from it outweighs the costs to be incurred. Daughters are educated to the extent that parents are willing to accept economic returns.

Psychological Costs

Apart from economic costs and benefits, there are costs involved at psychological planes well. The differential access based on the psychological perceptions is more firm and real threat. The factors herein include all such motives, which tend to make a parent reluctant to send daughters to school. One of the glaring factors is the concern for the physical and moral safety of a girl child which makes parents unwilling to let them travelling distances to school each day. The concern may vary urban-ruralwise as also the perceived crime rate in a given region.

Religion and socio-cultural factors such as those related to societal, economic, and familial roles of women strongly influence parents choice due to heavy costs imposed on non-conformist behaviour. This may have strong influence on schooling decision. Parents may tend to search for a school where only girls are admitted and the one where women teachers are employed. The concern rises when girls reach puberty. Parents may consider education itself a negative factor whether better-educated women make good wives. Education beyond the level of literacy for girls may be perceived as threat for their possibilities for marriage. There are perceptions running through society that higher educated women may not prove to be good homemakers. Therefore, as the work opportunities for women are increasing and more and more women are joining the mainstream, a constant tension is built up within families between adherence to social norms and its desire to benefit from the changing conditions. The researchable question here is that when the family responds to these shifts, and which families would do so. There is no definite theory about it; however, *prima facie* it suggests that behavioural adjustment is the response to change in incomes and prices that result from economic growth. For example, better education brings better labour market participation, which in turn means better wages and higher family income and, therefore, explains, increased investment by parents in daughter's education. The magnitude and speed of their response depends on acquisition of new information and on the price and income elasticities of their demand for education.

Opportunity Costs

Parents may not be able to afford the opportunity costs of educating their children. These costs vary by sex, tends to be heavier for girls because of their multifaceted and predefined responsibilities at home and in society. Studies suggest that in Indian household's seven-to-nine year old girls work as many as 120-150 per cent more hours than boys do. Naturally, girls who would work more than their brothers at home will have less probability of attending school. In a joint family, the possibility of increased opportunity costs in these terms will be more. The extended family will be more likely to have works related to childcare, household chores and petty miscellaneous works. The family may not be able to afford those costs if the girl child is sent to school. The cost is further likely to increase if the family is agriculture-based and has problem of fetching water from distance or no market nearby. Therefore, most likely, a poor joint family will have larger relative opportunity costs and lesser incentive for sending girl child to school. Does this mean when opportunity costs of educating girls and boys are identical, both will have equal chances of going to school? The answer, unfortunately, is no. Parents still keep girls at home to work and send their sons to school. Unless there are indications that daughters transfer part of their future income to their parents and marry late, there are not sufficient incentives for parents to send them school. Therefore, education after all is good for girls, which work for their betterment *via*, increased labour market participation.

Conclusion

Education is one composite single variable, which has the capacity to transform many odds turning in favour of girls. Therefore, an exclusive emphasis on girls' education is necessary. Education for adolescent girls is constraint due to many factors; the most prominent of them is non-availability of infrastructure and schools. Secondly, the travel time taken in reaching school when the school is far off. Therefore, it is not only the availability of school, which is important, but also its availability nearby is also important. Fear of crime and unknown eventuality would rise with the distance girl has to travel/walk for school; therefore, there must be more number of schools and colleges in rural areas. Since access to education is constraint by the distance of travelling/walking for school, provision of public transport exclusively for girl child is necessary.

Child marriages are very common in rural India, and the parents without the girls concern take this decision. It pulls back several dimensions of development. Therefore, a legal provision, would help rescue girls from the early marriages and open doors of development for them. In addition, certain Awareness programmes are needed which should focus on the importance of nutrition for a girl child and the dynamics of nutrition in physical and mental growth. Discrimination practiced at the household level is contributed a lot by the negative attitude carried by elder males towards girls. Such brutal mentality needs to be changed. While designing and conducting nutrition awareness programme, it is advocated that such programme should also include awareness for practicing parity, compassion and respect for adolescent girls. Both elder males and boys need to be persuaded through this kind of well-designed programme. However, it is to be reiterated at the end that girls need a lot of compassionate treatment and favour to enable them to lead a respectable and meaningful life, and in ensuring this, the role of family members and society is undoubtedly crucial and of prime significance. Change in the attitude of elders towards girls is urgently called for.

REFERENCES

Bezbaruah, Supriti and Janeja Mandeep Kumar (2000), Adolescents in India: A Profile, *UNFPA for UN System in India*, New Delhi.

Census of India, (2001), *vide* Economic Survey, GOI, Census of India-2001, New Delhi.

Dean, Angus and Dreze, Jean (2006), "Indian Food Puzzles: Growth,

Poverty and Mal (Nutrition)", *International Conference on Growth in India and the ICRIER*, New Delhi.

Department of Women and Child Development, Ministry of HRD, Government of India, *National Adolescent Girls Scheme*, New Delhi.

Dreze, J. and Sen, Amartya (1995). *India: Economic Development and Social Opportunity*, Oxford, pp. 167-175.

Government of India (2002). *Selected Educational Statistics*, New Delhi, Department of Education, HRD Ministry, GoI.

Government of India, Planning Commission (2001), *Report of the Working Group on Adolescents for the Tenth Five Year Plan*, New Delhi.

National Commission on Labour, (2001), *Report of the Study Group on Women and Child*, New Delhi.

National Institute of Public Cooperation and Child Development, (2000), *Adolescent Girls Scheme—An evaluation*, New Delhi.

National Commission for Women, Government of India, (1990), *National Commission for Women Act, 1990*, New Delhi.

National Institute of Public Cooperation and Child Development, (2004), *Statistics of Children*, NSSO's 60th Round Survey on Employment and Unemployment, January-June.

Panikar, P.G.K. (1980), "Inter-regional Variation in Calorie Intake", *Economic and Political Weekly*, Vol. 15, Nos. 41 and 43, pp. 1803-1814.

Parikh, Kirit S. (ed.), (1991), *India Development Report 1999-2000*, Oxford, University Press, New Delhi.

Planning Commission, (2001), *Report of the Working Group on Adolescent for the Tenth Five Years Plan*, New Delhi.

Planning Commission, (2001), *Indian Planning Experience*, New Delhi.

Sen, Amartya, (1992), "Missing Women", *British Medical Journal*, pp. 302.

Women and Child Development, Ministry of HRD, Government of India, (1998), *Report of the Committee on Prostitution, Child Prostitutes and Children Prostitutes and Plan of Action to Combat Trafficking and Commercial Sexual Exploitation of Women and Children*, New Delhi.

16

Current Status of Rural Education in India

Tomba Singh and *Rajesh Sharma*

Introduction

Under the Constitution of India, education is a concurrent subject, with a sharing of responsibilities (including legislation) between the Centre (Ministry of Human Resource Development) and States (Departments of Education). Management of schooling has been traditionally controlled by the mainstream state and district administrations. The last two decades have seen the emergence of a number of education-specific support institutions, such as the District Primary Education Programme (DPEP) and Sarva Shiksha Abhiyan (SSA) State Implementation Societies, State Councils of Educational Research and Training (SCERT), State Institutes of Educational Management and Training (SIEMAT), District Institutes of Education and Training (DIET), Block Resource Centres (BRC), Cluster Resource Centres (CRC), and, in rural areas, Village Education Committees (VEC), as well as an increased involvement of NGOs, that have acted as a counterweight to what is often an overly bureaucratic and hierarchical administration.

The last decade or so has also seen the establishment of the Panchayati Raj, or village council, and this body is playing an increasingly important role in education in rural areas across the country. There are broadly four stages of school education in India: namely, primary, upper primary, Secondary Education (SE), and

Higher Secondary Education (HSE). The combination of primary and upper primary schooling is termed elementary education. It is important to note that there is also a programme of pre-school education (for three to six years old), Early Childhood Care and Education (ECCE), mostly provided through the Department of Women and Child Development (DWCD), Government of India through *Anganwadi* Centre infrastructure. There are also a few others, government and private providers of pre-school and nursery education in rural areas.

Eighty-seven per cent of the schools in India are in the country's villages. Government statistics and independent surveys have revealed that over 90 per cent of the rural schools at elementary level are run by the government. Only in Uttar Pradesh and Tamil Nadu does that share drop to 73 and 74 per cent (Mehrotra, 2006). At the secondary and higher secondary levels majority of students are in government schools (55%), a large proportion are in private schools aided by the government (35%) with un-aided private schools accounting for the remaining ten per cent of places (World Bank, 2003). It is noticeable that in rural areas there has been an increase in enrolments in government SE and HSE schools in recent years with a corresponding decline in enrolments in the government aided schools (World Bank, 2003b).

Progress of Rural Education in India

There is no doubt that in terms of providing the benefits of education to the whole population the country could have done better, particularly in respect of Scheduled Caste (SC), Scheduled Tribe (ST), minority groups, the disabled and girls. There has been considerable variation in the progress made in education across Indian states, 'with some states lagging behind and others surging ahead' (Clarke and Jha, 2006). The rise in literacy rates and the expanding system of primary education is more in India. According to the National Sample Survey (NSS) estimates, the literacy rate has increased by about 13.17 percentage points in a period of ten years, from 52.21 in 1991 to 65.4 per cent in 2001. Given the rapidly increased enrolments in elementary education since 2001 it is possible that India will achieve universal literacy within the space of one more generation. This steady increase in literacy has been largely caused by massive growth in primary and upper primary schools and enrolments, particularly in rural areas.

Levels of Education in India

There are levels/stages of education in India. These levels are– early childhood, elementary, secondary and higher secondary education. The details status of these levels of education in rural area is mentioned below.

Early Childhood Education

The salient fact which emerges from the 47th and 58th rounds of NSS on Consumer Expenditure, Employment-Unemployment, Disabled Persons and Village facilities is the spectacular rise in the number of pre-primary schools available in rural India. The proportion of villages having pre-primary school facilities is seen to have increased from around 39 per cent to about 68 per cent in these eleven years. By contrast, the proportion of villages with primary schools has increased by only about 6 percentage points and the proportion of villages with middle schools by only 5 percentage points. The proportion of villages with secondary schools has increased by only about 1.5 percentage points.

The main provider of Early Childhood Education (ECE) in the countryside is the Integrated Child Development Services (ICDS), a Centrally Sponsored Scheme (CSS) managed by the DWCD that was launched in 1975. The ICDS programme adopts a multi-sectoral approach to child well-being, incorporating health, education, and nutrition interventions and is implemented through a countrywide network of 620,000 *Anganwadi* Centres (AWC) at the community level. Each AWC has an *anganwadi* worker who is responsible for delivering the services. It is estimated that *Anganwadi* workers are spending 39 per cent of their time on pre-school education and in 2003 the Government of India reported that the total coverage of the programme for children in the 3–6 age-group was nearly 170 million (MHRD, 2003). The ICDS programme runs *Anganwadi* centres in villages with a population above 1000 in selected blocks with a relaxed norm of 700 for tribal areas. MHRD is also supporting ECE through the auspices of the DPEP in Bihar, UP, Rajasthan, Orissa and West Bengal and in several other states through SSA and another CSS, Mahila Samakhya. In addition to these services the Fifth All India Education Survey carried out by NCERT in 1998 reported that there were 10,376 independent preprimary schools in rural areas, an increase of over 67 per cent in the previous ten years and it is likely that this number has doubled again in the last decade. The National University of Educational Planning and Administration (NUEPA) reports that in January 2006, 17 per cent of all schools in rural areas had pre-primary facilities (NUEPA, 2006). The UNESCO Education for All Global Monitoring Report 2006 reports that the Gross Enrolment Ratio (GER) in pre-primary education in India is 34 per cent (33.8% boys and 34.1% girls). The take-up of pre-school education and retention in primary schooling could be significantly increased if new *Anganwadi* Centres could be in or near primary schools and their timings could be synchronised with the timings of the schools. This is particularly important for ensuring that girls stay in schooling, as one of the major obstacles to this aim is the need for sibling care in many rural households.

Elementary Education

Most of what we know about the status of elementary education infrastructure in India comes from the District Information System for Education (DISE) data collected annually across all states (581 districts are currently covered) and collated, analyzed, and reported on by NUEPA. DISE is the most comprehensive information system in the education sector, improving with each passing year. Based on the NUEPA 2006 Report, we can assess the status of elementary education infrastructure in rural areas against a range of indicators, including school-based indicators such as the number of rural schools, the size of each school and the type of each school; facilities in school; enrolment-based indicators; and teacher-related indicators. NUEPA's report tells us that in 2004–05 there were 126 million students being taught by 3.1 million teachers in 0.9 million rural elementary schools for an average of 209 instructional days. As indicated above, 90 per cent of these rural schools are government schools. DISE also tells us that the percentage distributions of rural elementary schools by type of building are *pucca* (71%); partially *pucca* (9%), *kuccha* (2%), tent (0.11%) and multiple type 9 per cent. The average rural elementary school has three or less permanent classrooms (with 21% of schools having one or no classrooms). Sixty-five per cent are in good condition; 24 per cent are in need of minor repair; and 11 per cent are in need of major repair. In 2005, 48 per cent of India's rural elementary schools had no more than two teachers and only 25 per cent had five or more. Half of the rural schools having two or more teachers had no female teachers. These small rural schools with one or two mostly male teachers and three or less permanent classrooms have on average between 1 and 100 students (78% of schools have enrolments within this range) and 35 per cent of the schools have less than 50 students. Several different age-groups (often the whole school) are combined in one class and multi-grade teaching is the norm in such circumstances. The average student to classroom ratio in rural areas is 45. The average teacher to classroom ratio is 1.12 which indicates that a large proportion of teachers are teaching their students in classrooms shared with another class, or in alternative environments, such as the veranda of a school building, under a tree or beneath some other form of temporary shelter. The disaggregated data collected by NUEPA highlights the extraordinary growth in rural schooling that has taken place since 1994 (NUEPA, 2006). A total of 221,009 new elementary schools have been established in rural areas since 1994, this is one quarter of the total number of rural schools, largely as a result of DPEP and SSA. The growth in rural schools has been most pronounced in Andhra Pradesh, Chhattisgarh, Madhya Pradesh, Rajasthan, and Uttar Pradesh with these five states accounting for over half of the new schools. The majority of these new schools have been primary (159,240) and primary with upper primary (21,015). Well over 80 per cent of the new schools have buildings. A small number of rural elementary schools (less than 2%) are residential. Almost half of the rural schools have boundary walls and only 4 per cent have no building at all Chhattisgarh (13%) and Madhya Pradesh (14%) have the largest proportions of schools without buildings.

Gaps in Provision

Despite the significant resources that are being deployed annually by the government for rural elementary education, most critics point to the lack of infrastructure and incompetent teachers are being largely responsible for the poor state of schooling in India, particularly in the countryside. The most useful way of understanding this gap is to compare the Government's targeted level of provision of education with the actual reality as measured by DISE and other sources of data in Table 16.1. This table sets out some of the GOI's target ratios or norms for the provision of elementary education and compares these to the actual situation in rural areas. There exist sizeable gaps between target norms and actual provision in several areas of rural elementary education infrastructure and there is also significant regional disparity in provision, but it is important to note that these gaps are narrowing rapidly in almost all states except in Bihar.

The SSA programme prioritises good quality school buildings and facilities; improved quality of teacher training and teacher performance; longer time spent in school each day by students; higher levels of teacher motivation; re-energising academic support for and supervision of schooling; reorganization of the curriculum to reduce the learning load, imbibing local needs, and incorporating the concerns of the National Curriculum Framework 2000 (NCF, 2000) and, more recently, the NCF 2005 competency based and contextual teaching and learning materials; improved teaching and learning processes that are more child-centred and activity based; support for remedial teaching and enrichment programmes; formative evaluation and continuous assessment of student learning progress; participatory management of elementary education with community support.

The latest NCERT surveys of student learning achievement show low mean scores in all classes and subjects. It is also noticeable that SC children perform less well than other social categories. The ASER, 2005 report reveals low levels of student learning achievement and previous NCERT assessments have shown similar results. Nearly 50 per cent of students cannot read, write, or do basic arithmetic in spite of spending four or five years in school (Chavan, 2006). At least a part of the problem lies in weak foundation in the early years of primary schooling. Greater priority must be accorded to ensuring that all learners have acquired the basics of reading, writing, and numeracy by Class II so that a sound foundation is laid for the acquisition of higher levels of learning in later years. The SSA programme's milestones in adequate infrastructure for effective teaching and learning will undoubtedly help to improve the situation. These factors combined with the implementation of the NCF 2005 give us reasons to be optimistic about the future of elementary education in India, but the current emphasis of SSA on improved quality for all children must be maintained and translated into effective improvement strategies in all states. This then is the gap in provision based on current enrolments, but there are also large numbers of children that are not yet enrolled.

Secondary Schools

There has been considerable growth in the number of rural secondary schools and progress in secondary school enrolments over the last twenty years, but access to this level of provision is only a little over half that of elementary education. The current GER for secondary education in rural areas is 48 per cent with girls 14 percentage points behind boys in their share of these enrolments. According to 7th All India Educational Survey, 2003, the number of secondary schools in rural areas according to the type of school building, illustrates the recent acceleration in the growth of rural secondary schools: in the ten years from 1993 to 2002 the total number of schools grew by 33 per cent from 47,870 to 63,633. The number of secondary schools without buildings also grew by a factor of one-third, from 287 to 387 and over one-sixth of schools are without *pucca* buildings. The states with the fastest rates of growth are Andhra Pradesh (almost 50%), Chhattisgarh (more than 50%), Karnataka, Rajasthan, and Uttar Pradesh. In several states there has been relatively little growth in secondary schools; Bihar, for example, registers hardly any increase. In a few states, Goa and Kerala, for example, the number of rural secondary schools appears to have declined over this period. The ratio of rural upper primary schools to rural secondary schools, at the national level, appears to be close to 3 but the size of the challenge the Government will face in increasing equitable access to secondary schooling in rural areas in the future becomes more apparent when regional variations around this mean are taken into account. Only 65 per cent of villages have a secondary school within five kilometres. A school located beyond this distance from the village presents an enormous barrier to participation, a student walking over five kilometres to school and back each day would take over two hours, particularly if no road exists or there are

Table 16.1: Gaps in Provision

Targets/Norms	*Current Status (2004/05)*
Teachers	
One teacher for every 40 children in primary and upper primary	The average teacher: pupil ratio is 1:39.
GAP: Significant disparities exist between and within states: the majority of schools in Bihar, Jharkhand and UP, for example, have ratios well in excess of 40.8 per cent of rural schools have a PTR above 100 compared to 4 per cent of urban schools.	
At least two teachers in a Primary school	122,483 rural primary schools have only one teacher (19% of the total) and 9312 rural primary schools have no teacher (1.5% of the total)
GAP: As with all of the norms, while national mean average suggests progress is good, there are regional variations that need to be addressed.	
Primary School and Alternative School Facilities	
Within one kilometre of every habitation	DISE does not report on this norm specifically, but the PTR and Pupil: Classroom Ratio (PCR) suggests that this norm is close to achievement
GAP: As with all of the norms, while national mean average suggests progress is good, there are regional variations that need to be addressed.	
Primary School and Alternative School Facilities	
Within one kilometre of every habitation	Ninety-five per cent of the rural population living in the country's 826,000 habitations have a primary school or alternative school facility within one kilometre.
GAP: The gap is 5 per cent of the rural population at the national average level, but there are wide regional disparities.	
Upper Primary Schools	
There should be one upper primary school/section for every two primary schools	In rural areas there are on average 2.93 primary schools for every upper primary school. About 85 per cent of the rural population has an upper primary school within 3 km of habitation.
GAP: While the national average is now below 3, in eight states the ratio is below 2, in three states (Bihar, Jharkhand, and Meghalaya) the ratio is above 3.5. In West Bengal there are 5.3 primary schools for every upper primary school. The gap in access is therefore, wide in the larger northern states, particularly West Bengal.	
Classrooms	
A room for every teacher in Primary and upper Primary, with the provision that there would be two class rooms with veranda to every Primary school with at least two teachers.	The average teacher: classroom ratio is 1.12 Almost 80 per cent of rural primary schools have at least two class rooms and 81 per cent of rural primary schools have at least two teachers.
GAP: A gap of almost 350,000 classrooms exists in rural areas	
Free Textbooks	
To all girls/SC/ST children at primary and upper primary level within an upper ceiling of Rs. 150 per child. State to continue to fund free textbooks being currently provided from the State Plans.	Ninety per cent of girls, SC children and ST children at primary and upper primary level received free textbooks in 2005-06. In several states the government is funding free textbooks for all students.
GAP: A gap exists in some states for girls/SC/ST but this is closing fast. There are also gaps in respect of OBC, minority groups and children from the general population in many states.	
Teacher Grant	
Rs. 500 per teacher per year in primary and upper primary for Teaching and Learning Materials (TLM) with transparency in utilization	Over 65 per cent of schools received the ₹ 500 per teacher per year in primary and upper primary for Teaching and Learning Materials (TLM) in 2004-05.
GAP: There is still a gap in this provision, but it is closing fast—performance in 2005 06 is expected to be much better.	

Source: MHRD SSA Framework for Implementation, 2003.

rivers to cross, or it is very hot in summer and cold and rainy in the winter and so on. The number of institutions at school level makes clear the chronic shortage of institutions at higher levels of the education system in India. The General Enrolment of students at different levels of school is Primary 91 per cent, Secondary 49 per cent, Tertiary 6.4 per cent (NCERT, 2003).

The quality of the facilities in these secondary schools is difficult to assess on the basis of the little information. The World Bank has recently undertaken surveys of secondary education facilities in three states, however, (Karnataka, Orissa, and Rajasthan), while rural secondary schools are mostly equipped with adequate classroom facilities and the majority have electricity connections, latrines, and water, only half have access to science laboratory facilities and few rural schools have access to the internet or even computers. It appears that rural private schools are slightly better off than rural government or government aided schools in terms of telephones, more classrooms, and internet connections, but they have few co-curricular activities. In these schools about 6.8 million students were enrolled in 2002.

The gender disparity in enrolments rate is at this level of the rural education system. The secondary education level the gender disparities are significant: girls' share of enrolment at Class IX is 39 per cent and at Class X it is 38 per cent. These enrolment figures tell us nothing about the participation of the poorest households and SC, ST, and minority groups in this level of education. For this information we turn to household survey data and this shows that while rural secondary education enrolment has increased faster than urban enrolments and enrolments in the poorest quintile of the population are also increasing at a fast rate, there are large gaps in enrolment, relative to the general population, among the poor, SC, ST, and Muslim communities. There is also considerable variation across states with relatively high levels of enrolments in the southern states and extremely low enrolments in Bihar (20%), Uttar Pradesh (24%), Rajasthan (20%), Madhya Pradesh (24%), Chhattisgarh (22%), and West Bengal (21%), (NCERT, 2003).

Higher Secondary Schools

The GER in HSE (20%) is less than half that of SE (48%), equal to just a third of upper primary education (60%) and almost one-fifth of primary education (97%). At this level also there has been an incredibly fast rate of growth in rural areas: the number of schools has doubled in the ten years between 1993 and 2003 (Paul *et al.*, 2006 and Bray, 2004). There has also been a commensurate increase in enrolments (Chuard and Minger, 1986 quoted by Bray 2004). However, despite this growth, only a minority of villages have access to a higher secondary school within five kilometres. The number of rural HSE schools has doubled in the last decade and enrolments have grown dramatically. Gender disparity at HSE is only marginally larger than that at SE. Despite this growth GER remains only 20 per cent and there are extremely low levels of participation among SC, ST, and minority groups. The number of teachers has also grown over these ten years, 1993-2003, by an amazing 77 per cent. The student-teacher ratio in HSE is now 18. At this level the teachers' workloads are more important as all teachers are subject specialists. At SE and HSE levels the majority of rural students are in government schools (55%), a large proportion are in private schools aided by the government (35%) with un-aided private schools accounting for the remaining ten per cent. It is noticeable that in rural areas there has been an increase in enrolments in government SE and HSE schools in recent years with a corresponding decline in enrolments in the government aided schools (World Bank, 2003a).

Gaps in the Provision of Secondary and Higher Secondary Education

The report of the Central Advisory Board of Education (CABE) Committee on the Universalization of Secondary Education has been forthright in pointing out; there is a lot of disparity in schooling facilities in various regions of the country. There are disparities among the private schools, among private and government schools in the same state, between schools in central sector like KVS, NVS, Sainik Schools, etc. Also, there are no specific norms for secondary schools. No wonder, India hosts some secondary schools with magnificent buildings, library, laboratories, massive computer labs, cricket academy when majority of the secondary schools languish in dire poverty and deprivation. It must be appreciated that just the four-wall classrooms and teachers as per norms will not make a quality school. For providing universal and free access to quality secondary education, it is imperative that specially designed norms are developed at the national level and then disaggregated for each State/UT keeping in mind the geographical, socio-cultural, linguistic and demographic conditions of not just the State/UT but also, wherever necessary, of the Blocks (Report of the CABE Committee, 2005).

We would like to re-emphasize that significant disparities exist between urban and rural areas. The CABE Committee also recommended that the disparities among various categories of schools must be reduced. The Report acknowledges that this will require detailed planning of educational facilities and improved management of educational services. After long consideration, the Committee proposed a sample set of norms for secondary schooling that go way beyond the basic indicators adopted for elementary education under SSA. The recommended norms are in line with the large number of Kendriya Vidyalayas. For a large majority of the secondary schools, particularly the government-aided institutions in various states, however, the norms would appear to be Utopian because a large number of these schools do not have these facilities (Report of the CABE Committee, 2005). On imparting education in sciences at the SE and HSE levels, the first *India Science Report*, released in 2005 by the National Council of Applied Economic Research stated: 'although people in all sections of society want to study science, the poor and those living in the countryside miss out because it is too expensive and they lack the infrastructure, among other factors.' In India currently, while there has been a marked increase in access to secondary schooling in rural areas, the quality of this provision, certainly relative to the norms proposed by the CABE committee, leaves a great deal to be desired.

The pass rates of the various School Board examinations in Rajasthan, Bihar and Karnataka are below 50 per cent while those for other states are a little better. It is widely acknowledged that facilities and learning resources affect the quality of education. It is apparent that the provision of facilities and learning resources between different types of school and between rural and urban schools varies greatly with government secondary schools in rural areas receiving the lowest levels of provision. While the recommended norms for secondary education and a comparison with what is currently available in rural areas are important, this tells us nothing about the proportion of rural children in the age-group 15-19 years not enrolled in classes IX through XII. What is the gap in provision when these young people are taken into account? On the basis of the enrolment data we have for secondary education it appears, that approximately 60 per cent of the young people in the appropriate age range (15 to 19 years) residing in rural areas are not participating in secondary education, the vast majority of the young people out of school at this age are girls.

Bridging the Gaps (An Agenda for the Future)

The Union and State governments' education reform plans in many areas of the sector are already well advanced and the purpose of this final section is not to reinvent the wheel by suggesting new policies and strategies. Instead, on the basis of the analysis presented in this paper, some particular issues at each level of the rural education system are highlighted for attention within this overall reform context.

Early Childhood Education

Proposals for the reform of ICDS are currently being considered. With regard to ECE, among these proposals is one that the demand for pre-school education, and for feeding the older children, could be met by devolving these responsibilities to the Department of Education or to local authorities. The DPEP and SSA already deliver pre-school education services in some districts, and the feeding of four to six-year olds could become part of the National Mid-Day Meals Programme. In this manner, more of the AWW's time could be freed up for nutrition and health education and growth promotion, increasing the prospect of achieving better nutrition outcomes. If this kind of reform is not possible, there should, at any rate, be more emphasis given by the managers of primary education and ICDS to convergence between the two services. The potential benefits of greater convergence are enormous.

Elementary Education

Until the mid-to-late 1990s India's performance on basic education was less impressive than its policy statements. Lack of real political will, insufficient resources, bureaucratic complacency, and pervasive social exclusion kept over half of all children from completing a meaningful basic education. But recent years have seen better progress, mostly through increased public demand, improved sector management, and political and judicial pressure. With more money for programmes that target the most needy and with greater accountability to local communities, change is taking place. The record of SSA to date in increasing enrolment and retention suggests that empowerment and accountability are the key drivers of change that are enabling SSA to achieve the hitherto elusive goal of every child successfully completing basic schooling. SSA places special emphasis on particularly vulnerable groups, earmarking funds for their specific needs. They include both Scheduled Castes and Scheduled Tribes and other minorities, including Muslims and girls. In SSA terminology these groups are referred to as 'special focus groups' or 'SC/ST and minorities'. The SSA framework accommodates the needs of specific social and religious groups, through local planning as well as through special schemes such as residential courses for remote, working or migratory children, free textbooks and special innovation funds to meet extraordinary needs. The national policy commitments to girls' education are being implemented through SSA. SSA is working, in both the well-off states and in the poor, populous states: it is a good practice model of effective basic education programme delivery. It provides a sound policy framework for universalizing elementary education. It has enormous financial, political, and bureaucratic support behind it at national and state levels. It has popular support, it has within it partnership arrangements that function well, and it has the potential to ensure that every child in India gets a chance to go to school. This achievement will have global significance. In the course of the next five years SSA financing and implementation needs to contribute to:

1. Increasing the focus on those states, regions, and districts that are furthest behind (in particular Bihar, Orissa, Uttar Pradesh, and West Bengal);

2. Bridging the gaps for those social category groups that are most disadvantaged;
3. Giving greater emphasis to quality improving efforts; and
4. Developing and implementing activities related to increasing the accountability of teachers to the communities that they serve and strengthening broader school governance through the VEC.

During the course of the Eleventh Five Year Plan the gains and achievements of SSA must be locked in and their sustainability assured through coherent national policy and state policies and budgets that facilitate the continuation of educational development by the mainstream education administration after the mission mode has ended. As Clarke and Jha (2006) have stated, in respect of the gains of the 1980s and 1990s in Rajasthan education, alongside the mission mode of operations and such creative initiatives, it is important to address systemic issues in the education sector as a whole in the states, especially institutional and governance reform. To this end, it is desirable to put in place a mechanism for annual national reporting on education combined with regular independent assessments of learner achievement that report trends in achievement levels nationally and across districts and states. To ensure compatibility, the framework for these assessments, the core parameters and tools of these surveys should be uniform for the entire country and modular additions could be made by individual states and UTs. The states/UTs should have the freedom to adopt different parameters and tools for experimentation and innovation, in addition to surveys according to the national framework. National level capacity will need to be identified and built for this task among the MHRD and its associated institutions, such as NCERT and NUEPA.

Secondary and Higher Secondary Education

The plans that are currently being developed for secondary education must encompass the contribution of the private sector. With regard to PPP, the menu of possible choices and issues is wide-ranging and policy-makers considering further improvements to rural elementary education and the expansion of coverage of secondary and higher secondary education can follow the advice given in the World Bank's recent handbook on PPPs (World Bank, 2005). This Handbook suggests that after a comprehensive evaluation of PPP in the education sector, officials may more effectively consider and consult on the issue of private involvement in schooling. As well as making more effective use of the private sector there will also be a need to reform the grant-in-aid system. With regard to improving the quality of secondary education, it will be important to ensure alignment of the NCF 2005 with syllabus, textbook development, teacher training, and examination. There will also be a need to set national competency standards and to participate in international studies of student learning achievement for capacity building and benchmarking. The expansion of access will need to be managed carefully and school mapping will be necessary to facilitate effective planning and resource allocation. The lessons that have been learned in elementary education will be of use to the managers of secondary education in the years ahead, in particular, the way in which primary education was expanded, through DPEP before moving into a national expansion phase under SSA. This kind of gradual approach that involves piloting innovative ways in which to increase access and improve quality is likely to be more effective in the long run than a big bang expansion. The most important aim in expanding access to secondary education should be to eliminate gender disparity at this level of schooling within the shortest space of time and not later than 2015.

Conclusion

As education is the instrument for bringing changes to individual, rural society, economy, politics and nation at large. Quality education must be in rural education and it must be sustained, so that maximum population of nation will have benefit of quality education. Around 65 per cent of India's population lives in rural area. There should be proper execution of the provisions of education to all levels of education (early childhood education, elementary education, secondary education and higher secondary education). The rural students must not be deprived in terms of provisions of education which are already obtained in urban area of the country. India has huge human resource from rural population and it can be used for future development. So that

India should be the leading country in terms of education in the world.

REFERENCES

Bray, M. (2004). *The Costs and Financing of Education: Trends and Policy Implications*, Education in Developing Asia Volume 3, Asian Development Bank, Manila.

Chavan, M. (2006). 'On a New Slate: Quality Education, not just Education for All, is what is required in India.' *India Today*, 21 Asian Development Bank, Manila.

Clarke, P. and J. Jha (2006). 'Rajasthan's Experience in Improving Service Delivery in Education,' in Chand, V.K. (ed.) *Reinventing Public Service Delivery in India*. Sage, New Delhi.

http://gov.na/nic.in/aires

http://www.educationforallinindia.com/page119.html

Mehrotra, S. (2006). 'Reforming Elementary Education in India: A Menu of Options', *International Journal of Educational Development* 26, 261-77.

MHRD (2003a). *Education for All National Plan of Action*, Ministry of Human Resources Development, Government of India, New Delhi.

MHRD (2003b). *Early Childhood Care and Education. An Overview*, Ministry of Human Resource Development, New Delhi.

NCERT (2003) *7th All India Educational Survey*, National Council for Education Research and Training, New Delhi.

NUEPA (2006). *District Information System for Education*, National University of Educational Planning and Administration, New Delhi.

17

Education for Rural Transformation

In Interconnected World

Vandana Talegaonkar, Archana Tomar and *Valli Pillai*

Introduction

The Flat World (Friedman, 200) denotes a level playing field for development. It simultaneously announces that there can be no peaks and valleys of development. Cliched version of this is sustainable development. Addressing a particular section in the process of development is rural transformation. The 'why, what and how' of rural transformation requires deliberation. The authors of this paper explore the various contexts of rural transformation subsequent to which a model of education for rural transformation is proposed.

The word development is an elusive term. When it is considered in terms of social development, it can be defined as overall movement towards greater efficiency and complexity but with recognition of the concomitant problems (Hobhouse, 1924). Social development involves a process of change which is fostered through deliberate human action (Midgley, 1995). It is a process of planned social change designed to promote the well-being of the population as a whole in conjunction with a dynamic process of economic development (Midgley, 1995). It includes any and every effort towards the advancement of the interests of the community.

Rural transformation entails an important issue. It assumes that transformation is for the purpose of development. It indicates there is some entity which is not in proper form and needs transformation that is shift from current form to a renewed form. It is essential to raise a few questions about development and transformation. Who decides these? Are the ones deciding it entitled to do so? How are their notions of development and transformation received by those for whom these are intended?

Patkar (2007) observes very pertinently about this issue, "People who depend upon the natural resource base are finding that it has been unjustly acquired stripped from them and its natural wealth commodified to serve the interests of a consumerist elite, lands, water and forests are harnessed for the profit and benefit of those with power to purchase and invest nationally and globally. Local systems of government have been forced to 'adjust' in such a way as to intensify the pauperization of those who, in many societies, still represent considerable numbers even the majority people faced with loss of life, dignity and livelihood have no option but to fight for their survival. From the micro level, these movements connect to a global action demanding a major transformation of what development is and ought to be about."

Development of the Idea of Development

The idea of development is located in the West and not the developing world. It is a product of post colonial age. Though several thinkers like Mahatma Gandhi, Mao Zedong of China, Julius Nyerere of Tanzania have contributed to the idea of development. Yet, Black (2007) observes that its evolution in theory and practice has been driven by the industrialized world. Underdevelopment implied that every form of infrastructure was lacking which includes physical infrastructure, political, institutional, professional, financial, administrative, systems for health, education. These could not emerge spontaneously, courtesy of a transfer of funds, Western know how.

Inclusion policy would demand people to get together, move together and grow together and develop together. But where do we stand in terms of human capital.

According to McKinsey and company report, India will need to up-skill or re-skill 500 million people by 2020 to meet its growth requirements. However, at current capacities we can train barely 50 million—an astounding gap of 90 per cent will still exist.

Similarly, the Eleventh Five Year Plan points out that only 2 per cent of the existing workforce has skills training. Another report by Boston Consulting Group highlights that out of the 89 million people who are expected to join the workforce from 2009-13, over 14 million will be school drop-outs.

The UN Development Programme annually publishes a Human Development Index. Its list of what is necessary for successful development includes 'an improvement in living standards as well as access to all basic needs such that a person has enough food, water, shelter, clothing, health, education and so on.' What is human development?

In the rich world, social and psychological ill mounts even as 'standard of living' rise. The Human Development Index (HDI) was intended to counter crude economic indicators of development. Yet the table of countries with a high human development index diverges only slightly from that which measures economic success. The idea is powerful; yet its application is undermined by timidity and reluctance to depart from the definition made by the dominant powers of human purposes—which remains overwhelmingly economic.

In subjective surveys of the world, the people who express the greatest happiness live in Bangladesh. A 'world happiness survey' conducted by the London School of Economics in 1998 found India to be the fifth happiest country in the world, with Britain at 32 and the US at 46. Ghana, Lativia, Croatia and Estonia all came above the U.S. People in rich countries, including Austria, Netherlands, Switzerland, Canada and Japan were less happy than their counterparts in the Dominican Republic and Armenia. The least happy people were in Russia and other parts of the former Soviet Union, including Ukraine, Belarus, Moldova. Of course, there is a link between resources (or income) and happiness. In poor countries a small increase in income leads to a disproportionate improvement in lifestyle and life chances. Beyond a certain level, however, the direct relationship breaks down. Happiness in the rich countries depends on close personal relationships, good health and job satisfaction. Wealth is much more than just economy, wealth of experience, wealth of details, health is wealth, wealth of information, we all came into the world with nothing and will leave with nothing. Yet the monetary view of wealth has imposed itself upon all others.

After 20 years of economic reforms, India is recognized as one of the high growth economies with the potential. We have a large army of youth. But this demographic dividend can be encashed only if this large army is well prepared to handle posts, positions and workstations—in offices, on shop-floors and on sites across the nation and indeed the globe. In a situation of rapid change, this preparedness must be fast tracked to empower our people for the enormous opportunities that lie ahead of us.

In an increasingly interconnected world our talent must be best in accordance with the international benchmarks in terms of education, skills and training. We have seen and realized that any progress needs sustained intellectual input, creativity, problem solving, consistency and quality delivering and disseminating mechanisms. Unemployment has always been one of the grave concerns of independent India. A classic study by Blaug (1973) showed that higher education has expanded in the country despite high levels of unemployment among the graduates. This situation remains largely unchanged today.

According to the Economic Survey (2005-06) the unemployment rate went up during 1993-94 to 2004. According to the task force on employment opportunities, the number of job-seekers in the age-group of 20-39 years, which was approximately 77 per cent of the total number of job seekers in the age-group of 30 years and above had increased during the period 1991 to 1999 from 18.5 per cent in 1991 to 28.0 per cent in 1999. There is a steady shift from the lower (20-29) to the upper age (29 or more) from year to year, which indicates that job seekers face difficulty in securing suitable jobs at a younger age and continue in the registers of the employment exchange.

In this connection, various people's movements that merit attention are Zapatistas in Mexico, indigenous communities in the Amazon and in Canada, farmers in France, India and fisherworkers in Japan. These movements are struggle for a different conception of what development ought to be.

There are three things that affect country's progress —*hunger* (we have—food production) *disease* (accessibility to health and medical facilities) and *ignorance* (accessibility factor to education, right use of land, water and livestock—environment friendly). These blights of the society are common in urban or rural areas. In India government has given thrust to sustainable development and also concomitant development of urban and rural areas of the country. The divide between the urban and rural is quite marked in our country. The average percentage of urban population to the total population in India is 27.8 per cent which means 72.2 per cent of the total population are in the rural areas. One of the ways that India had tried to bring fair amount of improvement in rural areas is through extension programmes.

A Historical Perspective of Rural Development

The villagers were self-contained, self- sufficient and self-governed units and there was little need for social welfare. This was disturbed by the invasions of foreigners and Mughal rule. When people felt the need for rural reconstruction work, the panchayat system provided some of the facilities. The series of famines from 1875 to 1901 forced the government to appoint some commission. It recommended rural development work. It followed certain acts for the establishment of development departments like agriculture, animal husbandry and veterinary, irrigation, etc. In 1935, the rural development work was transferred as a provincial subject and as a result of this several provinces established their rural construction departments or village uplift boards. These boards or departmental programmes never emphasized people's participation, co-operation and involvement.

Initiatives for Rural Development: Extension Programmes

Extension programmes in India combines all the activities related to the promotion of all-sided development of village communities including political (panchayats and voterbanks), social (kaph panchayats and caste, class divisions, health and hygiene, roads and drainage, irrigation, selling of farm products), cultural (folk songs, drama, crafts and art work) and moral improvement (land relinquishment, honour killings).

In India, extension work had its beginnings with a few outstanding individuals of a philosophic and philanthropic bent of mind. The work of most of them was necessarily confined to relatively small areas.

One of the pioneers of rural welfare work in India was done by Rabindranath Tagore. He believed in both self help and mutual help and was one of the first to recognize the need for a change in the outlook of rural population as a pre-condition for improvement. Therefore, he urged every villager and his family should be educated.

Tagore's Sriniketan Institute teaches subjects like agriculture, village welfare, cooperation, scouting, village industries and education, attesting his insight into the needs of the villagers.

Extension by Agencies/Various Initiatives

Shantiniketan

In 1908 Rabindranath Tagore started youth organization in the villages, in the Kali-gram Pargana of his *Jamindari.*

In 1921 he established a rural reconstruction institute at Shantiniketan. A group of 8 villages was the centre of the programme.

Objective of the programme:

1. to create interest in people for rural welfare,
2. to study rural problems and to translate conclusion into action,
3. to help villagers develop their resources, and
4. to improve village sanitation.

Functions: Developing village leadership, organizing village scout called Bharati-Balika, establishing training centres for handicrafts and establishing demonstration centre at Shantiniketan.

The institute could not get much help from the government and it could not conduct research work. So, its work remained limited to the eight villages only. It has now been recognized as an important centre.

Gurgaon Experiment

This was organized by F.L. Bryne, Collector of Gurgaon district in 1920. He was prompted by the poverty and the misery of the people. The project emphasis was laid on increasing farm yields, curtailing expenditure on social and religious functions improving health standards and organizing welfare programmes.

Village guides were appointed in villages and they made extensive use of films, folk songs, dramas, etc., to approach the people. He also encouraged the education of women.

Village guides were not technical men, but they merely channels for information from outside.

The experiment remained dependent upon the initiative of a single person and when he was removed through transfer to another district, the people reverted to their traditional way of life. In 1933, Mr. Bryne was appointed Commissioner for rural reconstruction in Punjab and his work was further expanded. The Punjab Government aided the work financially in 1935-36. Later, it was transferred to the co-operative department and "Better living societies" were organized.

Shri Daniel Hamilton's Scheme of Rural Reconstruction

In 1903, Sir Daniel Hamilton had experimented with model village along co-operative lines in Bengal. This work continued with the organization of Central Co-operative Bank and a co-operative marketing society. This later offered training in cottage industries through its rural reconstruction institutes.

Christian Missions

The activities of these Missions can be accounted under three heads:

(a) Education,
(b) Medical services, and
(c) Rural reconstructions.

Education: Educational institutions run by these missions were about 2000 elementary schools 225 high schools and 38 colleges. In some of the colleges, there was a separate block attached to it for the extension work.

Medical services: There were mission hospitals, spread throughout the country which became effective centres for imparting in medicine, nursing, compounding and mid-wifery and many students after receiving training in these institutions have established themselves in village to carry on their work.

Rural reconstructions: Several agricultural demonstration centres, at Marthandam, Ramnad, Patanchary and other Y.M.C.A. and Y.W.C.A. Institutions have been doing useful work in rural areas.

Marthandam Attempt

This project was started by "Hatch" at Travancore state in 1921 under the auspices of the Y.M.C.A. He was an American agriculture expert. The objective of the project was to bring about a complete upward development towards a more abundant life for rural people in spiritual, mental, physical, social and economic fields. The working principles of the project were self-help with expert guidance, training person to improve their performance, making people conscious of other wants and needs and organizing reconstruction programmes to include the poorest. From the demonstration centre at Marthandam about 100 villages were covered through Y.M.C.A. centres in villages. Most successful projects like Egg selling club, Bull club, Weavers club, etc., had extensive social activities which could meet the needs of the villages. It arranged exhibitions, lectures and had a wide range of health programmes.

Gandhian Constructive Programme

Regarding development work in the country, Gandhiji emphasized that the "Salvation of India lies in villages". A key word of his economy are:

1. Decentralized production and equal distribution of wealth.
2. Self-sufficient of Indian villages.

He wanted to eradicate the class of middleman exploiters to that, the farmer could get the full price of his produce and he also wanted that the tillar should be able to programme which includes the promotion of village industries, adult education, rural sanitation, upliftment of backward tribes, women in education, public health, hygiene, economic equality, organization of *kissans,* labour and student.

Gandhiji created leaders like Vinoba, Nehru, Jayaprakash Narayan and Meeraben.

Etawah Pilot Project

This programme was conceived and born in 1947 at Etawah (U.P.). First 64 villages (later risen to 97) were covered under it. Albert Mayer of USA who came to India with American forces in 1944, was the originator of the project.

The main objectives of the project were to see what degree of production and social improvement, initiative and co-operation could be obtained from an average area.

The pilot programme included introduction of improved agricultural and animal husbandry practices, public health education literacy campaigns, improvement of cottage industries, training in rearing and evaluating agricultural implements and all-round village uplift activity.

Firka Development Scheme

It was a government sponsored scheme established at Madras State. It aimed at the attainment of the Gandhian ideal of *Gram Swaraj*. The scheme was launched in 1946, in 34 *firkas* throughout the states. In 1959, it was extended to another 50 additional *firkas*.

In order to effectively stimulate healthy competition between the official and non-official agencies engaged in constructive work. Five non-official agencies engaged in constructive work. Five non-financial agencies were selected and paid grants, for doing *firka* development.

1. Rural Reconstruction,
2. Drinking water facilities,
3. Sanitation,
4. Agriculture, and
5. Khadi and village industries.

Nilokheri Experiment

It was originally started to rehabilitate 7000 displaced persons from Pakistan and later integrated with the 100 surrounding villages into what came to be a rural-cum-urban township. In 1948, it was built round the vocational training centre that was transferred from Kurukshetra.

Sri S.K. Dey was the central figure of this project, late Union Minister of Community Development and Co-operatives up to 1965.

The scheme called "Mazdoor Manzil" aimed at self-sufficiency for the rural-cum-urban township in all the essential requirements of life the colony day school, farm polytechnic training centre, dairy, poultry farm, piggery farm, horticulture, garden, printing press, garment factory, engineering workshop, soap factory, etc.

Adarsh Seva Sangh, Pohri (Gwalior)

This plan of rural reconstruction was put into operation in 232 villages, falling in the *Jagirdari* of Col. Shitole which aimed to increase the per capita income of villages. In each village a village reconstruction society was formed and the important items of work were compost making, deep ploughing improved, breeding and management of cattle, etc. The sangh published a monthly journal "*Rural India*" which is devoted to planning and community projects.

Village Service (Indian Village Service)

Its founder Mr. Arther T. Mosher of New York and Shri B.N. Gunts established it in 1954. The objectives of this organization were to assist village people to realize the best of their own villages by developing individuals, volunteer leaders and local agencies and enable them to be effective in helping themselves and others. The objective also includes assisting government in developing villages.

For realization of the above objectives, the organization adopted techniques like personal contacts informal discussion groups, use of volunteers, demonstrations, use and production of periodicals, etc. it is financially supported by contributions and donations. The organization has branches in Lucknow and Etah (U.P.) and is affiliated to the Presbyterian Church in U.S.A. Residents of 15 villages are the beneficiaries of this organization.

Sarvodaya Programme

It was on Gandhian conception and evoked great enthusiasm in Bombay state. The main features were simplicity, non-violence scarcity of labour and reconstruction of human values. It ailed at raising the standard of living, a scientific development of agricuture, promotion of cottage industries, spread of literacy, medical and health facilities and the development of village panchayat.

Corporate initiatives: Indian Space Research Organization's (ISRO) commercial arm Antrix Corporation was awarded the globe sustainability research award 2010 set up by Stockholm-based Global forum for fostering sustainable development.

Tata Steel Rural Development Society (TSRDS), an organization involved in the steel major's community building initiatives, embarked on an initiative to empower communities by creating awareness on the Right to Information (RTI) Act at the grassroots level, in October 2009.

Lessons to be Learned from These Initiatives

The above initiatives talks about the focus of each agency in the task of rural transformation. It can be gauged from these that certain aspects like village leadership, sanitation, women education, scientific use of farm land, improving yield, marketing of produce, projecting local arts and crafts are being repeatedly mentioned. It indicates that these aspects are still in need of improvement and any rural reconstruction programme cannot overlook these. The proposed model of education encompasses these aspects.

Education for Rural Transformation

India has the advantage of a relatively large size of population in the working age-group. However, this advantage has not been exploited so far. If employment opportunities can be created and persons of working age are equipped with knowledge and skills we will be able to embark upon newer growth rates.

It is important to recognize that growth biased in favour of lower income groups would ensure stability since their consumption patterns are likely to be more stable. India can sustain high GDP growth and improve its position in the world GDP ranking, the moot question is whether this growth would be inclusive. Inclusive growth is not only desirable from the equity point of view, but is also important for ensuring stable growth.

Assumption in transformation is aimed at development.

Development symbolizes "betterment" from the present. What is the 'betterment' or 'improvement' needs deliberation.

Education for Rural Transformation should it be same as the urban education or should it be different from the so called urban education. The term urban also changes connotations as we look at the underdeveloped, developing and developed nations and their respective cities. Do we all need a universal design of education or should it be tailor made as per the requirement of the local communities.

Understanding Rural Development

These could be the specific objectives behind the rural development:

- to change the outlook of the villagers,
- to develop responsive village leadership,
- to develop village people to become self-reliant,
- to emphasize on improving and modernizing agricultural practices,
- to introduce new skills and occupations, and
- to provide health and medical facilities.

Steps in Organizing Development Programmes

In order to make development programmes run smoothly the following steps could be followed:

Establishing Rappc rt in the Community

Rapport is a condition of mental responsiveness that requires the knowledge of the people and ways of motivating them. In India each village is similar at the same time there are wide differences too. Right from the landforms that sustain the agricultural practices and sources of water and irrigation tne predominant crops and trees. Some are looked at with suspicion and distrust.

Identifying Problems and Needs

There has to be an understanding of the situation present there. The problems that are related yield of land or transporting the produce to places where it is demanded selling of their produce at reasonable price weather forecasts obstacles in the obtainment of water or in drainage of excess water taking care of livestock. The inputs in knowledge and skills will be required in these areas.

Planning the Programmes

What and how to transact the required knowledge and skills, when and where it can be conducted and who or who all will be involved. A year long or more than a year long programme can be planned.

Selecting Initial and Long Range Programmes

There might be areas which may need immediate attention in the economic and social areas and long-term planning concentrates on basic problems facing the community and there has to provisions for planning for emergencies or accidents.

Securing Participation of the People

The programmes become successful only when major decisions are made by the officials and the representatives of the community. Only organized approaches and efforts can only help in gathering their opinion and decisions.

Developing Effective Communication Channels

Communication is a conscious attempt to share information ideas attitudes. It is the act of saying the right things, at the right time in the right way to the right people on the right occasion for obtaining right results in the right direction.

Developing and using Existing Organizations

There might be farmer's organization youth clubs or women's organization.

Developing Adequate Community Leadership

Leaders initiate actions which help organizations to adopt improved practices.

Proposed Model of Education

Based on the philosophical basis of ideas and practices proposed by Gandhi, Freire, Gokhale and Mohammad Yunus a model of education for rural transformation is proposed. It has four aspects. The model is only indicative. Further, details can be worked out on locale specific demands.

ASPECT I

Entrepreneurship Skills: Certain areas in India thrive specially on certain type of tasks like the *bidi* work, carpet work, filigiri work, brass work, bangle work, etc., different areas specialize in different aspects. The need is to modernize and train the people in making of various things and also to see that they learn it in a systematic manner that can make them self-sufficient. It would include value addition, marketing, packaging and maintaining quality and appropriate supply chain.

Communication Skills/Information and Communication Technology (ICT) Skills: The expanding market needs to look for better avenues and sales so it is important to develop communication skills and also the ICT skills in the students coming in the fold of entrepreneurship skills programme.

Finance in Entrepreneurship Budget and Funds: Any business or activity would need to be planned, budgeted and financed. The people will have to be made aware about the variety of funding agencies and funding patterns available for them.

Collaboration with Institutions like National Institute of Design, National Innovation Centre Research and Training: Continuous and constant research and innovations are carried out, if the artisans are made aware about the researches and the market demands, how to modify and present the art which they have been making so far can make them understand the pulse of the market.

Centre for Tapping Indigenous Knowledge: A centre can be created to study the indigenous knowledge and its development.

Community center Sales and Publicity: Not all artisans may be well equipped with the publicity department. A community centre for sales and publicity could be worked out on a mutual basis to benefit the artisans.

Initially the Partners like NGO, Village Panchayat Institutions, financial institutions, banks, Corporate Social responsibility cell can help them.

Compensatory Education (so that the students don't have any complex): Compensatory education is also the need of the hour to bridge the gap between the skill inherent and skills acquired. Awareness of possibilities and chance available can also be built along with the compensatory programme. Sharing of success stories can also be a part of the programme.

ASPECT II

Human rights, choices, opportunities available, ethics, RTI, consumer rights, participation in public life, preservation of their cultural heritage.

Education for rural transformation needs to build awareness regarding ethics, human rights, right to information, consumer rights, etc.

ASPECT III

Academics: The option of general academics currently available in the urban areas can also be made available to the students.

ASPECT IV

Harnessing local/native physical/sports skills: Many areas also have native sports skills, wrestling, shooting, swimming, etc. Such skills can also be further developed and sports special sports academy can also be build in certain areas.

Conclusion

Wealth creation, wealth generation, wealth dissemination in monetary terms is not related to happiness. But at the same time monetary gains does bring improvement in the living standards of the community. At the same time there is need to make the rural economy self sufficient for sustainable development of any country it is an essential parameter of its development. The growth pattern of any country has to be inclusive the proposed model aims at building the needed self sufficiency pattern for the rural transformation. The area of rural transformation needs further deliberation though to indicate what exactly is rural. Any area is continuously growing, we for our paper have considered the Indian villages where there is scarcity of electricity, shortage of water, and other basic infrastructure facilities including health care, basic sanitation and educational facilities. Cities have expanded and the population and urban problems multiplied but the telltale of the rural sector remains to be same even after so many years of independence.

Anecdote: Shopkeeper, client and other sales persons.

Client to the salesman: Show me some material in cotton silk.

Salesman: Just a minute madam I will bring (bring a pile of cotton shades).

Client: I asked for cotton silk.

Salesman: this is it!

Shopkeeper: What happened you take care of other client I will look into the issue?

Shopkeeper: Madam sorry he is new, the stuff you are looking for is here.

Client: Yes, how many colours you have in this?

Shopkeeper: 5 shades in all.

Client: Why that boy did not show these before?

Shopkeeper: How will he know about fabrics? He studied in school and college.

One statement of the shopkeeper conveys a much deeper meaning indicating transformation of the curriculum to connect the students to the life and some basic things as simple as clothing.

REFERENCES

Black, M. (2007), *The No-nonsense Guide to World Poverty*, Internationalist Publications Ltd: Toronto, Ontario.

Kevin Watkins (2007), *"Human Development Report"*—Fighting Climate Change Human Solidarity in a divided World, published for the United Nations Development Programme (UNDP): New York.

Manwani Harish (2010), "Building Human Capital in India", *Economic Times*, 31st July: India.

Radhakrishna, R. (ed.) (2008), *India Development Report*. Indira Gandhi Institute of Development Research, Oxford University Press: Delhi.

Seabrook Jeremy (2007), *The No-nonsense Guide to World Poverty*, New Internationalist Publications Ltd.: Toranto Ontario.

Sharma, S.R., (2004), "New Perspectives on Extension Education", *Book Enclave*: Jaipur.

Venkataiah, S.V., (ed.) (2004), *Rural Education*, Anmol Publishers: New Delhi.

books.google.co.in/books/isbn8170 Hobbhouse in *Social Change and Social Research: An Indian Perspective*, Rann Singh Mann, Concept Publishing Company, New Delhi. Retrieved on 8/8/2010.

www.socwork.net/2008/ glossary/homfeld/reutlinger 8-8-2010.

18

Challenges in the Implementation of Right to Education Act, 2009

Vikas Modi

Basic education is a primary human need, J.P. Naik, an eminent educator of our country, has very strongly described the importance of primary elementary education in these words "The progress of primary education is an index of the general, social and economic development of the country as a whole." A well planned and properly implemented system of education at this stage plays a very significant role in laying down the proper foundation of child's cultural, emotional, ethical, intellectual, moral, physical, social and spiritual development. Primary education also contributes a lot to foster value of emotional and national integration studies have clearly established that countries which have made adequate provision for primary education are far ahead of those with inadequate provision.

Usually the terms elementary, basic education and primary education are used interchangeably. The National Policy on Education has used elementary education for class 1 to 8. The NCERT, in its publication entitled "National Curriculum for Elementary and Secondary Education: A framework" (1988), mention elementary education (8 years) divided into primary stage (5 years) and upper stage (3 years). The Ministry of Human Resource Development, department of education uses elementary education and under it includes primary classes (class 1 to 5) and middle (class 6 to 8). There is a good deal of class variation in the years of schools at the two stages. Generally speaking elementary education refers to the combination of two stages of education—primary stage of education covering classes 1 to 5 (age-group 6 to 11) and upper primary classes covering 6 to 8 (age-group 11 to 14). Thus the elementary stage consist of classes 1 to 8 and age-group 6 to 14.

The Right To Education Bill to ensure education to the young citizens of India falls in this category. How can education reach the last student? How can it be relevant to life? How can quality education be assured? Within these questions are contained issues of universal coverage, enrollment, retention, completion, future growth, skill education and training. They are also pointer to future issues that may arise with primary education. In present situations the need of strengthen our education system to make it competitive. India after independence had under taken commendable steps towards providing education for all. To large extent have been able to bring children to school, increase enrolment, and to reduce dropouts. For democracy to be meaningful, it is necessary that people in India are able to read and write. Proper education is the basic pre-condition for a democratic society. In this background Right to Education Act was passed in both the Houses of our Parliament in August 2009. The salient features of the right to education act are as follows:

- Free and compulsory education to all children of India in the age-group of 6-14.
- No child shall be held back, expelled, or required to pass a board examination until completion of elementary education.
- A child who completes elementary education up to 8th shall be awarded a certificate.
- Mandates improvement in quality of education.
- School teacher will need adequate professional degree within 5 years or else lose the job.
- School infrastructure to be improved in 3 years else recognition cancelled.
- Financial burden will be shared between State and Central Government.

No doubt many efforts have been continuously made by the government to achieve the goal right to education for every child but there are a lot of hurdles in the way of this noble target. These are as follows:

Increasing Population

Right to Education has brought many challenges, which we will have to face and the greatest challenge is posed by the fast growing population and other to the comparatively slower growing economy.

Lack of Awareness

Our government has passed the Bill quite enthusiastically, but most of the teachers, teacher educators, social activists and common men are not aware of the salient features of this Act. How they can be helpful in implementation and achievement of the targets set in the Bill.

Educational Deprivation

Educational deprivation has two dimensions:

1. Lack of schools and poor infrastructure; and
2. Poor quality of teaching.

Children with Disabilities

In the Right to Education all the children are supposed to be admitted in the nearby schools. But there is no provision for children with disabilities in every school. Special facilities and specially trained teachers are required. Regular school teachers are not sufficiently aware of the concept of disabilities and education of these children.

Illiteracy of Parents

Large number of population is still illiterate and is not aware of the importance of education for upliftment of human life. Therefore, a large number of our population is missing the opportunity of right to education.

Physical Infrastructure

To fulfil the targets of the Right to Education Bill, a number of school buildings, infrastructures, materials, classrooms, black boards, laboratories, libraries and furnitures are required.

If we want to overcome these challenges then it would be necessary to transform the entire education system and the following suggestions can be helpful:

- Teaching faculty should be strengthened with professional training and skill enhancement.
- Only qualified persons should be appointed for teaching.
- Children with disabilities should be provided extra facilities.
- A performance based evaluation of teacher should be done and efficient and innovative teachers should be rewarded.
- Teacher training should be school based and knowledge of the subject should be in detail.
- Regular training programmes and workshops should be organized for teachers.
- For quality education minimum infrastructure, administrative faculties, financial, curricular, and linguistic norms should be fulfilled.
- Parents should be educated about need of education in present era and material should be provided to create awareness among rural peoples.
- Women are the basis of family education, therefore, womens or mother should be educated through adult education.

In the last, I want to say that:

"Right to Education is every child's right
Your support can make it happen."

REFERENCES

Aggarwal, J.C. (2004), *Teacher and Education in a Developing Society.* New Delhi, Vikas Publishing House.

Aggarwal, Yash (2000), *Public and Private Partnership in Primary Education in India*, New Delhi, NIEPA.

Malik and Farwaha, Challenges in the Implementation of Right to Education Act, 2009. *University News*, Vol. 48(07).

NCERT (1993), Sixth All India School Education Survey.

19

Capacity Building of Head Master for Rural Transformation

Kishori Dash and *M.K. Pathy*

He who knows more is the Teacher of the other; Deserves he, Prestige of a Teacher. —Gangadhar Meher

Introduction

Despite geographical variation of land whether rural, urban or even tribal, role of a teacher assumes special significance for the development of the individual as well as the community where he resides. And his profession is considered as a mission. Dr. S. Radhakrishnan has aptly remarked, "Teachers place in society is of vital importance; he acts as the point of the transmission of intellectual tradition and technical skills from generation to generation and helps to keep the lamp of civilization burning." Children who are the potential wealth of a nation, are always exposed to the information and experiences of teacher. It is, therefore, necessary to realize that the emerging Indian society which is not to be found in its few cities but in 7 lakh villages located in different terrains, e.g. plain, hilly, deserts, swamps, costal and mountain regions, back water areas, tribal pockets, etc. can be transformed and achieved its wholestic development with the help of capable and committed teachers. Because education, whether formal, informal and non-formal is a process of transformation of the individual as well as the society for all round development. And teacher acts as an agent of transmission through his capacities and cherished values for social reconstruction. Head

Master, who is basically a teacher is not only the representative of the school and value system of the society, but also an architect par-excellence of new trends and values to help in the process of transformation.

Context

The rural societies of Brazil, China, India and South-Africa comprise 25 per cent of the world's population and more than 70 per cent of World's poor are rural poor. In India more than 72 crore people live in rural areas and are heavily dependent on agriculture. For which Agriculture contribute nearly one-fifth of the gross domestic product to the nation. Emergence of WTO has initiated globalization and changed the world economic order and has posed several challenges to the agricultural and rural sectors of economy, education employment and public health, etc. The process of globalization and the attitude of Multi National Companies (MNCs) and even the Government towards service and development in industrial sector have relegated agriculture to the backdrop. It has adversely affected the rural artisans too. Which have resulted in large scale unemployment in rural areas. For which they are undergoing a process of change unparalled in history whether in scale, speed or potential consequences for humanity as a whole. Such transformation is taking place in a context that is loaded with uncertainties; climate change; impact of growing scarcity of land and fresh water; the triple impact of food, energy and financial crisis; slow progress of education and whether the human race will have the wisdom, will and capacity to engage in local, regional, national and international collection to avert disaster. This rapid change in this context is creating conditions of enormous risk and vulnerability for rural people. At the same time whole new opportunities are emerging, for example to renewable energy, provision of environment services, food production and quality education, etc. This process of change needs to deal with the heavy inheritances: Poverty, high mortality, illiteracy, unemployment, injustice, lack of access to health and sanitation, education and other services, gender discrimination, insufficient public investment and other forms of inequality. Without dealing with these inheritances our hope for ultimate success based on the evidence of the impressive achievement in the field of economy, education science and technology, etc. will be a day dream. Because *Rural Transformation is about Human Development and is not limited to the Development of Things.*

Keeping in view the development of the rural people who are in fact the backbone of the nation. Government of India has planned and executed several programmes as follows:

1. **Introduction of Bharat Nirman (2005)**: It was a time bound business plan for rural infrastructure within four years action in the areas like: (i) Rural Housing, (ii) Rural Roads, (iii) Rural Water Supply, (iv) Rural Electrification, (v) Rural Communication Connectivity etc.
2. **Provision of Urban Ammenities in Rural Area *(PURA)*:** It was propagated by the former President of India Dr. A.P.J. Abdul Kalam in Vision 2020, argues: (i) Economic Connectivity, (ii) Physical Connectivity, (iii) Knowledge Connectivity, (iv) Societal Connectivity, and (v) Electronic Connectivity for the cluster of villages.
3. **Rural Development Plans by Panchayats:**
   (i) **Economic Aspect** like (a) Agricultural Productivity, (b) Land Improvement, (c) Minor Irrigation, (d) Animal Husbandary, (e) Fisheries, and (f) Minor Forest Product.
   (ii) **Social Aspect** like (a) Rural Housing, Drinking Water, (b) Rural Electrification, (c) Education, (d) Technical and Vocational Education, (e) Adult and Non-formal Education, (f) Family Welfare, and (g) Women and Child Development.
   (iii) **Spatial Aspects** like (a) Transport and Communication, (b) Small Scale Industries, and (c) Village and Cotton Industries etc.
4. **Rural Building Centres and Industrial Extension Services** (1988) established in Rural Areas with the goals and objectives of Technology Transfer from **Lab to Land** by Cost Effective and Environment Friendly (CEEF) Construction workforce and Building Activities.

Besides, various schemes and programmes like Minimum Needs Programme (MNP), Integrated Rural Development Programme (IRDP), National Rural Programme (NRP), Rural

Landless Employment Generation Programme (RLEGP), Jawahar Rojgar Yojana (JRY), Drought Prone Area Development Programme (DPADP) etc. were introduced to alleviat rural poverty, ignorancy, diseases and inequality of opportunities and providing better and higher quality of life for the rural population. Further, Sarva Sikhsha Abhiyan (SSA) as a National Initiation of Education For All was launched in 2001 as a historic stride in partnership with the State governments to achieve the long cherished goals of UPE by 2007 and UEE by 2010 with the following objectives: (i) Universal Enrolment of Children and their Retention and Achievement, (ii) Quality Enhancement of satisfactory type, (iii) Capacity Building of Teachers for Quality Teaching, and (iv) Bridging all Gender and Social Category Gap at Primary Stage.

Despite these efforts made by government and un-equitable improvements observed in the living standards of people over the past few years, poverty, illiteracy, hunger etc. are still realities mostly in rural India. Because Rural Development implies economic betterment, educational and scientific advancement of people as well as greater transformation. In order to provide the people with better prospects for economic development, increased participation of people from various sectors of live in the rural development programmes, decentralization of planning and mobilization, better enforcement of land reforms, greater access to credit and proper and sincere utilization of community resources need to be envisaged.

School as an agency of education is responsible for the wholestic development of the children and intends to change and develop the community through its teaching learning activities, active community participation and extension services, and Teacher who is the friend, philosopher and guide of the children are the counsellor of the community, therefore, needed to be deeply involved with the process of transformation in rural setting as change agent. The Headmaster who is parentally a teacher is a planner, administrator, capacity builder, director, evaluator and decision maker and above all a custodian of such a noble tradition of teaching and sharing of knowledge. And his capacity assumes special significance for the betterment of the child, school and the community. But so far, we have not been able to harness this useful manpower. This would be possible if his role is properly recognized and he is in a proper set of mind to understand the problems of the nation in general and community or society in particular. Therefore, he is to make understand about those serious problems and to build his capacities so that he can make since efforts to find out the solutions. In this context capacity building of headmaster assumes significant and an attempt is made by the authors to find out the answer of the strategic questions like:-

How to build-up capacity of the headmaster in rural setting? And what must be done for rural transformation?

Capacity Building

The necessity for capacity building arises when there is a goal to achieve and fulfil a mission. The goal or mission should prepare a person to meet the new challenges. For this he must build his present capacity to perform his job/work/duty in a better way than earlier. Because, *"capacity building is a conscious and purposeful process of achieving knowledge, skills, competencies and new trends or doing in a way that enables the individual to perform the job in a better way than earlier or in future."* While building capacity some resources are dedicated or invested to make things easier at a later time. Capacity is a relative term and the needs for its building is always changing according to new social order.

Capacity Building of Headmaster

It refers to the conscious process of acquisition of required knowledge, attitudes, skills, competencies and new trends on rural development by the head of the school along with his own teaching learning methods and activities so as to perform his social responsibilities in the changing and challenging new world of order. Through this capacity building he can make himself equipped than earlier and invest his resources properly to achieve the goal and fulfil the mission of rural transformation.

Strategies for Capacity Building

The following points need to be considered while building capacity and enhancing the knowledge, skills, attitudes and competencies of headmasters:

(i) ***Developing Professionalism***: Professionalism is a spirit of professional character exhibited by the headmaster who is also a teacher in his/her profession. A profession involves mastery of knowledge, skills, positive attitudes and values in a particular field. As a professional a headmaster must be well trained, skilled, proficient and contributing his best by enlarging his capacities. The enlargement of his capacity includes so many other qualities like monitoring, guidance and counselling, evaluation, resource mobilization, advocacy etc. which are necessary in dealing with rural people along with students.

(ii) ***Information and Communication Technology:*** The dimension of Headmasters' competency enlarges as per the advancement of Science and Technology and demand of the society. Technology proficiency is one of the latest dimensions of teacher competency. The use of ICT is unavoidable rather, highly inevitable to live, learn and work successfully in the increasingly complex and information rich society. The National Education Technology (NET-T) set in this regard to help the teacher and head of the schools to develop skill in using technology and their ability to integrate technology into teaching and extension work.

Further, it is observed that most of the teachers and head-masters are aware of the possibilities of integrating technology into teaching, research and extension services, but very few of them are capable of integrating ICT for the same. This integration is very negligible in rural setting than that of urban areas. The technology aware group can be easily motivated to integrate technology in to teaching and other activities of the school through appropriate orientation, training and short term courses. The technology unaware group needs developing strong motivation, counselling and intensive training in ICT.

(iii) ***Undertaking institutional as well as individual studies and Action researches*** related to curricular, innovation economic development and savings, environment protection, gender equity, community health, adult and continuing education etc.

Research culture is highly negligible in our country at school level. Some sorts of surveys and mini researches are rarely conducted mostly in urban schools. In some of the universities during pre-service training B.Ed. students undertake a very small research project. Mere submission of a very small research project at B.Ed. Level and an unpublished dissertation at M.Ed. level will not be sufficient enough to develop skills in undertaking innovative research projects related to school activities and rural development. Therefore, special orientation programme and refresher course on action research and innovative studies must be given priority for teachers and headmasters. Weightage must be given to the innovative research proposals on rural life and education. The research findings must be presented before the members of VEC and scholarly groups to share the experiences of the researchers and discuss them openly. Head masters and teachers of the rural schools must be given opportunity for the same. The best research projects may be presented at different levels of education. This will help the headmaster and the others to sustain the motivation level of teachers and other headmasters.

(iv) ***Understanding the Educational Needs of the Challenged***: Teachers training programme is the foundation for would be teachers and head masters and enriched curriculum with varieties of subjects is of great importance for developing their knowledge. Accordingly there should have a compulsory component of education of the challenged in the curriculum. But it is not so happened. A very little scope is there for learning, training and sensitization of the would be teacher and headmaster in this regard. Therefore, training programmes specifically on education for challenged to be organized for teachers and headmasters so that the procedure of identifying the severity of the challenged will be easily possible. Further, scope must be given by the authorities to discuss the maximum possible help that the school can render in meeting the needs of the physically, mentally, socially and educationally challenged children of the rural setting. Because there is very poor scope for the exposure and education of the challenged in rural areas. Above all, head master and his teachers should developed empathy and willingness to help such children by individual attention. This will be a step forward in fulfilling the cherished goal of Education for All.

(v) ***Reflective Practices:*** To initiate change towards progress one must examine his own behaviour carefully and monitor his own behaviour and assumptions consciously. As a human being the headmaster must do reflective practice. It is not restricted to teaching learning and administrative activities alone. It can be employed to any aspect of headmaster's job, as it is a continuous improvement of an action. The reflective practitioner has to put on a dual role; on the one hand he is the performer, and on the other hand the critic who watches and analyses the entire course of action and performance. Reflective practices can definitely help in empowering one. So, this has to be encouraged among the headmasters to over come many hurdles to development which are rooted in unexamined assumptions.

(vi) ***Preservation and Transmission of Rural Culture:*** Headmaster must develop attitude and skills in the integration and fusion of culture of the locality in the curriculum translation. He must motivate his teaching staff to do the same. This integration and fusion of rural culture demands the headmaster and teachers to be resourceful in the cultural component of curriculum. Therefore, talents of the local culturalists like singer, dancer, dramatists, artists, artisans, musicians, writer and others must be recognized and they should get involved with the school activities as **Resource Teacher** for students and teacher. The Head-master should act like a resource mobilizer for the same. So that rural culture which is basically folk based can survive and be preserved and transmitted by the students from generation to generation. Further, Indian culture reflected mostly in the rural areas encourages the practice of living together peacefully. This has also been advocated by International Commission (Delor Commission, 1996) on Education as Learning to Live Together. Developing a peace culture is of utmost importance in a secular country like India to avoid communal riots, terrorism, political rivalry, blasting of explosives for no obvious reason, brutality of Mous upon innocent people etc. leading to Mass Killing. Lack of peace culture in villages areas in the present day is also one the factor for rural underdevelopment. Curriculum should, therefore, interweave ample opportunities for inculcation of peace culture among students.

(vii) ***Exploration and Transmission of Traditional Vocational Skills and Culture:*** Traditional Vocations like agriculture, weaving, handicrafts etc. play a mojor role for the economic growth of villages. The process of globalization has adversely affected the rural farmers as well as artisans. Agricultural operation have also become highly cost prone. Lack of demand for the traditional rural industries, flow of foreign goods, high-tech production process have resulted in large scale unemployment. Therefore, steps must be taken to help the farmers and artisans and school must come forward in this regard by integrating traditional vocational culture in school curriculum through SUPW. Mere introduction of steaching, drawing or art in SUPW course will not fulfil the needs of the students for preparation of their vocational life. But if traditional vocational courses will be integrated and introduced, it will not only motivate the students but also encourage the artisans to keep them selves proficient. Headmaster should take a lead for this and motivate to involve the interested and capable teachers in this process. Orientation and training programmes on weaving, looming, scientific farming, tie and die, stone and wood carving, traditional painting (like *Pattachitra*) terracotta work, etc. can be organized in the school from time to time for the students and teachers. Local artisans, farmers skilled weavers and experts should be made involved as resource person or teacher of the trade. Provision to be made in the school for **workshop-cum-selling centre**. Mention may be made here as example that in the Western Region of Orissa (which is very famous for *Sambalpuri sari* (silk and cotton) and handloom cloth. Semi-skilled rural youth from weavers families (Meher family) are rushing over Andhra Pradesh, Chhattisgarh and Madhya Pradesh to prepare Pocchampoli, and Tusser and Cotton saries and and clothes getting good salary from the owner of the looms. This is so happened due to lack of exposures and opportunities of the rural youth to prove their talent. This human resources could have been utilized in the parent areas by involving them and building up their capacities for development of the community. Department of School and Mass Education in collaboration with industry, agriculture, rural development, etc. can make a move for the same and head masters should be given responsibilities to work accordingly.

(viii) ***Understanding the Educational as well as other Needs of the Community:*** Without understanding the needs of the people (including education) the headmaster will be a stranger in the process of human development. So he is to keep relationship with the community. For this, he has to be a part of the community and its activities whether cultural, religious or whatever it may be. His level of participation will motivate the people to join their hands for co-operation and in understanding the problems of the community and to find out their solutions.

Beside the mentioned strategies for the headmasters, the following steps must be taken at different levels for rural transformation:

- Developmental activities and programmes of the rural areas organised by concerned departments should be supervised and monitored by the headmaster or his representative teacher. Even evaluation of the said activities or programmes should be done by them.
- Rural schools are always facing the problem of scarcity of teachers and teacher-absenteeism. Therefore, many masters feel reluctant to spare themselves or the services of their teachers in developmental work of the community other than education. Therefore, adequate number of teachers must be appointed in those schools. Further, teachers, absenteeism should be strictly viewed.
- Quality of education depends on quality teachers. So headmaster should encourage his team to be updated

in content knowledge, advanced in Information and Communication Technology (ICT), development of positive attitude, skills and competencies in teaching methods curiosity for learning and listening to the problems of the rural students and above all sympathetic attitude towards poor children.

- Teachers, those who are basically from urban areas but posted in rural schools should develop interest to have knowledge about rural life and living style, rural economy, festivities, issues and problems etc. Head master must guide them in this regard, so that they can develop problem solving attitude and try to help the students and people in various ways.
- Special orientation programmes for the teachers of remote areas should be organized on the subjects like literacy development, environment protection, land and water literacy, resource mapping and mobilization, village infrastructure and health. And their potentialities should be dedicated and invested for development.
- Short-term courses should be introduced in the school specially for the training of small farmers, unemployed youth (both male and female) on scientific agriculture, maintenance of health and vaccination of cattles, caring of plants, use of pesticides, process of marketing, etc. Headmaster and his staff should co-ordinate and monitor the same.
- Like medical profession each teacher/headmaster should have to serve in rural areas at least for five years. This should be mandatory. Senior and promising teachers while getting promotion as head-master should be posted in the rural school first and they should be given all sorts of facilities like urban areas. Further, provision of rural allowance and medical facilities to be made for the teachers/head-masters of remote rural schools where communication and connectivity are still dreams. They should be giving responsibilities for developmental work for the people alongwith their normal work.
- Development of women in true sense will be possible

only when they will be made independent educationally, economically and mentally. SHG groups are formed in this country for this purpose. If we will go through the achievement levels of SHG groups, we will definitely get positive results. But if we analyse their achievement area-wise it will be shocking that SHGs running in urban areas are more successful than that of rural and tribal areas. It is also a fact that rural SHG groups of certain states like Tamil Nadu, Karnataka, Himachal Pradesh, etc. of our country have got success in empowering their women economically. But it is still to be successful in Bihar, South east part of Orissa, Jharkhand, Chhattisgarh, etc. on the country some of the SHG groups of western Orissa have got unbelievable success in this regard. Mention may be made here that "Radhakrushna" SHG group of **Belakula** village in the District of Angul (Orissa) have started co-operative weaving of Sambalpuri Sari (both cotton and silk) after learning weaving skills from the traditional weavers of their Meher society under the guidance of local school teachers. Further, Srujani Mahila group in the district of Bargarh are also doing the same with the dynamic leadership of the local school teachers. They are now been able to compete with the male weavers of Meher Society. Therefore, scope must be given for the upliftment of women artisans/weavers and artists of rural areas to prove their talent. Required infrastructural facilities, training, etc. must be provided to them by the Government through continuing programmes education projects. Headmaster and his team must take a lead for this endeavour.

- The National Adult Education Programme (1978) and National Literacy Mission (1988) were launched by Government of India to enable men and women to play active role in socio-economic and cultural sphere. Despite, the female literacy rate of rural and tribal women are found to be not satisfactory. Even male literacy rate of many states are not up to national level. GOI, therefore, has initiated the process of "Sakshara

Bharat" programme to arrest illiteracy from the nation.

In an agro-based developing society like India Literacy is virtually the pre-condition for an individual's evolution and development. This is also one parameter for social development. With little access to information, modernization and communication and virtually no access to survival tools the non-literates remain helpless, victims of poverty, deprivation and exploitation. Therefore, literacy and continuing education programme for the rural illiterates must be organized in an urgent basis in collaboration with various government and non-government organization. School should function like a nodal centre for the same. Further, women literary along with income generation programme should get priority and locally available raw materials should be utilized for the same for production.

Conclusion

The rural development debate of last few decades has thrown-up several new formulations regarding alternative designs for rural life and living, and has brought into sharp focus on a number of new concerns. The accent now is on human centred development, and not on growth rooted indication of GNP and National Income. This development will be incomplete without transformation of people living largely in the rural societies. It is possible only through the process of Quality Education and Active Participation of Rural Population in Productive Activities. Therefore, with the initiation of the headmaster and his team village school has to be made a Centre for Education and Information, Health and Nutrition, Production, Social Protection, Love, Affection and Humanization for Social Transformation.

REFERENCES

Chinapah, V. (2009). *Education for Rural Transformation in China and India: 53rd Annual Conference of the Comparative and International Education Society*. www.allacademic.com.

Krishna Kumar (2006). "An emergency for Rural Childhood", *Yojana*, Vol. 50, November.

Pawan Kumar (2006). 'Rural Infrastructure: Thrust area in Rural Development', *Kurukshetra*, Vol. 54, No. 9, July.

Rao, V.K.R.V. (1966). *Education and Human Resource Development*, Allied Publisher, New Delhi.

Report of the International Conference on Dynamics of Rural Transformation in Emerging Economics (April 2010), New Delhi, www.ruraltransformation.in

Report of the State Consultation Meeting of the Principals of the Training Colleges, (2005), Government College of Teacher Education, Kozhikode.

Singh, S.P. (2006). Sarva Siksha Abhiyan, *Yojana*, Vol. 49, September 2005.

20

English Language–A Stumbling Block for Rural Students

Challenges and Suggested Frameworks for Rural Transformation

M. Doss

Introduction

India lives in its villages. When anyone wants to develop India, he should plan for the development of villages first which is one of the vital factors for the growth of the Indian economy. Education for the Rural Transformation (ERT) is the only way to provide relevant, equitable and effective education of rural people for their upliftment in social life. English education was introduced in India to cater to the needs of the society. For increasing employability, English was studied as a second language to augment employment opportunities. This trend has been continued even now with a view to increasing the social status of the individual. Having seen the market demand for proficiency in English, many state governments have already policy changes in the schooling pattern to facilitate better learning of English. Countries like Japan, Russia and China, which lagged behind in English language learning and teaching, are now redoubling their efforts to teach English. These countries as do others, realize that English is needed in order to successfully meet the challenges of the emerging global reality which manifests itself in the twin process of economic globalization and cultural globalization (Kumaravadivelu, 2002).

English is a national language, an international language, link language, library language, language for higher studies, hybrid language, language for intellectuals, language for IT industry, language for social status and language for lucrative business. English is the language of opportunities because it takes one outside from one's own community to place where more opportunities are available for professional and economic growth. English is still a ticket but to a job market than to a cultural elite and one learns it in India on the basis of instrumental rather than integrative motivation (Probal Dasgupta, 1993; Sriraman *et al.*, 1995). It is empirically proved that English increases one's market value in the employment sectors in India, after the advent of IT sectors, Call centres, e-Publication and Editing and other Outsourcing units including Translation. The IAS turned Novelist Upamanyu Chatterji said that "English is an interesting subject but pseudo-methodology followed by the teachers makes it difficult and uninteresting. This leads to think that it's a nightmare for Indian students, especially students living in rural areas, though they have continuous exposure of English language starting from class one to class twelve. The people living in a lower strata or living in a remote area or living in a disadvantaged area suffer for want of right kind of teaching and apt motivation towards English language. At primary level, considerable number of children become drop-outs, because of difficult subjects like English and Mathematics and 40 to 55 per cent of failures in Public examination at SSLC level is in English alone in Tamil Nadu and Pondicherry. During 2009-10, result of Diploma in Teacher Education in Tamil Nadu was declared of which more failures in English were identified for various reasons. When students of SSLC and Higher Secondary level have arrears in English, they will become drop-outs after their second or third unsuccessful attempts and they will become employee of the local markets and factories. And the rural students who study English medium first time in science group may miserably fail or secure very low marks in the public examination because of lack of exposure to writing scientific materials in English first time in which they never get any sort of guidance either from the teachers or from any other sources, leading to more failures.

The teacher as a change agent should motivate students to study English for better employment opportunities by highlighting various employment opportunities in classroom teaching. "If a doctor commits mistake in the operation theatre, a patient will die; if a lawyer commits mistakes in argument, the period of case may be extended from five years to ten years probably; but if a teacher commits mistakes in the classroom teaching, the whole generation will be affected." In this connection, policy-makers should understand the needs of the societies before they design policies; curriculum planner should think about the achievement of educational objectives; textbook writers think about the development of competency of subjects pertaining to the syllabuses; educational administrators are to think about suggestions for the implementation of the scheme; and the teacher, the main backbone of the system, should translate everything highlighted in the policies through academic transactions in the classrooms.

This chapter attempts to explore the problems of rural students in learning English and problems of teachers in teaching English for rural students and remedy the challenges like unproductive teaching, using unsuitable methodologies, weak philosophical outlook, ignorance of selection of testing items, absence of effective communicative skills and lack of commitment in teaching of English for rural students. It requires some kind of systemic reforms to help rural students move upward vertical mobility.

Need of the Study

Rural students who are geographically disadvantaged may not be able to compete with urban children for their educational needs but at the same time system of education cannot prescribe a separate curriculum and English Readers for rural school children. However, educational authorities may train the rural teachers how to teach English with ease and confidence, by organizing in-service training programmes to them. It is the responsibility of the teachers who are working in rural areas to find out suitable methodologies that could work well among the rural students. Rural teachers, using translation technique can teach target language beautifully well, and with the help of Transfer of Learning technique, it can be transferred to other situations also.

Objectives of the Study

This study is undertaken with the following objectives:

- To understand the trend in teaching of English at rural level.
- To analyse the reasons for the backwardness of rural children in English language.
- To suggest suitable remedies for the effective rural transformation through English language.

Analysis

The analysis has been done on the basis of systemic changes starting from Policy of English Education, curriculum development, textbook writing, methodology for teaching, pattern of examination and organization of staff development programmes, etc.

Education Policy

Constructivism

Education was once thought of as a process of transmission but research has made it abundantly clear that the quality of teaching and learning is improved when students have enough opportunities to clarify, question, apply and consolidate new knowledge. There are many teaching strategies that can be employed to engage actively in the learning process. Students must do more than just listen: they must read, write, discuss or be engaged in solving problems (Chickering and Gamson, 1987; Meyers and Jones, 1993; Bonwell and Eison, 1991). Activity based learning, Competency based teaching, Joyful learning and Active learning methodology are some of the teaching and learning methodologies, derived from the philosophy of Constructivism. It is understood from the philosophy that educator strives to create a learning environment in which the student can learn to restructure the new information and their prior knowledge into new knowledge about the content and to practice using it. Student is assumed to be an intelligent participant in knowledge creation who can look up definitions and vocabulary before and after class independently. Hence, it is suggested that extensive training should be given to the teachers of English, working in the rural areas.

Competency Based Teaching

The first lesson entitled "Have your Garden" is written with dialogues, highlighting five competencies throughout the lesson. In this lesson, main focus is given on the language use, not on the content. Though this lesson has some content based questions, teacher should spend more time on the development of competencies introduced in the lessons. Ninty per cent of the teachers teach only the content of the lesson and dictate the question answers not the competencies which are inbuilt into the lesson. For instance, there are five competencies based on which the lesson "Have your Garden" is developed.

Competencies

- Listens to the teacher using phrase of polite requests and tries to use them.
- Listens to simple instructions and tries to carry them out.
- Listens to ask common relevant questions to his friends.
- Listens to ask for the purposes of common tools.
- Listens to express the purposes of common tools and objects.

At the end of the lesson, the students will be able to answer the following questions which are useful either in the classroom or outside the classroom. And it is pity that since most of the questions are text-based, the students are brought up with memorization skills in the system.

Questions for the first competency:

1. Could you give me a change?
2. Could you take me to the market?
3. Could you tell me how to plant the sapling?
4. Shall we go to nursery?
5. Could you take me with you?

Questions for the second competency:

1. Please, go to market and buy some vegetable.

2. Cross the road carefully.
3. Go and get the tool from our neighbour.
4. Dig a pit and plant a sapling.
5. Put it in the left corner.

Questions for the third competency:

1. Do you need any help?
2. What else can we do?
3. Why don't you raise your garden?
4. Where can we get the reader?
5. Where do we plant the drumstick cutting?

Questions for the fourth competency:

1. What is the crowbar for?
2. What is the spade for?
3. What are the tools we need?

Questions for the fifth competency:

1. It is for digging pits.
2. It is for digging ground.
3. It is for removing weeds.

Hence, it is suggested that competency based training should be given to the rural teachers who must understand the difference between competency based teaching and content based teaching.

Minimum Levels of Learning in English

Minimum levels of learning can be stated as expected learning outcomes defined as observable terminal behaviour. One can also state the MLLs in terms of learning competencies expected to be mastery by every child by the end of a particular class or stage of education. System of Education should recommend a syllabus which includes about eight functions, six rhymes and about one hundred words for the first standard and another eight functions, eight rhymes and one hundred words for the second standard. As for language skills, listening and speaking are taken up in the first two standards which will help the children read and write better in the third standard. Hence, the teachers working in rural areas should bear this in their mind. It is a national shame if any fifth standard student is not able to answer the question in English like: Who is your father? Where is your house?

Learning without Burden

According to Yaspal Committee recommendation, English reader has minimum number of lessons with maximum number of exercises because drilling helps children understand the pattern of the sentences and comprehend the matters in playful ways. It is suggested that teaching should be more activity oriented so that children will do all the activities joyfully. Hence, it is concluded that teaching through activities is more interesting than teaching through texts. In order to scare away the fear of English from the minds of the rural children, activity based teaching should be the only way.

Methodology

Decentralization in Teaching

After globalization, decentralization is gaining momentum in India. It could be better, if the concept of decentralization introduced in classroom teaching and learning process. Classroom is a miniature of a society, consisting of all kinds of pupils with different potentials. A sincere teacher after teaching of a particular lesson may fix responsibility with brighter children to re-teach certain concepts of what their teachers taught on the day. This is what we call 'Peer teaching or Peer tutoring'. Once India became very popular in 'Monitorial Teaching'. The British studied the monitorial system in India and used their understanding to revive their educational system. "The economy with which children are taught to write in the native schools, and the system by which the more advanced scholars and caused to teach the less advanced and at the same time confirm their knowledge is certainly admirable and well deserved the imitation it has received in England" (Bellary to Board of Revenue, 1983). In teaching of English, teacher may use of students potential to re-teach some text based concepts and their related competencies. For this, brighter children in the classroom, willing students from neighbouring classes, NSS volunteers, Monitors may be utilized for teaching English during rest hours. But at the same time, if the teachers of English in rural areas want to follow this approach, they should prepare the peers and volunteers how to go about this methodology with meticulous planning.

Computer Assisted Language Learning

In a disadvantaged society where disadvantaged learners are living, parents are uneducated who are not able to concentrate on children's education especially in English education. In this regard, corporate sectors may come forward to teach English for school children and soft skills for higher secondary and collegiate students, with a view to improving language proficiency among the rural students who are considered to be disadvantaged geographically. In this regard, specially designed mobile van fitted with 15 -20 computers along with co-ordinators and a few teacher educators should visit rural areas to improve proficiency of the children in English language through computer assisted learning, using educational CDs made by Corporate Sectors like Azim Premji Foundation. The above mentioned CDs which are either complementary or supplementary to learning are carefully prepared to cater to the needs of the children by a group of experts. This mobile unit with trained personalities will bring the children to the fold of education and moral values along with acceptable intervention strategies.

English for Specific Purposes

Students who studied everything in mother tongue at secondary level find very difficult to understand the scientific concepts in English. Though they are toppers at high school level, they fail miserably or score poor marks at post-secondary level not because of his inefficiency but because of the language and helplessness from the system or from the teachers. Rural students who are disadvantaged suffer for guidance in this regard. There are two ways to help the students: In English lesson, at least two lessons on scientific concepts may be introduced. As a remedy, it suggests innovative strategies in the following areas: production ot lessons with scientific concepts, word power in the technical fields, usage of appropriate structures, exercises for written communication in scientific field, oral communication and reporting and experimenting in the immediate environment—to be adopted for the inculcation of register based language proficiency for better and effective communication. Short-term in-service training for the teachers who are teaching English at secondary and post secondary level has been suggested, since this register based English course is comparatively different from teaching of English language.

And the second technique is that we select a unit from science and study the unit in mother tongue first and later study the same unit in target language. While doing so, one can understand the semantic level of the sentences in mother tongue and understand gradually how these sentences are constructed in English for communication purposes. Besides, they should note down some frequently used phrases and connective devices in scientific writing. Understanding followed by mechanical drilling will help rural students get through English confidently.

Teachers

Most of the teachers teaching English at high school level are non-English teachers, i.e. science teacher or social science teacher or mathematics teacher teaching English out of compulsion who have not studied English as a major subject and probably they may not have opted for Teaching of English at B.Ed. level. And at higher secondary level, most of the post graduate teachers teaching English have only literature background, i.e. M.A. English and probably they may have been promoted to the post of English teacher from various disciplines like physics, chemistry, zoology, etc. at undergraduate level. Many teachers are reluctant to accept that their job is to teach English language skills and not English literature (Mukerjee, Meenakshi, 1991).

Despite the lack of proficiency in English and training, every high school teacher is required to teach English. The result has been study erosion in the standards of teaching and learning English in the large majority of the government and state-funded schools. Admittedly, it is anachronism to assume that every graduate is sufficiently proficient in English to be able to teach it in high school classes, as was done in pre-Independence days. Moreover, as most of the in-service training programmes are organized like cottage industries with half baked teacher trainers, training centres do not create indelible impression among the teachers and hardly change their teaching behaviour. Hence, the teachers of English across the country behave like story tellers, translators of the texts in the name of teaching, ignoring the fact that they should develop language skills among the school children thereby making them competent in English to some extent. As a result of this system, the students become scapegoat and handicap in many respects.

Textbooks

With regard to textbooks, the size of the textbooks are warranting and threatening. The Chairman of Education Commission "Learning without Burden" Yasphalji suggested that size of the lesson should be small followed by more language based exercises inculcating language skills to be used for their day-to-day life. It is sad that textbook writers hardly follow these norms. Educational administrators should not have pseudo faith on the fact that size of the textbook should enhance the knowledge of the students. The size of the lesson with interesting materials, effective teaching methods, and competency based exercises, continuous and comprehensive evaluation, and in-service training centre in ELT with committed faculty members, monitoring mechanism and reformation in the system of examination will make the children learn English without aversion.

Unlike other teachers who enter the class with plants, flowers, chemicals with beakers and simple pendulum as teaching aids, the English teachers enter the class with English reader as the only teaching tool available to them in order to develop competencies in the target language. The practicing teachers have to understand the importance of contents and related exercises added at the end of the each lesson and how they are helpful in developing language competency. Education becomes a joyless burden in our schools because the quality of our curriculum, texts, teaching and examination procedures is so poor (Kumar Krishna, 2005; Yash Pal, 1993). A graduate applicant hardly writes correct English and a candidate for an interview are not able to speak four or five sentences fluently. The defects in teaching English may be ascribed to the following: lack of purpose, faulty methods, bad textbooks, unqualified teachers, faulty system of examination, unrealistic syllabus and defective outlook (Aggarwal and Shanti Swarup, 1963). The English Readers are also responsible for the present scenario.

The quality based English reader should be written with two fold objectives: it should be readable and it should be graded to the mental attainment of the pupil for whom it is written. In order to maintain educational standards, it is important to evaluate English readers whether the intended objectives are achieved or not. The English reader that is prepared with over expectation may be an academic burden to students and teachers as well. Hence, English reader should be prepared with clear educational policy, objectives of teaching, interesting contents, appropriate testing items and guidelines for evaluation, responsible for the development of language competency. There should be a link between objectives, contents and testing items. But, it is disheartening to note that only few textbooks have been prepared in tune with the factors as discussed above. This chapter attempts to study the structure and contents of the recently published English readers at secondary and higher secondary level and analyse the suitability of the testing items for the language development.

Examination

In the examination, memory power of the children is being tested across the country. Since English is considered to be skill oriented, at least 50 per cent of the language skills must be tested in the class room. Analysis of English question paper reveals that 85 per cent of the English questions starting from class VI to XII are based on memory and a few of them are skill based. This is one of the reasons why students after ten years of exposure to English, are not able to speak and write English in appreciable ways. Most teachers and students think that English is an academic subject which is meant for passing the examination not for practical purpose. This idea has to be discouraged.

Guidance and Counselling

Students need academic guidance because they study courses without knowing their future prospects. They become restless on the premises of the educational campus when they do not what they would like to become. Hence, educational institutions are supposed to organize guidance programme thrice a year to guide the students appropriately. When the following career Modelling designed by Dr. M. Doss (2009) was shown to group of collegiate students who are pursuing literature at undergraduate level in regular colleges, they had known only 8-10 per cent of the courses and the same was happened when it was shown to the group of teachers. Out of 33 job opportunities mentioned in the Career modelling, only 5-7 jobs were identified even by the teachers who are teaching English at higher secondary level. Some of them shared their views that if they had come to know about it earlier, it could have changed their life style.

English Course and Career Option

HSC

3 Years

B.A., English Literature
B.A., Functional English
B.Sc/B.A. Any degree
(with English as a Part I/II subject.)

2 Years

Integrated
M.A. English
5-years

M.A., English Literature
M.A., English Language Teaching
M.A., English Studies
M.A., Linguistics
M.A., Translation Studies
M.A., TESL
M.A., Functional English
M.A. English and Communication

3-5 years

1 year
M.Phil. Specialisations
British Literature
American Literature
African Literature

Ph.D. Specialisations
British Literature
American Literature
African Literature

Indian Fiction
Indian Writing in English
Linguistics
Computational Linguistics
English Language Teaching
Diaspora Studies
English Studies
Translational Studies
Comparative Literature
Journalism and Stylistics
Communicational Studies
English for Specific Purposes
Feminism

Indian Fiction
Indian Writing in English
Linguistics
Computational Linguistics
English Language Teaching
Diaspora Studies
English Studies
Translational Studies
Comparative Literature
Journalism and Stylistics
Communicational Studies
English for Specific Purposes
Feminism

Career Options for Those Who Studied English as Main Subject at UG/PG Level

- Teacher
- Lecturer/Assistant Professor in College/University
- Journalist
- Language Trainer
- Soft skill Trainer
- Freelance Writer
- Content Developer
- Call centre Supervisor
- Corporate Manager
- Public Relation Officer
- News Reader for T.V. and Radio
- Radio Jockey
- Editor for Electronic and Non-electronic Media
- Translator
- Interpreter
- Writer
- English Language Consultant
- e-Publishing and Editing
- Computational Linguists
- Linguists
- Communication Experts in Corporate Centres
- Receptionist in Hotel/Motel
- Announcer in Air India/Indian Railways
- Event Manager
- Tourist Guide

- Commentator/Compere
- ELT Book-Writer (Material Production)
- Lexicographer
- Civil Servant
- Administrative Officers

Suggested Frameworks

- English Readers prepared for secondary schools must have minimum lessons but more skill-based exercises for language development.
- English language training should be given to rural teachers with a focus on Activity based learning because activities and competencies are mutually exclusive.
- Speech practice should be provided through Computer Assisted language learning for better communication.
- Minimum Level of Learning (MLL) for English language must be fixed for each class at primary and upper primary level.
- The teachers of English should be informed well when to use translation method, Bi-lingual method and English to English approach for better understanding.
- Some basic concepts in teaching of language like 'Habit formation', 'Imitation', 'Pattern Practice', 'Contextualisation' should be taught to the teachers with proper examples while organizing in-service training to the teachers.
- Educational institutions should emphasis the teachers for language development rather than that of content development.

Conclusion

Education, whether formal or informal, contributes to the development of the individual directly and to the development of the nation indirectly. But the same kind of education especially English education is a burden to the geographically disadvantaged group in India. It doesn't mean that English education is not needed. Some kind of systemic reforms is essential to impart quality English education to the rural children. In this regard, this chapter has suggested a few policy and appropriate methodologies to make the rural children believe that English is an interesting subject. Consequent upon this, they should use English as instrument for effective rural reconstruction for peaceful living.

REFERENCES

Agnihotri and Khanna (1997). *Problematizing English in India*. New Delhi: Sage Publication.

Doss, (2004). "The Roll of Institutions, Teachers and Students in Developing Oral Communicative Competency among the Disadvantaged Learners." Paper presented in the UGC-Sponsored National Seminar, Organised by Erode Arts College, held in Erode, Tamil Nadu on 7th and 8th July.

Doss, (2008). "Survival Factors for Quality Technical Education in India." (ed.) by Dr. R. Hariharan in *Recent Trends in Technical Education*. New Delhi: MacMillan.

Krishnasamy and Sriraman (1994). *English Teaching in India*. Madras: TR Publications.

Kumaravadivelu (2002). "From Coloniality to Biobality: Visioning English Language Education in India." *IJAL*, 28:45-61.

Meenakshi, Mukerjee (1991). "The Debate in English Studies Today: A View from Within." *JEFL* 7 and 8: 30-40 Hyderabad, CIEFL.

MHRD (1991). *Minimum Levels of Learning at Primary Level*. New Delhi: NCERT.

MHRD (1992). *Learning without Burden: Report of the National Advisory Committee*. New Delhi: Government of India Press.

NCTE (1996). *Curriculum Framework for Teacher Education*. New Delhi: NCTE.

21

Nonformal Education for the Development of Rural Youth

Bharati B. Ganiger and *Ramesh M.*

Introduction

Different people have different ways in which they define education. Some believe that education can only be learned in state-run schools, colleges and universities. It is in those places where we may learn and gain our certificates that prove we have learned what we have learned. But education covers a broad spectrum, education is a lifelong process, and that we must learn every aspect of life as we grow. Education is such a process which starts from the minute we born and proceeds till we die, that is, from cradle to grave.

Swami Vivekananda had a deep and comprehensive conception of education. He said: "We want that education by which character is formed, strength of mind is increased. The intellect is expanded and by which one can stand one's own his feet". And ultimate goal of education is helping each soul manifest the potential divinity within it.

Gandhiji had said, "By education, I mean an overall all-around drawing out of the best in child and man, in body, mind, and spirit." This concept of education serves both goals at the same time.

There are some people who have never received a full-time education in any sort of school at all, but have learned the family ways, i.e. gone into a trade that may be has been passed down from one generation to the next. Such people can be found everywhere—from fishermen, artists, writers, musicians, fruit or clothes stall-holders, or antique collectors—to name but a few. A prime example of this can normally be found in the gypsy community, whose children do not attend full-time mainstream education. Rather, in the travelling community their trade is passed down over the years, (the trade being fairground rides). Many people may not have recognized educational certificates as such, but what they all seem to possess is a gift of some sort. This gift, or natural talent, means that they can get by in life just fine, without having the certificates one needs to gain mainstream employment as we know it, be it in an office or bank. Education does not mean any one thing, but rather it encompasses a whole range of subjects. Indeed, many people just seem to be naturally gifted in one subject or another and will naturally navigate towards that. This does not mean that any one person has the right to put down another, simply because they have not had a school, college or even a university education. Rather, it is each to their own. The definition of education is a broad spectrum that covers a whole range of ideals and subjects. Educational certificates, although they may be very useful in gaining employment in an office, or court of law, or any other mainstream employment agency, are useless when it comes to working, on stalls, or creating a piece of art using wood, or metal, or communicating with people in the right way.

Types of Education

Most of the general population assumes that education and schooling are interchangeable terms and education occurs only in School, i.e. formal way. But Learning takes place at formal, Nonformal and Informal ways of educational setting and learning experiences will be equally powerful in all these settings.

Formal Education

Formal education is associated with schools and it is always organized and structured and has certain set of learning objectives more precisely. Formal education is the hierarchically structured, chronologically graded educational system running from primary schools through the university and including in additional to general academic studies, a variety of specialized programmes and institutions for full-time technical and professional training (Coombs, 1973) example: Schools, Colleges and Universities.

Non-Formal Education

Non-formal education occurs in other than the traditional schooling. And it is also more learners centred than formal education. Non-formal education lies in between formal and informal learning settings. Any intentional and systematic educational enterprise usually outside the traditional schooling in which content is adapted to the unique needs of students in order to maximize learning (Klies, 1973). Non-formal Education is more flexible when compared to formal education and these are less structured. Examples: Extension Education and Vocation and so on.

Informal Education

It is everyday experience one can get, which are not organized or planned. When these experiences are interpreted by elders or peers they constitute informal education. These are pervasive, ongoing and incidental. When infants and young children are learning to speak they do by listening and imitating so it is informal learning. Example: Home, School, Community, and society in total all the surrounding environment will give the experience that is informal education.

Present Status of Education of Rural Areas in India

Gandhiji said that India lived in her villages 80 per cent of population living in rural areas and most of them are below poverty line. India's prosperity lies in the prosperity and well-being of rural population but in rural areas most of the people are illiterate and even children continue to be deprived of quality education. And these children are lacking all kind of opportunities as getting by the rural children because rural areas are having limited number of schools, in competent, untrained teachers, lack of proper teaching materials, lack of infrastructure, lack of cooperation from the communities and so on. Overall enrolment in primary and middle schools are very low 50 per cent of children living in rural areas leave school before the 5th grade because of lack of interest, for working at home and fields. A large percentage of drop-outs are females forced by their parents. As these children grow into adults they remain illiterates, in future they are also reluctant to send their own children to school because of their failure in the education system. This in turn create demotivating environment for the children.

In view of such concerns the government is undertaking various schemes and programmes under which they intent to improve the practical infrastructure, providing source materials, providing training the teachers for example; Sarva Shiksha Abhiyana (SSA), legislative frameworks (Art.21-A, 51-A, 46). With all the possible formal and non-formal views of education for rural people including youth.

Non-formal Education for Rural Youth

Rural Youth

Age and location are the two key defining characteristics of rural youth. Usually, we know that age of youth vary quite considerably from 15 to 24. The 2007 world development report, which focuses on 'The next generation', expands definition of youth to include all the young people aged between 12 to 24. Youth are in a period of transition from childhood to adulthood. The transition is multifaceted it involves their physical, mental, sexual maturation, growing autonomy, social and economic independence from parents and other careers. In developing countries like India the rural children become adults quickly mainly because the transition from school to work usually occurs at the early age and his transition completed in a short space of time. The same is true for the poor young rural women with regard to marriage and child bearing. Lack of alternatives is the major reason given for every high level of marriage and child bearing among rural adolescent girls. Rural survival strategies demand that young people fully contribute to meeting the livelihood needs of their households from an early age. Consequently, youth as a transitional stage barely exists for large majority of rural youth and poor in particular.

Another related attribute of rural youth is that they tend to lack economic independence or autonomy. The rural household is a joint venture, and the gender division of labour is such that full, individual control of the productive process is virtually impossible for women. Large proportions of rural youth are subordinate members of usually large extended households, they largely dependent on their parents for their livelihood needs. As youth grow older, the autonomy of males increases but contracts for females. Moreover, in most of traditional and poorest population girls typical marry shortly after menarche or when they leave school.

Rural youth are very heterogeneous since their age is differs from one to another. A 12 year old boy may be attending primary school, and a 24 year old single mother of 4 children working for existence, vending on streets of large rural village. The youths livelihood needs also differs from one another.

Current Situation and Needs of Rural Youth

The total youth population in the world today is estimated about 1500 million and is projected to grow 2 billion by the year 2050 (Bennel, 2007). All of that growth will be in the developing world, where it is projected that in the future eight of every nine youth will be living in a developing country. Although, the total number of youth will remain greater in rural areas over the next 10 to 15 years, all future growth in numbers of youth will be in the cities. By year 2025, it is estimated there will be over 1 billion youth living in the cities, with only 700 million remaining in rural areas. For most developing countries the last decade one of the increasing difficulty declining in living standards, unemployment, deteriorating services, social unrest and political instability. We see people still live in absolute poverty with a diet to poor to allow enough energy for work. Children and youth will constitute largest proportion of the population in developing countries compared to around one-third of the population in developed countries. Rural youth accounts for around 55 per cent of the world youth population. They are among the disadvantaged of the groups. Often they have limited access to educational programme that are geared to their situation and needs not surprisingly, many rural people drop-out of school at an early age. Class work is often geared more towards academic accomplishments and to the urban areas than to learning skills useful to rural life, and preparing for adulthood. There is a genuine need for the young person's labour on the form or in the home adding yet another reason, why parents see little reason to keep their children in school. Women have even greater difficulty than young man as they are often not given the same opportunities in education, training and involvement in rural development activities. Rural youth are facing problems in various ways like health, sanitation, unemployment, malnutrition, drug abuse, violence, discrimination, lack of knowledge due to lack of educational opportunities, low standard of living and so on.

Main Issues Affecting Rural Youth

There are many issues affecting rural people in general youth in particular, like:

- Education and Training
- Agriculture
- Employment
- Rural to Urban Migration
- Health Issues
- Support Services

Education and Training

Education and Training is an issue of critical importance for the rural youth. Lack of skills and opportunities and training programme are a major reason for increasing unemployment. Rural people do not receive quality education. Rural young women receive still less education than man. There are fewer opportunities for vocational training in the rural areas. Formal education is not reaching entire village children, and it is mostly restricted to primary levels. It is not helping schools drop-outs of rural youth. Education system has not kept pace with the needs of rural young people, so the young ones are not prepared to face the fruitful life. The negative result of this has been that rural young people who acquired degrees are pushed out of the job others who have higher degrees and skills. The reduction in the formal sector job opportunities during the recent years has particularly affected educated rural youth. Nearly 140 million youth in developing countries are classified as 'illiterates'. More generally, the preparation of rural youth for productive work is poor. Even though there are many vocational training programmes they are not finding place in the rural areas.

Needs of Rural Youth in Education and Training

1. Rural youth are in need of education in terms of knowledge, skills and at application levels.
2. Rural youth are in need of vocational training, industrial training and basic skill development in all possible places, namely agricultural productive works, building, carpentry, electrical repairing, motor mechanics, plumbing, printing, sewing and so on.
3. Rural youth are in need of motivation to work and develop in the rural areas itself. They need innovative schemes, projects, workshops in the areas of agriculture, literacy, population, health, and environment.
4. In rural areas the formal education system should work more functionally in collaboration with non-formal and informal education systems.

Agriculture

India is a country of villages; the village economy is mainly depending on agriculture. It is widely recognized that rural diversification will be the lynchpin of successful agricultural transformation in the future. Where rural diversification is not economically feasible the alternative will be the transition of economic activity from the rural to urban areas. Whatever, the outcome rural youth will be at assets, most notably land and sector is seen as the ladder from underemployment in low productivity, small holder production to regular wage employment in the local economy and from their jobs in the formal sector. As rural farmers believe in the traditional notions of agriculture the crop production is very low. And rural youth are increasingly disinterested in small holder farming which is viewed as 'dirty work' they feel agriculture as inferior so this leads to stagnation of development in the agricultural sector. Lack of knowledge and information regarding innovative agricultural methods for high productivity is also a concern. For many rural youth who wish to remain on the land, the obstacles include the lack of new arable land for cultivation and poor infrastructure, land pressure often results in marginal and unsuitable land being used for cultivation leading to soil degradation and erosion, deforestation and other environmental problems of the region because of this now-a-day's rural youth are migrating to urban locality in search of better work than agricultural work, hence the labour scarcity has become common issue in this sector.

Needs of Rural Youth in Agriculture

1. Vocational education and training programmes on various modern methods of crop cultivation and extension services.
2. High price for primary products, improved marketing services and infrastructure.
3. Use of technology, credit services, subsidies, etc.
4. Proper training in various productive agricultural methods like, poultry, dairy, goats, fisheries, horticulture, etc.

Employment

In the view of stagnant industrial development and public sector employment during the past decades, the traditional peasant farm sector has absorbed most of this growing labour force mainly through the intensification of farming. However, the relatively decreasing contribution of agricultural production towards GDP, suggests that this has been achieved with reducing per capita income and increasing underemployment. Rural youth are not creative at mind to find their self-employment activities youth are not concentrating on productive agriculture, youth have negative attitude towards manual work and life. Among youth there are no youth organizations, and no training programmes on agriculture and other skills. As most of the rural youth are illiterates, school dropouts they do not have capability to think beyond traditional method of agriculture. They are fully dependent on agriculture when natural calamities occur, years together they do not find work. In rural areas some of the youth even they think for innovative opportunities for the employment but they are not getting any motivation and financial support from the community.

Needs of Rural Youth in Employment

1. Enhanced infrastructure development.
2. Enhanced marketing system.
3. Vocational training programmes in productive agriculture, namely poultry, dairy, sericulture, and small scale industries to process agricultural products, etc.
4. Availability of rural financial credit system and subsidies schemes.

Rural to Urban Migration

In the rural areas youth do not find proper education and environment. Urban areas lifestyle looks to be very attractive to rural people who are taught urban values through the education system and see the limited employment opportunities in the rural areas. This migration may be seasonal because of floods, draughts and natural inconveniencies occurring in the rural area. For many youths agriculture is thought of as a low status job and a last resort, which adds to the pull urban life. Average earning is high in urban areas compared rural areas leads to urban migration.

Needs to Prevent Migration

1. Agriculture and rural industries needs to established.
2. Improvement of rural infrastructure and services including education, health, social and recreational facilities.
3. Implementation of national poverty alleviation strategies.
4. Education and training services.

Health Issues

In rural areas there are various set of circumstances which are placing youth at higher risk, namely malnutrition, sanitation, malaria, drug abuse, HIV/AIDS, violence, discrimination, broken families and high birth rates among adolescent girls. Lack of awareness and educational opportunities and limited possibilities standards of living. Often youths are persuaded into negative behaviours and actions by friends *via* peer pressure make some of the youth to attempt for various bad health issues like drinking, smoking, drug abuse, suicide, etc. Involvement of rural youth in pre-marital sex relationships without preventive measures. Because of adaption of improper lifestyle the rural people are suffering from various diseases. Unavailability of well equipped hospitals and professionally trained doctors.

Needs to Mitigate Health Issues

1. Organizing health awareness programme.
2. Enhancing youth participation in health related projects.
3. Development and dissimilation of health related practical information.

Support Services

In rural areas when youth however motivated to do some small scale business or any innovative works at village the social and the financial support will not be given to them by the community instead it will discourage and de-motivate them. There is no availability of secure new market opportunities leads to low price for the agricultural products. Lack of proper guidance in using improved technologies. And youth in these areas do not constitute an organized and vocal constituency with the economic and social power to lobby on their behalf.

Needs to Provide Support Services

1. Government and Non-government intervention programme to improve physical, natural and financial assets and job related capitals through skills training.
2. Development of human resources in the agricultural sector.
3. Enhance and improve coordination of developmental

efforts and support offered by different government and NGOs.
4. Secure new market opportunities.

Role of Non-formal Education (NFE) for the Rural Youth Development

Non-formal Education (NFE) is conceptualized as an organized educational activity occurring in the traditional framework of formal education system. Formal education is highly structured and rigid one. The NFE includes lots of flexibilities in terms of organization, timing and duration of teaching learning, clientele groups, and age-groups of learners, condensed methodologies of instruction and evaluation procedures. All these features made NFE a critical mode for reaching out to the hardest to reach groups of children and youth, both rural and urban India.

The NFE Includes Certain Objectives Regarding Rural Youth

1. To provide youth with education in terms of ideology and morality.
2. To enhance the skill and knowledge of youth in areas of science and technology.
3. To provide youth with vocational training, employment opportunities and skills training.
4. To support the youth in maintaining good physical and mental health to prevent destructive social behaviour.
5. To set up and strengthen the structure of youth organization.
6. To develop methods and techniques to improve youth and child related activities.
7. To generate income for youth and child development and to cooperate with international youth.

Non-formal Education (NFE) Includes Both Curriculum and Materials, the Content of Curriculum Includes

1. All youth should become cultured, educated and self-respected citizens.
2. Youth scientific temper should be inculcated.
3. The habit of self-learning should be encouraged.
4. The poverty in youth life should be countered by enabling

them to organize their work systematically and learn new skills.

5. Youth should become aware of social conditions around them as well as the need for social change.

Non-formal Education (NFE) programme in India launched by government during 1979-80 the NFE policy help those students who are school dropouts, working children and youth and children from areas without easy access to school. NFE is being reached to rural youth by both government policies, projects and also by NGOs. Government policies must support rural youth programming efforts without organization. National efforts, youth activities will continue to be limited, fragmented and ineffective. Food and Agricultural Organization will continue to play an active role in supporting Seminars, Workshops, and other activities which have favourable influence on national youth programme policy. Existing rural organization whether government or non- government will be the most effective means of reaching out of school rural youth.

Education and Training

For the rural youth development, youth's need should be fulfilled. The rural youth are in need of various facilities. The NFE will help the rural youth in making them educated and responsible citizens. As tnere are many school drop-outs, adult illiterates for them NFE has become boon. In rural areas NFE is providing various vocational and training centres through government and NGOs. They are engaging rural youth in various activities, namely training in agricultural methods, industrial training, training for the improvements in traditional occupations like, carpentry, weaving, pottering, sewing etc.

Non-formal strategies present a very broad spectrum in terms of magnitude and scope, management structures, governmental control and supervision, NGO involvement, community participation, local government support, curricula, pedagogy, linkages with the formal system and attention to gender equity. Yet, at their core, there are several commonalities that set them apart and give them a distinct identity of their own.

Non-formal education should have a linkage with the formal system. This, of course, is advisable and often critical. But here again, existing practices vary widely. Many NFE programmes are conceived as an end in themselves. Their aim is to impart basic education and general awareness so as to bring students to a level of functional ability. Others seek equivalencies so that they can perform certification tasks for at least the earlier grades ranging from I to V. Still others go a step further, with the objective of putting students back into class and giving them a chance to pursue their educational careers. There are also, more often than not, close collaboration in the areas of teacher training. Planning, curriculum preparation, certification, teaching-learning material, accommodation sharing, etc.

In training, orientation is just as important as training. Hence, the two are combined in short bursts. The importance of refresher training at periodic intervals is generally stressed. Great reliance is placed on the job learning. Naturally, this involves closer supervision and monitoring.

According to National Policy on Education, 1986, the Non-formal Education Programme, meant for school dropouts, for children from habitations without schools, working children and girls who cannot attend whole-day schools, will be strengthened and enlarged. Modern technological aids will be used to improve the learning environment of NFE Centres. Talented and dedicated young men and women from the local community will be chosen to serve as instructors, and particular attention paid to their training. All necessary measures will be taken to ensure that the quality of non-formal education is comparable with the formal education. Steps will be taken to facilitate lateral entry into the formal system of children passing out of the non-formal system.

Effective steps will be taken to provide a framework for the curriculum on the lines of the national core curriculum, but based on the needs of the learners and related to the local environment. Learning material of high quality will be developed and provided free of charge to all pupils. NFE programme will provide participatory learning environment, and activities such as games and sports, cultural programme, excursions etc. The Government will takeover all responsibility for this vital sector. Voluntary agencies and Panchayati Raj Institutions will take much of the responsibility of running NFE programme. The provision of funds to these agencies will be adequate and timely.

The establishment of vocational courses or institutions will be the responsibility of the Government as well as employers in the public and private sectors; the Government will, however, take special steps to cater to the needs of women, rural and tribal students and the deprived sections of society. Appropriate programme will also be started for the handicapped. Graduates of vocational courses will be given opportunities, under predetermined conditions, for professional growth, career improvement and lateral entry into courses of general, technical and professional education through appropriate bridge courses. Non-formal, flexible and need-based vocational programme will also be made available to neoliterates, youth who have completed primary education, school dropouts, persons engaged in work and unemployed or partially employed persons. Special attention in this regard will be given to women. Tertiary level courses will be organized for the young who graduate from the higher secondary courses of the academic stream and may also require vocational courses. It is proposed that vocational courses cover 10 per cent of higher secondary students by 1995 and 25 per cent by 2000. Steps will be taken to see that a substantial majority of the products of vocational courses are employed or become self-employed. Review of the courses offered would be regularly undertaken. Government will also review its recruitment policy to encourage diversification at the secondary level.

The new pattern of the Rural University will be consolidated and developed on the lines of Mahatma Gandhi's revolutionary ideas on education so as to take up the challenges of micro-planning at grassroots levels for the transformation of rural areas. Institutions and programme of Gandhian basic education will be supported.

Agriculture

NFE is working hard to resolve the problems existing in agricultural sector in rural areas by taking various initiatives. National Agricultural Policy (2010) aims to attain output growth rate in excess of 4 per cent per annum in agriculture sector based on efficient use of resources. It seeks to achieve this growth in a sustainable manner and with equity. The Policy resolution than describe in detail the strategy and policy alternatives which are grouped under the heads: Sustainable agriculture, Food and nutrition security, Generation and transfer of technology, Inputs management, Incentive for agriculture, Investment in agriculture, Institutional structure, Risk management etc. There are various training programmes for the vocational training in the sub-areas of agriculture like involving youth in dairy, poultry, aquaculture, promoting rural women in finance, agro business, marketing etc. Training also includes awareness programme related to importance of agriculture, innovation and technology in agriculture for high yield and improvements in the traditional notions of rural people's professional works. Government of India is providing credit flow for promotion and development of agriculture, small-scale industries, cottage and village industries, handicrafts and other rural crafts. It also has the mandate to support all other allied economic activities in rural areas, promote integrated and sustainable rural development and secure prosperity of rural areas through National Bank for Agricultural and Rural Development (NABARD).

Employment and Rural to Urban Migration of Youth

Non-formal Education (NFE) is playing vital role in providing various employment opportunities for the rural youth, by various schemes, like Training of Rural Youth for Self-Employment (TRYSEM). As supporting component of IRDP, the scheme TRYSEM was launched with the aim to provide basic technical and entrepreneurial skills to rural youth from the families below poverty line to enable them to take up self-employment and wage employment in the broad fields of agriculture and allied sectors, namely industries, services and business activities. The target groups comprise of rural youth between the age 18-35 years. Prime Minister's Rozgar Yojana (PMRY) for Educated Unemployed Youth. The Scheme has been formally launched on 2nd October, 1993. The PMRY has been designed to provide employment to more than a million person by setting up 7 lakh micro enterprises by the educated unemployed youth. It relates to the setting up of the self-employment ventures through industry, service and business routes. The scheme also seeks to associate reputed non-governmental organizations in implementation of PMRY scheme especially in the selection, training of entrepreneurs and preparation of project profiles. At the most general level youth employment policies should focus on increasing the demand for labour in relation to supply, increasing the integrability of disadvantaged youth so that they can take advantage of labour market and other economic opportunities when they arise.

In the rural areas as there will be less opportunities for employment, low standard of living are the reasons for youth to migrate to urban areas. NFE through various schemes should provide self-employment opportunities to the rural people to prevent the problem of migration.

Non-formal Education (NFE) in Health of Rural Youth

Various organizations through NFE are attempting to improvement of the health in the rural areas particularly of rural youth, by conducting awareness camps related to hygienic conditions of houses and the surrounding environments, diseases, like malaria, cholera, HIV/AIDS, etc. According to National Rural Health Mission (2005-2012), it adopts a synergistic approach by relating health to determinants of good health, viz. segments of nutrition, sanitation, hygiene and safe drinking water. It also aims at mainstreaming the Indian systems of medicine to facilitate health care. The Plan of Action includes increasing public expenditure on health, reducing regional imbalance in health infrastructure, pooling resources, integration of organizational structures, optimization of health manpower, health centres into functional hospitals meeting Indian Public Health Standards. Also NRHM provides strategies like Training and enhancing capacity of Panchayati Raj Institutions (PRIs) to own, control and manage public health services. Promote access to improved healthcare at household level through the female health activist (ASHA). Health Plan for each village is implemented through Village Health Committee of the Panchayat.

Support Services

Education and training of NFE is alone contribute to self-employment in rural areas. But there should be certain support services in terms of micro finance, integrated packages of inputs (credit, training, advisory support and other facilities). For example, formation of Self-Help Groups, the government or NGOs should provide micro finance for the initiation of this organization.

Such organizations have created movements in the lives of women in the rural areas, they have gained the sense of confidence and cooperation intern they become the support for the family and others. Youth groups like scouts, agricultural cooperatives, young farmers club, religious societies, etc. should find place in the rural areas with the assistance of village panchayats. Considerable influence is exerted by the government, community on rural youth development. Many kinds of mass media like radio programmes, particularly radio drama, tape and video-audio visual vans and other types of mass communication media should be used as communication and support materials for the rural development.

Initiatives by the Corporate Sectors and NGOs

The corporate sector has not lagged behind in contributing its bit for achieving rural development in India. Some of the current initiatives in this regard are e-choupal by ITC, Rural BPOs by Lason India and Byrraju Foundation, Gram IT by Byrraju Foundations etc. Similarly, NGOs have made significant contribution for rural youth development in the country. Notable amongst these are MV Foundations, Naandi Foundation, Basix India, Byrraju Foundations, Sanghmitra, Grameen Sahakari Vikas Society, Swayam Social Welfare Organization, Dr. Ambedkar Buddhist Charitable Trust and many more are trying hard for the rural development in India.

Conclusion

India faces challenges of building the young generation for the new millennium. The future of the country depends on the youth of today. The youth represents the national strength, vitality and vigour. The youth can be called as *Yuvashakthi*—the real strength of nation. But rural youth are unaware of their capability to transform the rural areas in turn the country. The rural youth have to be properly trained and moulded to be the custodian of India's national pride, champion of our culture, and to work for the development of the country. The high return on resources invested in youth today has both immediate and long-term benefits. The society has the challenge to provide the youth with the right education, vocational training, awareness programmes etc. Non-formal Education plays very important role for the rural development. Rural youth programmes play an important role in building life skills of individual young people: strengthening families and communities; and working towards sustainable agricultural and rural development as a major contributor to overall progress of a country. Formal and Informal education systems, government and non-governmental organizations, communities, Parents, youth groups should come forward to make a joint venture for the challenge of rural youth development by considering the all possible youth developmental programmes according to the needs and aspirations of various groups of rural youth.

REFERENCES

Bennel, P.S. (2007). *Promoting Livelihood Opportunities for Rural Youth. Knowledge and skills for Development*. Geneva. ILO.

Coombs, P. (1973). *New paths to learning for rural children and youth.* New York; NY: International Council for Rural Youth and Development.

Food and Agriculture Organization (FAO), United Nations, www.fao.org.

Improving health of Young People (2010). World Health Organization (WHO). Geneva.www.who.nt.

Iredale, R. (1978). Non-formal Education in India: Dilemmas and Initiatives. *Comparative Education.* 14(3).

Kleis, J., Lang, L., Mietus, J.R.(1973). *Toward a contextual definition of nonformal education.* Non-formal education discussion papers, east Lancing. Michigan: Michigan State University.

National Policy on Education (1986). Ministry of Human Resource Development, Government of India.

Nayar, D.P. (1979). Nonformal Education and Rural Development in India. *Community Development Journal.* 14 (1).

Patanjali, P.C. (2005). *Development of nonformal education in India.* Shree Publications.

Reddy, D.N. *et al.*, Rural Transformation in India. Institute of Human Development in India, New Delhi.

UNESCO (1972), *Learning to be.* Paris: UNESCO.

World Bank (2006), *2007 World Development Report: The Next Generation*, Washington D.C., World Bank.

22

The Role of Education in the Social Transformation in the Militancy Infested Areas of Jammu (J&K)

D. Rajeev Rattan

About Jammu

Jammu and Kashmir region is segmented into North and South parts by the Pir Panchal Range. South of which is situated the Jammu Division comprising presently of nine districts—Poonch, Doda, Rajouri, Ramban Udhampur, Reasi, Samba, Jammu and Kathua. Out of these Poonch, Rajouri, Doda, Reasi as well as Ramban and Udhampur touch the Pir Panchal Range from West to East in that sequence major parts of these four districts are drained by mighty Chenab river and its tributaries notably the Ans river. Unlike Kashmir, Jammu's demography is a linguistic and religious mosaic. It is 66 per cent Hindus, 30 per cent Muslims, 1 per cent Sikhs and others. Though Rajouri, Poonch, Doda, and Ramban districts are Muslim dominated but have sizeable Hindu population. Jammu, Udhampur, Reasi, Samba and Kathua are Hindu dominated. It is not a simple Hindu-Muslim divergence but Muslims of Jammu do not identify themselves to Kashmir. People of Jammu did not support quit Kashmir movement for an end to Dogra rule. When Sheikh Abdullah favoured accession to Indian Union the Jammu based Muslim Conference and Hindu Sabha supported Maharaja's desire to remain independent. Muslims of Jammu nurture strong feelings of grievances to

Kashmiri leadership. The border areas of Jammu region are quite backward, less developed. The problems of the entire belt from Poonch to Kishtwar along the South eastern side of Pir Panchal are aggravated by under-development, growing number of educated unemployed youth and lack of communication. Being at the periphery their grievances are not represented even in Jammu's regional politics. Their share in political power is not adequate. Their voice is not represented and articulated even at regional level. If not alienation there is huge discontent in the Muslims of Jammu.

Cause of Militancy in Jammu

Jammu region has its strategic location and has greater proximity to Line of Control (LoC) and International Border (IB). The Poonch and Rajouri districts share a long border of over 200 kilometres in the form of LoC. This is a soft border as a large number of people from this region have migrated to Pakistan. People have close relationship to the people of other side. The Muslim dominated areas of Jammu region are linguistically, ethnically and culturally similar to those residing across the Line of Control. Jammu's topography is far more complex than that of the Valley. Rajouri, Poonch Reasi, Ramban and Doda districts of Jammu region are mountainous and thickly forested. The terrain is punctuated with rivers, ridges and ravines. This provides the militants a perfect cover. Many parts of Jammu are thinly populated and difficult to access. There are parts such as the Hill Kaka region in Surankote that can be reached only after 2-3 days of tough trekking. Militants have set up bases in such inaccessible areas without being detected for years. After 1995, the new thrust area of Pakistan's political and militant offensive is the Muslim majority belt in Jammu, from Poonch to Kishtwar, which is tending to feel religiously insecure, starved of its ethnic urges and suffering from a sense of discontent. The main objective of the new thrust of militancy in the Muslim majority part of Jammu is to provoke communal violence and create a sense of insecurity in the minority to encourage migration.

From the very beginning Pro-Pak rather than Pro-Azadi militants have been active in Jammu region. While in valley Pro-India Muslims and members of establishment were the main targets of militants. In Jammu region the targets are not political but communal.

In the recent times, many of the micro studies conducted in these border areas which clearly reflect that due to non-availability of the schools as well as the other job opportunities, the persons living in these border areas fall easy prey to the anti-national elements, thus aggravating the cause of militancy among the locals. The problems which could be localized in these areas are the following:

(i) Lack of schools in these border areas.
(ii) Non-availability of the teachers in these schools.
(iii) The nomadic life style of the majority of the population.
(iv) Very less job opportunities despite of the Reservation for Scheduled Tribes/residents of the backward areas/ residents of actual line of control.
(v) Being in the far off areas, the role of the religious bodies are very important to motivate them for any cause.
(vi) Most of the girls are semi-literate and never prefer for the jobs unless available in the area itself.
(vii) Very less exposure to the social educational issues like of population control, environmental degradation as well as early marriages.
(viii) Not a single village has the community based compulsive learning system.
(ix) No exposure to the latest technological gadgets like of the use of ICT in the educational settings.
(x) Traditional schooling and no emphasis on the vocationalisation of the education.
(xi) Students generally drop-out of the schools due to the petty disputes of land, etc.
(xii) Girls are allowed for the education within the local area.

Out of these problems, most of the problems are related to the sect of the Muslims. The population of the Muslims is in majority in the areas on border with the Pakistan. It is one of the pertinent reason that many of the teenagers who are either out of the schools or the drop-outs or even in their late twenties fall an easy prey in the hands of the anti-national network to work against the interest of the Union of India on the pretext that religion is under threat and the *Jihad* is the solution.

Proposal for the Rural Transformation

Looking in the above context, it is proposed that a massive drive of rural transformation may be initiated in these border areas at the level of the education. Although, the Government of Jammu and Kashmir in league of the Government of India is setting up the schools in these areas but the real fruits of transformation from these schools is yet to take place in reality.

Hence, it is proposed that on **experimental lines** a **TEN** schools may be termed as **Mobile Schools**, to start with for all such persons who are of school going age but are not yet attending the schools, in all such areas bordering Pakistan in which besides the basic compulsive education the national values in the context of the National sovereignty and integrity as well as the ills of the Militancy will be the thrust areas.

As it is going to be an experimental study, it is proposed that the curriculum may be framed in the context of the locale which would further integrate them in the real situations.

Objectives of the Study

The study shall focus mainly on these objectives:

(i) To study the impact of the Mobile Schools in bringing a change in the educational index of the population.

(ii) To study the impact of these schools for inculcating the national as well as international values among the masses despite of the religious and the *Jihad* beliefs.

(iii) To initiate an educational drive of the elders to find the benefits of the education and to promote through education the betterment of the Girls lifestyle, restricting the family make up as well as promoting the cause of the ecology.

(iv) It will also be endeavoured to create the self-sufficient employment opportunities among these compulsive literates like of cottage industry to bring in them the self-respect as well as self-confidence among the others to do better.

Although these are some of the broad objectives which will be undertaken besides many of the other offshoot objectives which will be detailed later on.

The further details of this programme, like the research design and the tools, will be worked upon further and it is hoped that the results will be positively significant and shall be able to set forth the pace of transformation in the most crucial areas of the Indian society.

23

Education for Rural Transformation

A Case Profile of the Rishi Valley Institute for Educational Resources (RIVER)

Sakesh Genni, Sandeep Kumar and *Meera Subramanian*

Introduction

India lives in its villages (M.K. Gandhi, 1995). It means, to develop India, the villages in India must developed, Education for Rural Transformation is only way to achieve this. Education is the primary agent of transformation towards increasing people's capacities to transform their visions for society into realities. The dynamics of rural transformation in the "globalized" world has created new educational imperatives that call for a re-evaluation the role of education for rural people from new perspectives. Education teaches individuals how to make decisions that consider the long-term future of the economy, ecology and equity of all communities. The challenge of Education to serve rural transformation must become one of the main aims of Education for All. Educational programme have to become a vital part of transformation through committed partnerships of governments, communities, business organizations and civil society as a whole.

The rural transformation seeks to convey a vision of proactive and positive process of change and development of rural communities in the context of national and global changes in which education is a key instrument for shaping and fulfilling the goal of rural transformation. Responding to the diversity of rural situations is a key measure in making education relevant to rural transformation. The critical concern is to link educational activities to diverse needs of building skills and capacities for seizing economic opportunities, improving livelihood and enhancing the quality of life (UNESCO, 2001). The RIVER model made this into reality by combining their curricular content and learning materials with locally developed supplementary content in its educational programmes. This responds to specific changing opportunities for bringing rural transformation. Rishi valley is committed for the Education for the rural people. Rishi Valley Education Centre (RVEC) has made the bridges to the local village population through various programmes such as rural education, rural health, reforestation, bio-diversity conservation and watershed management. Hence, this paper focuses on the profile of RIVER as a model for rural transformation.

Context of the Rishi Valley Institute for Educational Resources (RIVER)

Rishi Valley is situated in the rural interior of South India, in a chronic drought area in the state of Andhra Pradesh—600 kms from Hyderabad. Krishnamurti Foundation India (KFI) set up in 1928 as a charitable institution by Jiddu Krishnamurti and Annie Besant, started the Rishi Valley Education Centre (RVEC) in the 1940s in Madanapalle, as a small residential fee-paying school with an independent entity, for students from middle class families. RIVER project works for the improvement of Primary education, as Primary education plays a key role in the rural transformation. If improvement and changes needs to occur in the villages, rural education needs a revamping. Referring to Andhra Pradesh, the fifth largest state of India, much of the state's population continues to depend on agricultural production for survival. As in many other states, therefore, the economic disparities between urban and rural areas are marked. Nearly, 49 per cent of schools in the state have enrolment of 50 or fewer students (DISE, 2006: 61, Figure 2.30), and the average primary school enrolment is 87 students. (DISE, 2006: 63, Figure 2.33). In 2004-05, just over 83 per cent of schools in the state were located in rural areas, representing 71 per cent of total student enrolment (11,122,940 students, DISE 2007a and 2007b). With an average drop-out rate across the five grades of primary education at just over 22 per cent, Andhra Pradesh also has the nation's highest drop-out rate at the primary level (DISE, 2006: 139, Table D28). Keeping these NGOs are working on this line. Riṣhi Valley Education Centre has been working to improve the primary education in the rural areas of Andhra Pradesh.

Many factors contribute to lower educational participation in rural areas. On the demand side, rural children may be less interested in attending school. First, the opportunity costs of attending schools are often higher in rural areas (Lockheed and Verspoor, 1991: 158). Many rural households are dependent on their children for help at busy times of the agricultural year such as harvest time. Schools are usually designed to follow rigid schedule both in terms of time of the day and term dates, and often expect children to be in school during busy periods in the agricultural calendar (Taylor and Mulhall, 2001: 136). Second, parents in rural areas often have a lower level of education, and may attach a lower value to schooling. The perceived lack of relevance of schooling may be enhanced by a rigid curriculum, often designed for a context (and sometimes culture) removed from that in rural areas. Rural schools rarely adapt the curriculum to make use of local examples, or to link the curriculum to local needs (Taylor and Mulhall, 2001). Third, even where parents place a value on schooling, they may not be able to participate in children learning. Parents in rural areas are less likely to be educated themselves, and so have less ability to provide support for their children. Some report that they are embarrassed to discuss school topics with their children, because of their own lack of knowledge. Further, homes in rural areas are often ill equipped to meet the needs of children to study, and often lack facilities like electricity (Taylor and Mulhall, 2001).

The Rishi Valley Institute for Educational Resources (RIVER) has developed a unique multi-grade, multi-level integrated learning methodology for classes 1 to 5. RIVER offers practical training programmes of varying lengths for teachers, resource persons, educators and administrators, in order to help transpose the programme. The educational programme of the school evolved through several phases that include pioneering innovations in educational practices, infrastructure building, a widening circle of students and teachers, and the working out of a meaningful curriculum that is regularly reviewed and updated.

The rural education programme enabled the evolution of a multi-grade learning system that addresses many of the entrenched problems of rural education with the support of Government of India grant. Centre has collaborated with many agencies (including UNICEF and various state governments) in training teachers and propagating this method of education in several regions across the country.

The RIVER model is based on continuous and progressive decentralization and localization of education, as opposed to the globalizing and homogenizing forces currently in vogue. In this model, good schooling means schools as resource centres for the community and not isolated institutions. Children viewed as members of a community, this conviction meant replacing a syllabus-centred, textbook oriented, teacher-directed mono-grade approach with one that met the multiple learning needs of them.

Programmes have been extended to formal and non-formal schools in states of Tamil Nadu, UP, Jharkhand and several districts of Andhra Pradesh. More recently, under the auspices of UNICEF they have entered into a 'Quality Improvement Programme' for 6 states of India. The programme will ultimately result in the setting up of 1000 multi-grade schools in one district in each of these schools.

In summary, children in rural areas may be considered more difficult to educate. They are likely to have less parental encouragement to go to school, and more alternative demands on their time, such as helping with agricultural tasks. When they attend school, they may find the curriculum less relevant to their lives, and find less support for their learning from the home environment.

Need for Multi-Grade Schools

In response to domestic and international pressure to achieve Education for All and the Millenium Development Goals (MDGs), the numbers of primary schools have increased. Small schools are a significant feature of rural India. Common features in these schools are poor educational quality, student disillusionment, high rates of drop-out and low rates of retention. Mono grade model of schools in the rural areas are extremely difficult if not impossible to achieve due to teacher ratio. So multi-grade schooling is essential. Multi-grade is often dismissed by policy makers and educators as a second-class option, there is growing evidence from around the globe that explicitly chosen and well-supported multi-grade techniques can result in positive educational experiences and outcomes (Ames, 2006; Aikmen and el Haj, 2006; Small, Multigrade Schools and Increasing Access to Primary Education in India Psacharapoulos *et al.*, 1993). In multi-grade schools, the teachers are often left with only minimal support in facing the challenges of multigrade management, and educational quality suffers as a result. In this view, RIVER has emerged as a model.

Aims of RIVER

RIVER establishes linkage through community curriculum, mothers committees, sharing of real life experiences with children. Rishi Valley Education Centre aims at to establish rural education centres as learning centres for the whole rural community: children, teachers and the parents alike through RIVER model. The functions of The RIVER model are as follows:

(i) To provide free basic education, nutrition and health care for children from local villages.
(ii) To draw working children into the school system.
(iii) To train teacher trainers in multi-grade classroom methodology.
(iv) To publish instructional material for village schools.
(v) To create a green space around the school campus for the conservation of bio-diversity in general and medicinal plants in particular.
(vi) To establish adult literacy classes in the school premises.
(vii) Raise awareness of health, nutrition and sanitation.
(viii) To actively involve the community in the day-to-day management of the school.

Structure of RIVER

Rishi Valley Institute for Educational Resources promotes rural education through two attached multi-grade model schools; a Back to School Programme and a Middle School that caters to students from Satellite schools, with an emphasis on a girl child.

The Multi-Grade Methodology

The RIVER model of multi-grade methodology is a unique structure for village education. Educators at RIVER developed set of materials that would be appropriate to the language and local customs of the community, as well as for teaching in a multi-grade classroom. The existing state textbook was deconstructed, and the required subject content of each chapter reorganised into a set of activities. The material presented in these activities drew on local folk and oral traditions. For example, local stories or images were used as tools for learning to read, to understand new vocabulary, or to make calculations. The activities are arranged in a sequence of five types—introductory, reinforcement, evaluation, remedial and enrichment, which students follow at their own pace. The end of each sequence (nominally a chapter of the nationally mandated textbook) denotes a 'milestone', and a series of milestones forms a 'learning ladder'. There are four sets of learning ladders, which cover the primary curriculum from class 1 to class 4, with separate ladders for language, mathematics and environmental studies at each level. Teaching and learning in class 5 is organised slightly differently, however, with about half of the work using activity based learning techniques and the other half organised in a more traditional textbook mode, in order to begin preparing students for the transition to government upper primary schools. The academic curriculum is integrated with activities aimed to promote conservation, sustain local culture and graded for individual levels of learning and grounded in up-to-date information through the education kit called 'School in a Box'. It has carefully designed 'study cards' and 'work cards', which are supported by a pictorial 'achievement ladder' that gives a clear sequential organization to what are essentially self-learning materials.

The cards allow children to learn at their own pace by selecting, with the help of the 'achievement ladder', the appropriate 'study card' for their level and performing the necessary follow-up activities or exercises contained in the 'work cards'. The work cards supported by teaching aids are prepared in such a way that children are actively involved in what she is doing and the possibility of her sitting "dreaming" in front of an open book is reduced to the minimum. Children at different levels within a single classroom share the same kit. A textbook in each subject for each child can be dispensed with or used as enrichment material.

This method encourages silent self-study and individualized learning, though teacher instruction. The group work is also a necessary part of the learning process. It gives ample room to the fast-learner as well as the slow-learner to progress at their own pace. Student absenteeism is not a problem in schools because a student is able to simply take up where he or she had left off on returning to school after a period of absence. Learning by rote and dry comprehension exercises are not practiced in support of activity-based learning.

Given the rich folk tradition in which villages are steeped, folk art, folk songs and local stories and legends are also incorporated into the curriculum. Education is seen not as a process of trying to bring every educated person's competencies to one homogenized level, thereby alienating the child from his own roots and ironing out cultural differences, but as a tool for deepening an understanding of herself, of her traditions and roots, while also exposing her to a wider cultural and knowledge base. This value-based model of education communicates ideals such as tolerance for other cultures, protection of the environment, preservation of folklore and local medicinal traditions.

The model of rural education provides a practical and attractive alternative to traditional education in villages, based on the one teacher per class, mono-grade, mono-level model.

Satellite Schools

These are small one-teacher schools, located at the centre of the village. Each Satellite School serves as resource centre for the villages to which it belongs. In this, adult literacy programmes, integration of local traditional arts in the form of puppet shows, health and nutrition projects are organised. For example, Valmikivanam established in Rishi Valley is one of them. Satellite Schools are gradually extending their reach by interacting with Government-run Schools, and helping organize reading workshops, metric melas among other joint activities.

Back to School

This programme is meant for the child labours of the surroundings and to get them back to school and provide education. The objectives of the programme are to ensure that every working child is schooled and ensure that at least 10 per cent of students enrolled in the programme will be mainstreamed each year after passing the Andhra Pradesh State Board Examinations. After that, students will be mainstreamed in a maximum two-year period; no child will participate in the academic programme for more than two years.

Students live and study on campus, with the willing consent of their parents. The students, the youngest of whom is seven years old, attend a "bridge school" that will prepare them for entrance to the local government schools. After their schooling at Rishi Valley, when they reach academic standards commensurate with their age they transfer to common schools for continue their education.

Designers Workshops—'School in a Box'

A collection of multi-grade, multi-level cards called 'School in a Box' is made available in Telugu, a dialect variant of Telugu used in the tribal belt of A.P., Hindi, Malayalam, Tamil and Kannada. RIVER has designed and published the Telugu and Hindi kits, and assisted in the design of materials in Tamil, Malayalam and Kannada.

The systematized process of "trans-creation" requires a team of resource persons—educators, storytellers, writers, and illustrators—to work in tandem with the RIVER team. These recourse persons ideally are people who are steeped in the culture of their language and who can build upon this rich background to create songs and stories for children.

Centre offers a variety of programmes for agencies that wish to learn about the multi-grade, multi-level schools: (a) one-day exposure visits acquaint visitors with an overall sense of the programme, (b) three-day workshops for administrators provide insights into organizational structure and working of the programme, (c) fifteen-day workshops for trained teachers give them hands on training in the multi-grade, multi-level methodology and orient them in classroom management, and (d) long-term designers workshops are offered for creating multi-grade, multi-level learning materials in languages other than Telugu.

Advantages of RIVER

RIVER has its own advantages to the rural children, parents, teachers and the community.

Classroom Interaction

The graded curriculum supplements the textbooks with interesting self-learning materials to make learning individualized, child-centred and interactive. It bridges attainment gaps in children so that all children achieved mastery of minimum levels of learning. Students of varying age and ability levels circulate learn together helped by the peer. Thus, this programme increased the access to primary education in the rural area.

Teacher Commitment and Involvement

This system enhances teachers' creativity and competency by ensuring teacher participation in developing, implementing and reviewing leaning materials. It has great support systems through constant monitoring and guidance of the teachers. The accountability of teachers ensured through development of transparent monitoring and evaluation materials. Teachers using the RIVER methodology thus have a significantly different role to that commonly noted in primary teachers in India (Sarangapani, 2003). Rather than taking an authoritative role as the holder of knowledge and facts which must be passed on to students (Freire, 1972), teachers become facilitators and create an environment in which students can learn and ask questions freely. RIVER views its teachers as having a much wider role in the communities in which they work. Teachers are expected to draw on local resources to enrich the curriculum and to plan learning activities outside the school, including field trips, village surveys, and metric melas.

Teacher Training and Multi-grade Teaching

In-service teacher training programmes provide teachers to teach in child centred multi-grade classrooms and prepares teacher trainers who can be mobilized to train other teachers. It also develops teachers to adopt innovative curriculum, which is locally appropriate to create a good learning environment for multi-grade teaching. Provides a school based mechanism for regular meetings of teachers for sharing experiences. To avoid the high absenteeism of teachers in the rural schools, RIVER recruits and train young people with minimal qualifications living in the villages. Thus, it helps in the teaching learning process.

Community School Linkage

Community school linkage established through community curriculum, mothers committees, sharing real life experiences with the children. The curriculum is enriched through the village resources and cost effective models are prepared without diluting the quality. There is an in-built replicating strategy moving in partnerships and capacity building capabilities are developed.

Summing Up

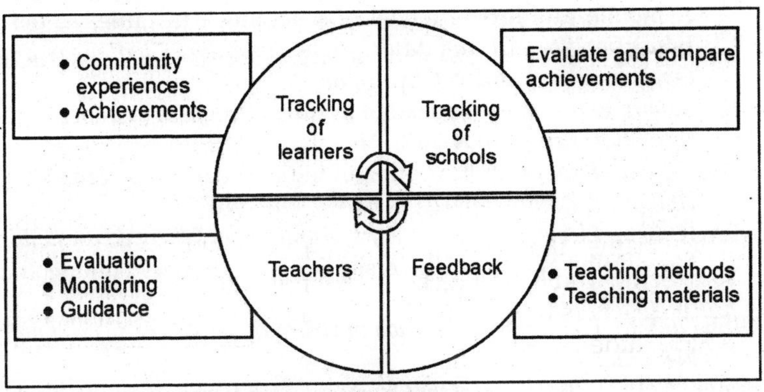

Fig. 23.1: Represents overview of RIVER

The innovative and proven methodology of the RIVER model has acclaimed globally and given a positive direction to primary education. The impact of this model has helped not only children but to the hundreds of teachers that are regularly trained through RIVER model, and the schools that access this learning from different parts of India.

The child-friendly approaches of the RIVER model has empowered and benefited many teachers across the country in enriching their teaching learning skills and their vision towards a common sense quality school. The positive social impacts of the model, includes growing community involvement in the schools, which has resulted in marked improvement to adult literacy rates, health and welfare in the villages. (Rao and Rao, 2006). The RIVER model rural schools have benefited mainstream education programmes all over the country and is a great contribution to high quality rural education.

REFERENCES

Ames, P. (2006). "A Multigrade Approach to Literacy in the Amazon, Peru: School and community perspectives". In Little, A. (ed.) *Education for All and Multigrade Teaching: Challenges and Opportunities*. Dordrect: Springer.

Aikmen, S. and el Haj, H. (2006). "EFA for Pastoralists in North Sudan: A mobile multigrade model of schooling". In Little, A. (ed.) *Education for All and Multigrade Teaching: Challenges and Opportunities*. Dordrect: Springer.

DISE (2006). Elementary Education in India: Progress towards UEE, *Analytical Report 2004-2005*. New Delhi: NIEPA.

DISE (2007). Elementary Education in India: Progress towards UEE, *Analytical Report 2005-2006*. New Delhi: NIEPA.

DISE (2007a). *Elementary Education in Rural India: Where do we stand?* New Delhi: National University for Educational Planning and Administration [NUEPA].

DISE (2007b). *Elementary Education in Urban India: Where do we stand?* New Delhi: NUEPA.

Freire, P. (1972). *Pedagogy of the Oppressed*. Middlesex: Penguin Books Ltd.

Gandhi, M.K., (1995). *India of My Dreams*, Ahmedabad: Navajivan Publishing House

Lockheed, Marlaine and Verspoor, Adriaan (1991). *Improving Primary Education in Developing Countries*. Oxford University Press, World Bank.

Psacharapoulos, G., Rojas, C. and Velez, E. (1993). 'Achievement Evaluation of Colombia's Escuela Nueva: Is multi-grade the answer?' *Comparative Education Review*, 37(3): 163-276.

Rao, Y.A.P. and Rao, A.R. (2006). *Community-based Education at Rishi*

Valley. Paper presented to the International Conference on Local Governance, Texts and Contexts: Perspectives from South Asia. 1-2 February 2006, Lahore, Pakistan.

Rishi Valley Education retrieved from www.rishivalley.org/ rural_education/overview htm

Sarangapani, P. (2003). *Constructing School Knowledge: An Ethnography of Learning in an Indian Village*. Thousand Oaks, California: Sage Publications.

Taylor, Peter and Mulhall, Abigail (2001). 'Linking learning environments through agricultural experience—enhancing the learning process in rural primary schools'. *International Journal of Educational Development*, 21, 135-148.

UNESCO, (2001). *Education for Rural Transformation towards a Policy Framework*, Paris: International Research and Training Center for Rural Education (INRULED).

Index